D1348561

GEORGE MACKAY BROWN AND THE
SCOTTISH CATHOLIC IMAGINATION

Scottish Religious Cultures *Historical Perspectives*

Series Editors: Scott R. Spurlock and Crawford Gribben

Religion has played a key formational role in the development of Scottish society shaping cultural norms, defining individual and corporate identities, and underpinning legal and political institutions. This series presents the very best scholarship on the role of religion as a formative and yet divisive force in Scottish society and highlights its positive and negative functions in the development of the nation's culture. The impact of the Scots diaspora on the wider world means that the subject has major significance far outwith Scotland.

Forthcoming titles

Poor Relief and the Church in Scotland, 1560–1650
John McCallum

The Catholic Church in Scotland: Financial Development, 1772–1930
Darren Tierney

Miracles of Healing: Psychotherapy and Religion in Twentieth-century Scotland
Gavin Miller

www.edinburghuniversitypress.com/series/src

GEORGE MACKAY BROWN AND THE SCOTTISH CATHOLIC IMAGINATION

LINDEN BICKET

EDINBURGH
University Press

Edinburgh University Press is one of the leading university presses in the UK. We publish academic books and journals in our selected subject areas across the humanities and social sciences, combining cutting-edge scholarship with high editorial and production values to produce academic works of lasting importance. For more information visit our website: edinburghuniversitypress.com

© Linden Bicket, 2017

Edinburgh University Press Ltd
The Tun – Holyrood Road
12 (2f) Jackson's Entry
Edinburgh EH8 8PJ

Typeset in 10/12 ITC New Baskerville by
Servis Filmsetting Ltd, Stockport, Cheshire,
and printed and bound in Great Britain by
CPI Group (UK) Ltd, Croydon CR0 4YY

A CIP record for this book is available from the British Library

ISBN 978 1 4744 1165 3 (hardback)
ISBN 978 1 4744 1166 0 (webready PDF)
ISBN 978 1 4744 1167 7 (epub)

The right of Linden Bicket to be identified as author of this work has been asserted in accordance with the Copyright, Designs and Patents Act 1988 and the Copyright and Related Rights Regulations 2003 (SI No. 2498).

Contents

Acknowledgements

There are many people who I would like to thank for their help and generosity in bringing this book to completion. *George Mackay Brown and the Scottish Catholic Imagination* stems from doctoral research undertaken at the University of Glasgow from 2008 to 2011; I would like to thank Professor Kirsteen McCue and Professor Gerard Carruthers for all their enthusiasm, guidance and advice during my time in Scottish Literature. Much of this book was written during my postdoctoral fellowship at the Institute for Advanced Studies in the Humanities at the University of Edinburgh from 2013 to 2014. I would like to thank those at IASH for their friendship, and the good conversations which enriched my own Catholic imagination during this time. I am especially grateful to Professor Jolyon Mitchell, former Academic Director of IASH, for his support and encouragement. I have also found conversations with colleagues, students and friends in the School of Divinity at the University of Edinburgh to be invaluable.

This book would not have been possible without the support of Morag MacInnes, Jenny Brown, Maggie Fergusson, Elizabeth Bevan and the late Archie Bevan – to whose memory the book is dedicated. I would like to thank Drs Theodora Hawksley and Tom Farrington for their careful proofreading and stimulating comments. I am especially grateful to Gillian Sargent for her encouragement and advice. And I would like to say a special thanks to my family, for all their warmth, love and support. Thank you to my parents, David and Elizabeth, for teaching me to love stories. Thank you to Eloise, Lorna and Isabel for all your support and reassurance. My greatest thanks and love go to my husband, Michael John O'Neill, who proofreads patiently, loves me unceasingly and makes every day joyful.

Quotations of George Mackay Brown's unpublished writing, works currently out of print and archival materials (including correspondence) are by permission of the Literary Estate of George Mackay Brown. Poetry is reproduced by permission of John Murray Press, an imprint of Hodder and Stoughton Ltd. Quotations from George Mackay Brown's works which are currently in print are by permission of Polygon Birlinn Ltd. Quotations also appear by permission of Steve Savage Publishers Ltd. An earlier version of the discussion of Robin Jenkins in Chapter 1 first appeared in *Some Kind of Grace: The Fiction of Robin Jenkins* (Brill, 2017), eds Douglas Gifford and Linden Bicket. An earlier version of Chapter 3 first appeared as 'George

Mackay Brown's Marian Apocrypha: Iconography and Enculturation in Time in a Red Coat', in *Scottish Literary Review* 5.2, 2013 (Glasgow: Association for Scottish Literary Studies). I am grateful to the editor and the ASLS for permission to reprint this material.

Abbreviations

A – *Andrina and Other Stories*
CP – *Collected Poems*
FI – *For the Islands I Sing*
G – *Greenvoe*
H – *Hawkfall*
LfH – *Letters from Hamnavoe*
LoL – *The Loom of Light*
M – *Magnus*
MF – *The Masked Fisherman and Other Stories*
OS – *Orkneyinga Saga*
OT – *An Orkney Tapestry*
RaD – *Rockpools and Daffodils*
SN – *The Sun's Net*
TK – *A Time to Keep*
TRC – *Time In A Red Coat*
VoB – *The Voyage of St Brandon*
WT – *Winter Tales*

EUL – Centre for Research Collections, Edinburgh University Library
MFA – Maggie Fergusson Archive. George Mackay Brown materials owned by his biographer
NLS – National Library of Scotland
OLA – Orkney Library and Archive

CHAPTER 1

The Scottish Catholic Literary Imagination

I. 'A monk at his devotions': George Mackay Brown the Catholic Artist

Pray for us Catholics here in Orkney, dear Sister Margaret. There was a great faith here in the pre-Reformation centuries; the light continues to burn.[1]

George Mackay Brown

In a letter written late in life to his friend Sister Margaret Tournour, a member of the Society of the Sacred Heart, George Mackay Brown (1921–96) reiterates his deeply held belief that despite centuries of beleaguerment and trial, Catholic faith and culture never really vanish. His intimate and cherished correspondence with Sr Tournour – herself a trained wood engraver and book illustrator – reveals the extent to which Brown felt relaxed enough to write freely about his literary craft, and also, frequently, about his adopted Catholicism, the religion to which he converted over thirty years earlier in 1961. Despite Brown's usual reluctance to speak openly about matters of faith, in this set of letters there is no suggestion of guardedness or caution, though there is evidence of autobiographical myth-making in his discussion of the pre-Reformation settings for many of his stories and poems. Brown self-consciously depicts a monkish life of solitude and prayer, in what he calls 'this little hermitage of mine', and 'my own little candle-lit cloister in Mayburn Court'.[2]

Many of the studies of Brown which have appeared since his death in 1996 have been eager to dispel the prevailing image of him as a sombre, isolated figure, cut off from the mainstream of late twentieth-century Scottish cultural circles, and practising an ascetic devotion to his craft. His fifty-two years of writing, spanning journalism, poetry, short stories, novels, plays and children's fiction, have lately been subject to a spate of reappraisals, retrospectives and reprints, due in most part to Maggie Fergusson's award-winning biography of Brown (2006).[3] Fergusson's biography not only restored a much-needed and balanced view of Brown's life – rendering it neither in hagiographical nor condemnatory terms – it also rescued this author from his 'odd maverick status' as a Scottish Catholic convert writer, and one, moreover, working in the apparently peripheral and Presbyterian environment of Orkney.[4] Brown's collusion with years of literary marketing, which presented him most often visually as a remote islander, and his own summation of his life as a 'gray, uninteresting thing', had to a large extent obscured the little-known but fascinating aspects of his biography, which Fergusson's work sensitively revealed.[5]

While the picture of Brown's busy cultural life, his relationships, and his influence from, and on, other religious people has been made even clearer by recent critical and biographical studies, Brown's literary Catholicism is something that is still often met with hostility or perplexed incomprehension in mainstream Scottish literary criticism. In fact, the idea of a Scottish Catholic imagination is one that has been almost completely submerged in studies of Scottish literature to date. Scotland's Reformation, and subsequent writing about this turbulent period in Scottish history, has powerfully shaped the literary canon. Ironically, it is the by-now dominant orthodoxy of early twentieth-century literary critical writings, with their fierce, hostile resistance to Scottish Calvinism, which have sealed a Calvinist imagination as the defining characteristic of the Scottish novelist. The critical anxiety to diagnose the doctrinal cast of Calvinism as haunting the mind of the Scottish author has led to the exclusion of other literary religious imaginaries, so that the idea of a modern Scottish Catholic writer can barely be countenanced. Brown, and most especially his early teacher, the critic and poet Edwin Muir (1887–1959), are not innocent of this charge.[6] Indeed, Muir is the main proponent of such criticism.

Douglas Gifford writes: 'it seems to me – and I freely admit here that such comparisons are odious – that compared with Sharp, or, say Crichton Smith, [Brown] is *too* fixed in a *prescriptive* vision.' He continues:

> [Brown's] Catholicism – a strange Orkney hybrid of pagan celebration and reaction to the bleakness of the Reformation – compels him to a predictable denouement, and increasingly in the later work – as with the explicit miracle that ends *Magnus* – an artless obviousness and repetitiveness of situation and image. Tentatively I suggest that his case is the sad one of a truly great writer who has chosen to live in a room with only one view from its single window.[7]

It is worth questioning why Gifford comes to this conclusion so 'tentatively'. His analysis can be situated within the broad tendency of Scottish literary criticism to distrust religion, but also, and more crucially, it is part of wider commentary on Brown that finds his Catholicism strange, or unorthodox. The clear suggestion that Brown's Orkney setting constrains him artistically is in evidence here, as is the charge of paganism – both oft-dispensed Scottish critical judgements on Brown's creative artistry. The identification of paganism and the charge of heterodoxy is frequently the conclusion arrived at by Brown's critics, if they address his Catholicism at all.

This chapter pursues three lines of enquiry stemming from the diagnosis of Brown's writing noted above: first, a watchful investigation concerned to cultivate a more complete understanding of the Scottish critical tradition's response to religion and literature in the twentieth century; then, tracing the forgotten literary Catholicism of a Calvinist country by recouping the faithful fictions of a number of neglected Scottish Catholic writers; and last, an assessment of Brown's locus within a Catholic literary culture, which is committed to the specifics of place and nation, but which can also be thought of as global, or transnational, in its shared themes and religious imagination.

This last point is a central principle of this book: the Catholic imagination in literature is far more nuanced, and geographically and culturally determined, than is often allowed in studies of fiction and poetry. In his seminal study of the Catholic novel in British literature, Thomas Woodman criticises the accepted definitions of British Catholic fiction, arguing that this genre 'presents its own problems of definition'. He notes: 'the context of Scottish Catholicism is very different from the English version'.[8] More recently, Richard Griffiths has argued that 'British Catholic literature' is so wide a term that it is virtually 'an artificial and meaningless concept'.[9] J. C. Whitehouse has been keen to stress that Catholic literature 'is not a single and homogenous corpus', while Patrick Sherry agrees that 'it has wider geographical frontiers than some critics appreciate' and that critics are often 'faced by the danger of coming to a premature generalisation about Catholic novelists, based on too restricted a canon'.[10]

The study of Scottish Catholic fiction is still uncharted territory, but it is time for this rich, diverse and experimental body of work to leave the footnotes of Catholic literary history, and be understood as a major chapter in the story of Catholic artistic and cultural production across the globe. The work of George Mackay Brown has never before been understood as part of a Catholic literary imaginary in twentieth-century Scotland, but in fact Brown's writing can be read and situated specifically within this little-known body of work. Viewing Brown's writing in this light challenges some of the salient critical orthodoxies that dominate our understanding of his fiction and poetry. Moreover, cultivating a more complete understanding of modern Scottish Catholic writing by using Brown's work as a contextual academic study in turn illuminates the Catholic fiction that is still being produced in Scotland. In recent years, there have been a number of new proponents of Scottish Catholic fiction. Writers including John Burnside, James McGonigal, Anne Donovan and Andrew O'Hagan share a powerful desire to interrogate the construction of their identities as Scottish Catholics. Their work, which reaches towards the numinous in newly creative ways, demonstrates that Catholic writing is not simply a historical phenomenon, confined to the Oxford Movement of the mid-nineteenth century, or the later novels of Waugh, Greene, Lodge, et al. Scottish committed literature of recent decades points to a very particular set of cultural influences and a unique spiritual heritage: its 'light continues to burn'.

II. The 'Knox-ruined nation'? Twentieth-century Scottish Literature, Criticism and Religion

In 'Prologue', the first poem of Brown's debut collection, *The Storm* (1954), Brown sets out an artistic manifesto that is at once defiant and full of future poetic purpose:

> For Scotland I Sing,
>   the Knox-ruined nation,
> that poet and saint
>   must rebuild with their passion.
>
> For workers in field
>   and mill and mine
> who break earth's bread
>   and crush her wine. (*CP*, 1)

It would be another seven years before Brown officially entered the Catholic Church, but here he allies the creative work of the artist with God's holy men and women, the saints, in the shared task of national reconstruction. Scotland, 'ruined' by the catastrophic legacy of sixteenth-century Knoxism, must be rebuilt as part of a Godly project for the common folk who till the soil. These are the folk who Brown's early mentor, the poet and critic Edwin Muir, mentions just over a decade earlier in his poem 'Scotland 1941', where he despairingly depicts the 'blighted' and 'starving' Reformation. In Muir's view, Scotland's harmonious medieval Catholicism is demolished by the Protestant Reformers 'Knox and Melville [who] clapped their preaching palms / And bundled all the harvesters away.'[11] Brown's response to Muir's historiography determines not only to restore poetry to the artistically bereft nation, but also, significantly, the Eucharist – the Real Presence of Christ which Scotland's people have been denied for centuries. In this way, Scotland will at long last be artistically and spiritually nourished. It is no wonder that Muir found Brown's first collection of poetry so beguiling. He writes in his introduction to this work that 'grace is what I find in all these poems' (*CP*, x).

In his reading of Brown's 'Prologue', Berthold Schoene disregards the intertextual references to Muir's original lament. Instead he notes: 'As the pagan imagery in the second stanza illustrates, Brown's Catholicism is far from orthodox. On the contrary, it has much in common with pagan nature religions, sharing their belief in an observable immanence of the divine in the processes of nature while assigning great significance to a semi-sacred quality of agriculture.'[12] Setting aside the fact that Brown had not yet been baptised (although he had been thinking of becoming a Catholic for many years at this point), a reading which privileges a 'pagan' interpretation of the sacramental world view and Eucharistic symbolism in this poem seems especially peculiar. But Schoene is not unique in his identification of Brown's paganism. As noted earlier, Douglas Gifford too has shared this view, calling Brown 'religious, perhaps, rather than Christian; for the pagan elements often sit closely with the Christian'.[13] Elsewhere, Brown has semi-seriously been called a 'pagan pape'.[14] It would seem that, reluctant to identify the religious-artistic project which is proposed as an antidote to centuries of Calvinism in poems like 'Prologue', critics decide that Brown should be read as unorthodox and saved from religious didacticism by an earthier, more flexible pantheism. Far better that he should be a quasi-Catholic, part-pagan poet of the land than a proselytising preacher, displaying what Douglas Dunn calls his 'highly unfashionable religious impulse'.[15]

It may be, however, that these critics are trying to extend the critical parameters of Brown's work to new dimensions, because the 'Knox-ruined nation' is one that is depicted in twentieth-century Scottish literature and criticism with astonishing frequency. The famously embattled high priests of this proposition, Edwin Muir and his poetic rival Hugh MacDiarmid, were, at first, strikingly at one when it came to pointing the finger at the cultural bogeymen who caused what they deemed to be Scotland's artistic malaise. In 1928, MacDiarmid bitterly laments the 'peculiarly unfortunate form the Reformation took in Scotland', which was 'anti-aesthetic to an appalling degree', and was the root of 'the general type of consciousness which exists in Scotland today – call it Calvinistic or what you will'.[16] Muir's view is even more despondent. Dedicated to MacDiarmid, his *John Knox: Portrait of a Calvinist* (1929) plants the blame squarely at the feet of 'Knox, the Reformers, and the Covenanters' who 'have made Scotland what it is'.[17] According to the Muir-MacDiarmid thesis, early twentieth-century Scotland is a gloomy place, its creativity and once-homogenous national culture thwarted by violently iconoclastic, divisive puritans. Moreover, according to this thesis, Protestant theological cultures since the sixteenth century have reimagined the nation as a vale of tears. As a result, Scotland is a nation that is characterised by distrust of the fallen, material world, and which has been left sternly resistant to artistic and cultural production.

With some justification, Muir argues that because of the puritanism of Scotland's Calvinist Reformation, the nation's theatrical tradition never flourished. He continues:

> For its imaginative literature [Calvinism] was confined more and more to the Old Testament, and though the Old Testament contains some splendid poetry, it has at all times been over-praised at the expense of greater works. Calvinism, in short, was a narrowly specialized kind of religion, but it was also a peculiar religion – a religion which out-raged the imagination, and no doubt helped, therefore to produce the captivity of the imagination in Scotland which was only broken in the eighteenth century.[18]

His diagnosis of Scotland's inhibited imagination famously leads Muir to decide in *John Knox, Portrait of a Calvinist* that 'what Knox really did was to rob Scotland of all the benefits of the Renaissance'.[19] As late as 1980, Muir's former student George Mackay Brown was to leaf through the pages of this volume again, and writes to a friend: '[Knox] was a dreadful man altogether. How can fear and terror be so emphasized at the expense of charity and goodness and peace. I'm glad I didn't live in those bleak days ...'[20] Despite the fact that Brown's writing began to be published in the 1950s, and went far beyond the parameters of the 1920s and '30s 'Renaissance' moment and into a postmodern world, the 'Knox-ruined nation' – an idea he learned from Muir – remained lodged in Brown's imagination throughout his literary career.

But Brown was not alone in imagining Scottish culture to be historically menaced by a destructive, life-denying religion. Muir and MacDiarmid's view has been so powerfully persuasive that hostility to supposed Calvinist misery has utterly shaped the canon of Scottish writing. Many of the critics who diagnosed the diseased Calvinist imagination in the early twentieth century were themselves influential, canon-shaping cultural critics and literary historians. In her cultural essay 'Mrs Grundy in Scotland' (1936), the novelist Willa Muir notes that 'the Reformation was a kind of spiritual strychnine of which Scotland took an overdose'.[21] Alexander Scott, the poet and academic who was instrumental in establishing the first department of Scottish Literature at the University of Glasgow, also responds to Edwin Muir's suggestion that the Reformation was a miserable nursemaid to Scottish culture, stunting its growth from the offset. Muir's claim in 'Scotland 1941' that 'out of that desolation we were born' is taken to its logical conclusion in Scott's poem 'Calvinist Sang' (1949), where Scott notes sardonically that to survive in modern Scotland you need a heart and hands 'dour as the diamant, cauld as the starns'.[22] And Muir's view is also a clear influence on the poet and critic Tom Scott, who writes in his introduction to the *Penguin Book of Scottish Verse* (1970) that 'the seventeenth century [was] a poetic wasteland, few birds being heard to sing, although the jackdaw clacked loudly enough in the pulpit'.[23] Again, Scott borrows images from Muir's poem of absolute despair, 'Scotland 1941', particularly in his appropriation of the image of Calvinist clerics as sinister crows. It is in this poem that Muir first describes the 'rusty beak' of the covenanter Alexander 'hoodicrow' Peden.

The poetry of the Gaelic Renaissance is no kinder in its depiction of a frightening, fanatical Calvinist evangelism in the Highlands. In his 'Am Bodach-ròcais' ('The Scarecrow'), Ruaraidh MacThòmais (Derick Thomson, Professor of Celtic at Glasgow University) presents an almost gothic vision of the Highland minister – tall, thin and dressed in black. A chilling spectre, he drifts into a ceilidh house and ends a game of cards, halts a folktale so that the words freeze in the teller's lips and, the speaker tells us, 'took the goodness out of the music'. The gifts of this clerical scarecrow are 'fragments of the philosophy of Geneva' and a 'searing bonfire' in the breasts of the people of Lewis.[24] Along with poets including Iain

Crichton Smith and Sorley Maclean, MacThòmais (1921–2012) offers a searing portrait of Calvinist theology. This simultaneously spirit-chilling and hellfire-raising religion is the scandalously oppressive cause of cultural and spiritual decay in the Gàidhealtachd, from Lewis' mid-nineteenth-century Evangelicalism to the present day. In its alien philosophies of predestination and total depravity, this 'philosophy of Geneva' is notably foreign – an aggressive species of religion that has colonised and destroyed the formerly gentler devotions of Celtic Scotland.

Plenty of other influential criticism and poetry reflects Muir and MacDiarmid's view. Maurice Lindsay, one of Scotland's most prodigious cultural commentators, writes in his poem 'John Knox' that the reformer 'stripped windows with a fanatic's delight, / raved sermons to the baffled poor', and was, ultimately, 'a fiery terror and the Lord of War!'[25] This idea can also be traced in his groundbreaking *History of Scottish Literature* (1977). Here Lindsay argues that, though the sixteenth-century makar and creator of the masterful Reformation play *Ane Satyre of the Thrie Estaitis*, Sir David Lyndsay, 'had something in his temperament of that haranguing preacher's disease said to be endemic in every Scot', he at no time 'incited violence or advocated bigotry'. These are actions which Maurice Lindsay attributes very firmly to the Reformers, claiming: 'the distinction of approving violent tactics to help achieve allegedly desirably partisan ends belongs to Knox, Melville and their less celebrated heirs and successors'.[26] So Lindsay deftly identifies the Scottish character as rather miserable, clerical and prone to hellfire sermonising, while characterising the Reformers – the progenitors of these national characteristics – as vicious tyrants. It is little wonder that Kenneth D. Farrow has observed the discrepancy in the treatment of Reformation culture in writings by Scottish historians and literary critics of the early twentieth century. While the former 'have expended much ink and effort on the period', as far as a balanced picture of Knox is concerned, 'the Scottish literary critic has not proved himself quite as ready to follow suit'.[27] Knox, Melville and other Calvinist clergy haunt Scottish critical writings and poetry of the early twentieth century like eerie wraiths and menacing thugs.

But there are mitigating circumstances for this strongly negative strand in the work of 'Scottish Renaissance' critics and poets. The early decades of the new century were marked by post-war economic collapse, the decline of heavy industries and mass unemployment. A sense of powerlessness was inevitable, particularly because of the decline in Britain's imperial prestige, and war losses which were hardly compensated by declining markets, industrial action and extremely high levels of emigration. Social problems like sectarianism in industrial areas of the west coast of Scotland with historically high levels of Irish immigration were only intensified by mass unemployment and labour market discrimination. The Muir-MacDiarmid stance, reacting against entrenched anti-Catholic attitudes in Scotland, was perhaps refreshingly counter-cultural, representing a search for more humane values, and was received by Scottish artists as a convincing thesis for the supposedly broken tradition that Scotland had inherited in the Depression era.

Certainly, the weight of evidence for anti-Catholic feeling, Catholic disempowerment and explicit sectarian violence is overwhelming in the 1920s and '30s.[28] In 1921, the year of George Mackay Brown's birth, there were some 600,000 Catholics (many of them Irish-descended) in Scotland. This Catholic population was seen within the Church of Scotland to have 'most abominably abused the privileges which the Scottish people [had] given them'.[29] The 1918 Education Act, which permitted the state funding of Catholic schools in Scotland, was much despised for allowing the spread of 'propaganda' by the Catholic hierarchy, and Irish Catholic men were seen to be 'seducing innocent Scottish girls into mixed marriages, in which the girls were brought "to betray the faith of their fathers and also [to] betray their country"'.[30] Much has been written about the Church of Scotland's encouragement of ethno-religious bigotry in this period. Its report *The Menace of the Irish Race to Our Scottish Nationality* (1923) has received a good deal of attention, so shocking now is its depiction of impoverished Irish immigrants as an immoral, religious and criminal threat to the native Scottish population. But the Kirk was not alone in encouraging sectarian feeling, and it worked with other organisations against the Irish 'menace'. Anti-Catholic political parties attracted huge support in Scotland's central belt in the 1930s. Alexander Ratcliffe's Scottish Protestant League held meetings that were attended by Church of Scotland and United Free Church ministers. The anti-Catholic agitator John Cormack's party, Protestant Action, sparked anti-Catholic riots in Edinburgh in the spring and summer of 1935.

George Mackay Brown missed these riots, as he did not matriculate at Edinburgh University until 1956, but Brown did witness Cormack's public speeches during his student days. Though his 'influence had waned' in Edinburgh by the late 1950s, Cormack still preached sectarianism publicly, 'at the Mound, Edinburgh's open-air arena, [. . .] guarded by a bunch of toughs' (*FI*, 118–19). Brown writes in his autobiography that his Edinburgh landlady had been a member of the Women's Orange Order, but 'had left the order in anger and disgust when she heard McCormack's [sic] jeering remarks about a boat-load of Irish fisher-folk who had been drowned in a storm' (*FI*, 119). And Brown himself witnessed Cormack's 'long bitter sneer' and degrading remarks in a speech about Margaret Sinclair, a Poor Clare nun from Edinburgh whom many Catholics considered holy. He was later to reflect that, at the height of Cormack's popularity, 'It was the nearest Scotland ever came to Fascism, with Catholics instead of Jews as scapegoats' (*FI*, 119). Brown may have thought, as he felt his way towards conversion in 1950s Edinburgh, that Muir and MacDiarmid's diagnosis of cultural brokenness due to a fierce, violent Protestantism had real power. MacDiarmid's writing on this subject, like Muir's, is strongly persuasive:

From the Renaissance point of view the growth of Catholicism, and the influx of the Irish, are alike welcome, as undoing these accompaniments of the Reformation which have lain like a blight on Scottish arts and affairs [...] It is necessary to go back behind Burns to Dunbar and the Old Makars – great Catholic poets using the Vernacular, not for the pedestrian things to which it has latterly been confined, but for 'all the brave translunary things of great art' [...] There has been no religious poetry – expression of 'divine philosophy' – in Scotland since the Reformation. As a consequence Scotland is singularly destitute of aesthetic consciousness. The line of hope lies partially in re-Catholicization, partially in the exhaustion of Protestantism.[31]

MacDiarmid's cultural and political nationalism, which allied the greatness of Scotland's medieval art with its former status as an independent polity, would have been part of a galvanising and convincing call to conversion for Brown – especially in its inclusive acceptance of Irishness in the call for a new Scottish republic of 'diversity-in-unity'.[32] Even if Brown was not politically nationalist himself (he gave no hints of this in his writing and usually avoided political comment), MacDiarmid's argument would have had considerable strength in light of the sectarianism of Brown's Edinburgh surroundings. The barbarism of Reformation iconoclasm would have seemed all the more extreme to a writer interested in both his home islands' past, and in the pre-Reformation literature of Orkney – particularly the magnificent, compelling Icelandic sagas. In 1960, Brown confirms his outrage at the cultural effects of the Reformation in a letter to his friend, the Orkney historian Ernest Marwick. He writes, 'Last week I did a short story with an Orkney setting for the fourth centenary of the Reformation, in which of course the whole sordid conspiracy is shown up in repellent detail. I hope to get an X certificate for it – maybe a trial at the Old Bailey.'[33] Brown was received into the Catholic Church just over a year later.

The view of Scotland as the culturally bereft inheritor of a broken tradition due to the iconoclasm of the Reformers continues to be a dominant trait of more recent criticism. For Marshall Walker in *Scottish Literature Since 1707*, Calvinism is 'toxic'.[34] Carl MacDougall buys wholeheartedly into the Muir-MacDiarmid thesis when he writes, 'in early times our writers' imaginations soared with divine inspiration. But since the Reformation, literary flights of fancy have been darkened by Calvinism.'[35] Andrew O'Hagan, the author of a number of novels which are themselves shaped by his own Catholic imagination, writes: 'The great Calvinist effort to stamp out art would offer lessons to the Taliban [...] To make literary experience a kind of witchcraft, or something beyond the pale, something outside of the higher order of religious thinking has been a terrible legacy in Scotland.'[36] And perhaps most controversially, the composer James MacMillan's public remarks during his lecture ('Scotland's Shame') at the Edinburgh International Festival in 1999, in which he launched a searing attack on what he saw as Scotland's continued, endemic sectarianism, can be traced straight back to Muir's critical narrative. MacMillan faced a huge public and media outcry in response to his lecture. He later re-emphasised his belief that the Reformation was a 'cultural revolution' which 'involved a violent repudiation of art and music from which it could be argued that we have not fully recovered'.[37] But crucially, he also noted the influential critic whose poem had helped him form this view, claiming: 'The reasons for dismissal of artists is something that goes right back into the Scottish psyche and Scottish history. Edwin Muir, a great hero of mine, has written about this in his prose work and his poetry.' MacMillan responds directly to 'Scotland 1941', saying:

> [the poem] is regarded as a thing of genius, but only through gritted teeth [. . .] Muir has been maligned, both living and dead. He was someone who was willing to speak his mind and say uncomfortable things and say things that didn't fit with a self-gratifying, self-congratulatory, self-absolving view of Scottish identity.[38]

It is not the task of the present study to prove whether or not the Reformation was as scandalously damaging to the development of Renaissance humanism and subsequent Scottish art as MacMillan and his forebears have argued. But it is important to note that all of these arguably overwrought displays of distress about the state of Scottish cultural production today have their genesis in the incredibly persuasive but also highly negative writings of the early twentieth century. It is remarkable how much weight Muir's 'Scotland 1941' in particular continues to have in shaping the view of the nation's religious and artistic traditions.

Seeing pre-Reformation Scotland as a kind of independent zenith of literary creativity, and the ensuing centuries up until the eighteenth-century 'Vernacular Revival' as a wasteland marred by the strictures of Calvinism, has meant that, ironically, critics have occluded Catholic voices from the literary canon. Curiously, the first Renaissance in Scotland does something quite similar, as Sarah Dunnigan points out in her study of the censorship of pre-Reformation Scottish literary voices by subsequent canon-builders, editors and critics.[39] Dunnigan's is just one example of a much more balanced and finely textured number of works on Scottish culture and religion that have begun to emerge in very recent years. She argues that in order to create a strongly defined national literary heritage, or coherent cultural narrative of national identity, the two Scottish Renaissances both erase and remake Scotland in cultural and historical terms. In their identification of a tradition fractured by nagging Scottish puritanism in literary texts over the last four hundred and fifty years, Muir and the other critics of the twentieth-century Renaissance have reshaped history. The Scottish religious imagination, now broadly conceived to be Calvinistic, has become part of an essentialist version of Scottish identity, along with the use of 'Scots vernacular, unpretentious writing, patriotic themes, and a democratic viewpoint'.[40] Anti-Knoxism and hostility to Scottish Calvinism has come to define the religious imagination in Scottish literature, leaving very little room for works of a modern Protestant ethos or, ironically, of the Catholic imagination.

Crawford Gribben and David George Mullan's important study *Literature and the Scottish Reformation* (2009) has also reconsidered the relationships between literature and the Reformation period, allowing Protestant writers to be seen for the first time as the authors of cultural projects not suppressed by anti-art religious tyranny. Muir and MacDiarmid's critical narrative has, according to Gribben, 'achieved its worst success', and Knox has become 'a very necessary "other"', if not a cultural and historical villain of the worst kind.[41] Gribben argues that 'Scottish Studies still needs the "creative recovery" that will understand devotional or religious works as literature.'[42] However, this area of study also desperately needs the creative recovery of silenced and excluded Catholic voices in Scottish literature. These voices have been denied canonical recognition, and, just as with Protestant works, have been the victims of erasure from collective memory and critical writings. Catholic fiction has suffered even more neglect, as (despite its antagonistic relationship with Calvinism) Scotland's mostly Protestant tradition of literary criticism has until very recent times been reluctant, or unable, to recognise Catholicity.

The work of George Mackay Brown is a particularly useful exemplar of this critical erasure. While his writing attracts more and more in the way of public and critical admiration, he is still seen to be a quasi- or mock-Catholic writer of fiction and poetry. His own hostility to the Reformation has been acknowledged by several critics, including Alan Bold, who writes that 'the Reformers stalk like servants of the devil in [Brown's] poems and stories'.[43] However, Brown's convincing depictions of popular religion in the medieval period, where pagan elements of worship are gathered into Christian liturgical practice – as they were throughout Europe into the early modern period – have been misread as his own 'unorthodox' or confused Catholicism. Moreover, Brown's analogical view of the world (a recurrent feature of Catholic fiction, as we will see) has not been recognised, and this has led to puzzled commentary on his supposed interest in nature religions.

Proponents of the Muir-MacDiarmid thesis, so disappointed to see 'Scotland, cursed to cultural sleep by the bad fairy of Calvinism' but so eager to have her reawakened by the kiss of a 'Hibernian prince', failed to admit that many of the nation's most canonical texts have been produced by writers of Protestant formation.[44] William Drummond of Hawthornden, James Thomson, Robert Burns, Robert Louis Stevenson, Margaret Oliphant, George MacDonald, Nancy Brysson Morrison and, recently, James Robertson are all part of a literary tradition which is strongly influenced by Protestant theology and spirituality. Only the most stubborn of critics could accuse these writers' imaginations of being inhibited or creatively stunted. But the Scottish critical tradition has also been slow to recognise the bountiful fictive and poetic possibilities represented by the interaction of Catholic and Protestant literary imaginations. These imaginaries need not be seen as oppositional, aggressive enemies, but mutually enriching, artistically inspiring sites of interaction and exchange. Brown – the Presbyterian child and adult Catholic convert – may have argued that in the sixteenth century 'Knox brought all down in his wild hogmanay' (*CP*, 35). But perhaps only Brown, a writer committed to exploring his new faith within the craft of fiction and poetry, could see the opportunity for 'new ceremonies' in a future Scotland, after 'the crucifixion of the seed' (*CP*, 35). It is to the subject of Scotland's submerged Catholic fictions that this chapter will now turn.

III. Scottish Faithful Fictions: Literary Catholicism in a Calvinist Country

In his series of essays *The Sign of the Cross: Travels in Catholic Europe* (1995), the novelist and critic Colm Tóibín records his impressions of religion in modern Scotland. His essay 'The Language of the Tribe' sees Tóibín travelling to Glasgow, and viewing Scotland through the lens of ethno-religious tension and sectarian division in Northern Ireland. 'When I went to Glasgow in 1993 I carried with me all this baggage about conflict between Catholics and Protestants', writes Tóibín; 'my view of the place was profoundly affected by my experiences in Northern Ireland. It is possible that I asked all the wrong questions.'[45] Viewing Glasgow as a simulacra for the nation as a whole, Tóibín speaks to a number of journalists, academics and an unnamed Scottish poet. He then records his increasing astonishment at finding very few Catholic writers in Glasgow. One journalist mentions Muriel Spark's name when he is asked about Scottish Catholic writers, but Tóibín rejects this suggestion:

> She was a convert, I said, that was different. Do you mean, I asked him, that all of the writers, with their street credibility and their working-class heroes, are Protestants? Yes, he said. And do you mean, I went on, that no one has ever raised this matter? Correct, he said. And do you mean that most people do not think it is a significant fact? Correct, once more.[46]

Why Spark's convert status makes her 'different' is never really made clear by Tóibín. Regarded by her biographer Martin Stannard as one of the 'grand triumvirate of Catholic-convert novelists' in twentieth-century Britain along with Graham Greene and Evelyn Waugh, Spark is a fascinating example of a Scottish Catholic writer who exploits a cosmopolitan exchange between Calvinist and Catholic theology in her writing.[47] But she is not authentic enough for Tóibín. Spark is too complicated a writer: her Jewish father, Anglican mother, Edinburgh upbringing, conversion to Catholicism and international settings render her too complex to fit the desired mould. It is clear from 'The Language of the Tribe' that Tóibín longs to discover a small but industrious cult of Irish-derived Catholic writers, writing their essentialist version of Scottish (or Glaswegian) identity with a strongly pan-Celtic flavour:

> ... surely, I thought, there were stories to be told: the arrival of unskilled and unlettered men and women from Donegal in Ireland into this strange world of factory-work and mines and labour politics; the slow melting into Glasgow of these outsiders; the adherence to Celtic football club; the pub life of the city; the idea for the generation which benefited from free education that they belonged in the city and were outsiders at the same time. I could not understand why there were no Catholic writers in Scotland.[48]

No one is able to tell Tóibín during his visit to Glasgow that, in fact, these stories do exist. Their authors have written about popular piety, politics, social conditions and the cultural identity of the Irish in Scotland since at least the final decades of the nineteenth century. The pages of numerous magazines and newspapers tell the stories that Tóibín seeks to hear – most notably the *Glasgow Observer*, the newspaper of the Irish Catholic diaspora, established in 1885. This newspaper is one example of an outlet for Irish-Scots writers who composed popular poetry for a late-Victorian Irish migrant community interested in maintaining links with the culture of home, while exploring a new Scottish cultural and linguistic context.[49] However, these stories have only recently begun to be recovered in Scottish studies, and they are mostly confined to anthologies which are by now out of print, or remain within the pages of historical newspapers, so it is perhaps no real fault of Tóibín or his sources that Victorian Irish-Scots writers and their works are largely forgotten. But it is strange that the comparatively much better-known Patrick McGill (1890–1963), the 'navvy poet' of Donegal, escapes Tóibín's notice.

McGill's first three autobiographical novels of emigration and urban deprivation were hugely successful. The first, *Children of the Dead End* (1914), which dramatised McGill's own experience of nomadic labour in Kinlochleven, sold ten thousand copies in a fortnight in Britain and the USA, outstripping sales of Joyce's *Dubliners* that year (Joyce sold only 499 copies, and bought 120 of these himself).[50] The second novel, *The Rat Pit* (1915), picks up the tale of Norah Ryan, the young Donegal girl from *Children of the Dead End*. This novel details God-fearing Norah's descent into prostitution, and her early death in Glasgow. McGill's tales of poverty, injustice and socialism were enjoyed by a huge transatlantic readership which transcended religious denomination; George Mackay Brown writes that despite the lack of books in his childhood home in Orkney, McGill's novels 'impressed [his father] very much', as '[h]e was always on the side of the poor over the wealthy and over-privileged' (*FI*, 18).

Tóibín does not learn of these fictions, and so his exaggerated disappointment with the paucity of Catholic writers in Scotland remains. But his essay does point to a key element of the limited discussion concerning Catholic writing in Scotland to date – that it must surely be Irish-derived and dated exclusively from the mid-Victorian period. The only general study of modern Scottish Catholic writing in recent times is Patrick Reilly's very valuable article 'Catholics and Scottish Literature 1878–1978', which identifies three groups of Catholics interacting with Scottish writing: Scoto-Irish refugees from famine; Highlands and Islands Catholics; and converts (sensibly, given their immense contribution to Catholic writing). But Reilly's more generous, systematic approach to uncovering Scottish Catholic writing is still (arguably) simplistically Irish-centred. Reilly argues that '[t]he most crucial event in the history of the Catholic Church in modern Scotland occurred in Ireland', and he notes the Great Famine from 1845, and the subsequent Restoration of the Scottish Hierarchy from 1878 as the starting points for his discussion of Scottish faithful fictions.[51]

Although evaluations of Irishness in modern Scottish writing have added much to our understanding of the nation's literary heritage in the last two hundred years, Scottish Catholic writing should not solely be read as the product of Irish emigration, or as one and the same thing as Irish-Scots writing.[52] Woodman writes that 'Catholicism is a rich and complex system, and there are many different ways of being a Catholic'; this is no less true in Scotland than elsewhere.[53] Although the focus of this book is the twentieth century, it is worth tracing a very broad historical trajectory of devotional literature in Scotland – highlighting some key examples of texts which keep the Catholic tradition alive, particularly in the decades leading up to Brown's first published work in the 1950s – to demonstrate that Catholic writing is not simply confined to the peaks of Scotland's medievalism and nineteenth-century Irish emigration, while floundering in the troughs between. This new cartography of Catholic fictions in Scotland cannot be covered in any more than a very broad way here. The works of Brown's near-contemporaries in the early decades of the twentieth century will receive most attention, as they point to a newly energised Catholic literary network at this time. Nonetheless, this broad map adds detail to the barren cartography of MacDiarmid and Muir, and points to a fascinating story of faithful literature which has not readily been told by the Scottish critical tradition. Exploring this entirely understudied field of Scottish Catholic writing is an exciting new prospect. It opens up opportunities for a major revision and re-evaluation of the way that religion and Scottish literature have been considered in critical writings up to now.

The Triumph Tree, the virtuosic anthology of Scottish poetry from 550 to 1350, demonstrates that Catholic devotional writing existed in early medieval Scotland in a variety of languages – Latin, Welsh, Gaelic, Old English and Norse – and from a complex range of perspectives and poetic traditions. This anthology provides an incredible catalogue of true Celtic Christianity (rather than later nineteenth-century confections of Patrick

Geddes, William Sharp and other Celtic Revivalists) and sets out a powerful claim for the linguistic plurality of Scottish religious writing. Although the wealth of later medieval Scottish religious poetry does not match the size of English collections (it has been suggested that this corpus has been lessened by the effects of the Reformation), the cultural flowering of this period is undeniable, again with many languages – Older and Middle Scots, Norman French, Latin, Gaelic and Norse – all stitching threads in the tapestry of cultural production. The 'sophisticated, international outlook' of medieval Scotland drew strongly from European philosophy, poetry, romance and fable, to create what Alessandra Petrina calls 'the golden-age of a poetry-making community'.[54] The virtuosic poetic talents of the medieval makars Henryson, Dunbar and Douglas in an aureate high style, plain middle style and bawdy low style persuaded MacDiarmid that 'there has always been a considerable native Catholic population, and most of the finest elements in our traditions, in our literature, in our national history, come down from the days when Scotland was wholly Catholic'.[55] Conversely, the fact that the clergyman Dunbar was able to compose glorious, complex hymns of Marian veneration while also producing scatological bawdry would have fed the Reformers' idea of Catholic hypocrisy.

As we have seen, the Scottish critical tradition has often viewed the ensuing periods of Reformation and Renaissance through to the eighteenth century as literary wastelands, but this is simply not the case. Although a strikingly new Protestant purity of expression and form can be traced in the Reformed poetry of the mid-sixteenth century, Reformation did not strike all at once and break every tie with Scotland's Catholic past; rather it extended slowly over several decades. As Sarah Dunnigan points out, the religious allegory of the Catholic convert Alexander Montgomerie (1550s–1598), *The Cherrie and the Slae* (1597), is poised between the 'opaque, visionary world in which the dreamer learns to taste the healing, "merrie" consolations of the "Cherrie", perhaps emblematic of the Catholic faith – "Since for it onely thou but thirsts" – [and] the "poysond SLAE" of Reformed faith'.[56] Similarly, the Calvinist allegory *Ane Godlie Dreame* (1603) by Elizabeth Melville (1599–1631) proclaims the falsity of Catholic doctrine, but also 'recalls pre-Reformation, feminised visions of Christ'.[57] Dunnigan notes too that William Drummond of Hawthornden's (1585–1649) religious sonnets 'seem the poetic equivalent of the shadowed, sensuous flesh of European Baroque art', while medievalism and Petrarchism meet and coalesce in the love poetry of Jacobean court culture – notably in William Fowler's (1560–1612) *Tarantula of Love*, 'where a Protestant sensibility wrestles with the Catholic apotheosis of Petrarch's sequence'.[58]

It is not until a post-Union of the Crowns Scotland that a kind of Counter Reformation or anti-Reformation outlook can be discerned in the nation's literary production. This can be seen most forcefully in the Episcopalian, Jacobite and Scoto-Latinist Dr Archibald Pitcairne's bitingly satirical play *The Assembly* (1692), which takes aim at the General Assembly of the Church of Scotland and the hypocrisy of Scottish Presbyterianism – a theme that would be vigorously explored in Scottish poetry over the next century and beyond. Pitcairne's outlook was embodied in the first volume of James Watson's later *Choice Collection of Comic and Serious Scots Poems both Ancient and Modern* (1707). An Edinburgh printer and one of Pitcairne's circle, Watson was also a Catholic Jacobite. His *Choice Collection* was to become a seminal eighteenth-century poetic anthology, offering readers Scoto-Latinity, poetry in Scots and, notably, republication of Montgomerie's earlier *The Cherrie and the Slae*. Watson was part of an Edinburgh book culture that printed poets like John Dryden – another Catholic – and it can certainly be argued that this Catholic and Episcopalian book trade helped lead the way to the eighteenth-century 'Vernacular Revival', which was energised in 1710 by Thomas Ruddiman's republication of Gavin Douglas' *Eneados* (his translation of Virgil's *Aeneid* of 1513). The republication of *Eneados*, writes Leith Davies, was an attempt 'not only to assert [. . .] Jacobite sympathies but also to connect Scottish writing with the classical tradition in Europe'.[59] Indeed, the international reach and exchange that Scotland's Catholic writings exhibit, alongside their lively interaction with a society defined by the ideals of Presbyterianism and the coming Enlightenment, demonstrates that these Scottish faithful fictions have been an overlooked wellspring of creativity through the centuries.

A continuing story of Jacobite, anti-Unionist eighteenth-century poetry unfolds with the emergence of Allan Ramsay, Robert Fergusson, Alexander Ross, Alexander Geddes and, of course, Robert Burns. Ross and Geddes have been lost from this most canonical group of Scottish poets, but they are an important part of the story of Scotland's submerged Catholic literature. Ross (1699–1784) married a Catholic woman and produced the longest poem in Scots of the eighteenth century – *Helenore, or the Fortunate Shepherdess* (1768). Geddes (1737–1802), another vernacular language poet, was a Catholic priest. He published his translations of the psalms and the Bible for English Catholics, as well as translations of the satires of Horace, and a poetic sequence published in Latin and in support of the French Revolution. In 1792, the Scottish Society of Antiquaries published his *Three Scottish Poems with a Previous Dissertation on the Scoto-Saxon Dialect*. As Gerard Carruthers notes, '[t]he Tory, anti-Presbyterian, Jacobite sensibilities of Ramsay and Fergusson were increasingly "written out" by the nineteenth-century Scottish mentality that begins to see the apotheosis of the eighteenth-century Scots revival as the Presbyterian, peasant poet, Robert Burns'.[60] This mentality ensured that there was no room left for poets like Geddes, who still deserves extensive assessment and a seat at Scottish literature's canonical table.

Burns' own great ecumenical energy, which brings religious satire as well as the Stuart icon Mary Queen of Scots into his poetry, might be said to encourage the beginnings of the nineteenth-century interest in antiquarianism and Catholicity in Scottish culture. With the nineteenth century, a strong Catholic presence began to emerge in Scotland's literary culture. The reasons for this emergence included Irish immigration from 1845, but also, crucially, the historical novels of Sir Walter Scott. A favourite author of the great thinker, theologian and convert John Henry Newman, Scott undoubtedly contributed to a literary taste for gothic, neo-romance and medievalism, alongside the attractive and nostalgic vision of Catholicism that can be seen in later Pre-Raphaelitism. In 1839, six years before his conversion from Anglicanism to Catholicism, Newman – himself the author of two novels – was to write of Scott:

> During the first quarter of this century a great poet was raised in the North, who, whatever were his defects, has contributed by his works, in prose and verse, to prepare men for some closer and more practical approximation to Catholic truth.[61]

In this ringing endorsement, Newman virtually anoints Scott as one of the founders of the Oxford Movement – the small but tremendously important Catholic revival which reverberated in English literature for over one hundred years and of which he was a leading light. Certainly, many Tractarian members of the Movement – a great number of whom were converts and novelists – read Scott's works enthusiastically. Perhaps as a consequence, they 'looked with deep sympathy upon the Scottish Episcopal Church', which Scott had called 'the ancient but poor and suffering Episcopal Church'.[62] Indeed, Stewart J. Brown notes that in the collection of poetry *Lyra Apostolica* (1836), Newman described Scottish Episcopalians as 'our brethren of the North . . . cast forth to the chill mountain air'.[63]

In his discussion of Scotland and the Oxford Movement, Stewart J. Brown also reveals that despite the overwhelmingly Presbyterian nature of religious life in Scotland in the 1830s (between 85 and 90 per cent of the Scottish churchgoing population worshipped in Presbyterian churches), there were Tractarian priests in Scotland, and a movement that would result in the creation of eighty-eight new Episcopal churches between 1840 and 1860.[64] There were also high-profile conversions to Catholicism, most notably that of the landed aristocrat John Patrick Crichton-Stuart, 3rd Marquess of Bute (1847–1900). Crichton-Stuart's conversion was fictionalised in 1870 by Benjamin Disraeli, in *Lothair*, the first hugely successful novel written after his first term as Prime Minister. The hero of *Lothair*, like Bute, is a wealthy, orphaned Scottish aristocrat of Presbyterian background, who becomes increasingly drawn to the richly sensuous beauty of Catholic ritual. The novel's settings of London and the St Jerome family estate, Vauxe, mirror something of Bute's surroundings during his student years at Christ Church, Oxford. While the titular hero of *Lothair* comes close to conversion to Catholicism, he ultimately chooses the Church of England as his eventual spiritual home. Nonetheless, Bute's sensational conversion in 1868 is not to be underestimated in terms of its literary influence on Disraeli, and in its religious effect on others. In choosing

Rome, Bute opened the door to many other literary converts and tales of conversion. Compton Mackenzie's trilogy of conversion novels after his own reception into the Catholic Church in 1914 might well be considered relatives of Disraeli's novel about Bute, and of Newman's tale of conversion from Anglicanism to Catholicism, *Loss and Gain* (1848).[65]

Literary conversion should not be underestimated in its importance to the history of Scottish, English and other European Catholic literature. As Thomas Woodman notes, the late Victorian period was one which 'saw the most extreme refraction of Victorian aestheticism and the most exhibition-ist way of opposing bourgeois Victorian values, the *fin de siècle* movement'.[66] The 'attractively exotic and unpuritanical' Catholic Church appealed to, among others, the literary converts Aubrey Beardsley, Frederick Rolfe (who in 1889 was a student at Scots College in Rome) and, eventually, Oscar Wilde.[67] Wilde's friend (who was reputed to be the inspiration for *The Picture of Dorian Gray* and was presumed to be Wilde's lover), the poet John Gray (1866–1934), is most pertinent among this group to the history of Catholic writing in Scotland. His conversion in 1890 and training for the priesthood at Scots College, Rome led him eventually to serve as a priest in Edinburgh – first at St Patrick's Church in the Cowgate, and, from 1906, at St Peter's in Morningside, where he would remain for the rest of his life. Gray's last work, the futuristic fantasy novel *Park* (1932), details the strange pilgrim's progress of a priest, Mungo Park, whose name should point us to St Mungo, or St Kentigern, as well as to the Scottish explorer of West Africa of the same name. Park dies but awakes to find himself in a futuristic society, which is ruled by the Catholic Church and inhabited by a black hierarchy (the white population now live underground). *Park* is a deeply strange novel; as Richard Griffiths points out, 'though it has a religious theme, it does not seem to have a discernible message'.[68] But it is fascinatingly eccentric nonetheless, and is full of references and allusions to other Catholic works, liturgy and symbols of timeless Catholic beauty, which the novel strongly suggests will always survive the assaults of time. This idea is something that can be traced throughout the history of Catholic fiction in Scotland, perhaps because of what was seen as Scotland's uniquely ferocious Reformation. The image of the Church of Rome, battered and wounded, but ultimately triumphant in the face of erosion and neglect, has been a powerful thematic strand in this writing.

Concurrent with the decadent movement in Wilde's circle and beyond, the French Catholic literary revival of the late nineteenth and early twenti-eth centuries began to flourish. Developing out of the neoromantic forms of French literature which took aim at Enlightenment philosophy and the anti-clericalism of the French Revolution, writers including Georges Bernanos, François Mauriac, Léon Bloy and Charles Péguy used the symbolism and experience of Catholicism as part of a muscular theological critique of the decline of religion in modernity, and of the 'reigning ideology of bourgeois, materialist French society'.[69] The artistic alternative provided by these writers was the French Catholic novel, a genre in which David Lodge has traced the classic formula of 'the idea of the sinner "being at the heart of Christianity" (Péguy's phrase), the idea of "mystical substitution" [. . .], the implied criticism of materialism, [and] the tireless pursuit of the erring soul by God, "The Hound of Heaven" in Francis Thompson's famous metaphor'.[70] Also important, as Mark Bosco points out, is 'the conflict between the corrupt flesh and transcendent spirit, usually devised as sexual tension between male and female protagonists, ascending to a spiritual suffering that finds its reference in Christ's crucifixion'.[71] These novelistic ingredients can readily be found in the novels of the English converts Evelyn Waugh (especially in his *Brideshead Revisited* of 1945) and Graham Greene – an apt pupil of the French Catholic novel and of Mauriac in particular. Waugh and Greene's reactions against what they saw as the bourgeois, liberal values of 1930s England took on a similarly combative role to their French forebears, despite the different context of Catholicism as a minority religion in inter-war England. Indeed, while writers of the French Catholic novel reacted strongly against secularism, later English novelists of the Catholic imagination rebelled against their Protestant surroundings. While as converts, Waugh and Greene may not have been representative of ordinary, English cradle Catholics of the time, Woodman agrees that their work reveals 'the use of Catholicism as an ideological weapon against the status quo'.[72] In this respect, their writing and the work of other converts articulated 'even in exaggerated form, something of the experience of the whole community' of Catholics, who made up a small and embattled minority in England.[73]

The experience of Scottish convert writers of the 1920s and '30s makes for a fascinating comparison with these canonical authors of the golden age of English literary Catholicism. This chapter has already made reference to the novels of Patrick McGill, the Irish 'navvy poet' of Donegal who left Ireland to work in the potato fields of Ayrshire and then as a labourer, or navvy, on the Caledonian Railway. But quickly, and in tandem with the rise of the Muir-MacDiarmid thesis of Scotland's cultural brokenness, there emerged a number of new works, and literary converts, who began to write about the condition of Scotland and the place of Catholicism in it.

MacDiarmid and Muir's horror at the effects of Calvinism has already been covered here, but they did also attempt to create their own Catholic-sounding works. In the October 1922 edition of his magazine *Scottish Chapbook*, MacDiarmid published his 'Five Sonnets Illustrative of Neo-Catholic Tendencies in Contemporary Scottish Literature', including 'The Litany of the Blessed Virgin'.[74] In Muir's *Scottish Journey* (1935), he writes that the Catholic grotto of Carfin outside Motherwell (the creation of Canon Thomas Taylor in the 1920s) was 'the only palpable assertion of humanity that I came across in the midst of that blasted region'.[75] Muir's response to this grotto, a shrine constructed by unemployed miners and dedicated to Our Lady of Lourdes, is strikingly different to his writing about the other sites of Scotland's industrial heartlands. Muir finds Edinburgh a city divided between the bourgeois respectability of Princes Street and the 'mouldering and obnoxious ruin' of the Canongate.[76] Glasgow 'festers', and Muir condemns both Port Glasgow and Greenock, which 'comfortably stink and rot, two of the dirtiest and ugliest towns in Scotland', as well as Dundee – 'the dirtiest and ugliest of all'.[77] For Muir, the little grotto at Carfin is a beacon of gentle Marian devotion dramatically at odds with the mechanisation and grim industrialism of Depression-era Scotland. His later impressions of Marian devotion in his autobiography, and his poem 'The Annunciation' (discussed in Chapter 3 of this book) extend his appreciation of Mariology into something approaching crypto-Catholicism. In his reaction to Carfin, a site of devotion seemingly untouched by central belt industrialisation, Muir echoes something of contemporaneous English Catholic fictions, in which writers 'were repelled by the social dislocations and ugliness spawned by industrialism and appalled by the greed and materialism unleashed by unfettered capitalism'.[78] However, while for a writer like Waugh the antidote to the materialistic 'age of Hooper' lay in romanticising the English Catholic aristocracy and turning politically to the right, the mood in writings of the Scottish converts was quite different.

Returning momentarily to the discussion of Glasgow in Colm Tóibín's essay 'The Language of the Tribe' helps to account for the mood of Scotland's literary converts in the twentieth century's early decades. Alongside his lament that there are 'no Catholic writers in Scotland', Tóibín writes:

> Irish nationalism was constructed by writers as much as by politicians or revolutionaries; some of these – Yeats, for example, or Lady Gregory, or Synge – were Protestants but they had offered their power and support to a Catholic nation. In Northern Ireland writers like Brian Friel or Seamus Heaney, both Catholics, were essential aspects of the nationalist community's sense of itself, even when they did not write about politics. In the Republic, writers like Patrick Kavanagh and John McGahern had named our world for us. Maybe it was my problem: but I could not imagine coming from a nation, or a community or a place which did not have writers.[79]

Again, it would appear that no one is able to help Tóibín trace the strong connections between nationalism and conversion to Catholicism in interwar Scotland. There were many literary conversions in this period and it is striking just how many of the writers who turned to Rome were also writing revisionist histories of Scotland from a Catholic perspective, and becoming involved in nationalist politics. As Colin Kidd points out:

> since its formation in 1934 the SNP has been a party of poets and novelists, and so too were the organisations that preceded it – the Scots National Movement of the 1920s (led by the Celtic mythologist Lewis

Spence) and the National Party of Scotland, founded in 1928. [. . .] Literary figures contributed disproportionately to the electoral fortunes of the NPS. The nationalists' first major victory at the polls came in 1931 with the election of the novelist Compton Mackenzie by the student body as the rector of Glasgow University.[80]

Although Mackenzie (1883–1972) was born in West Hartlepool in England, he was fascinated by the Scotland of his ancestors from an early age – an attraction he attributed to reading Sir Walter Scott's history of Scotland for children, *Tales of a Grandfather* (1828). Though Mackenzie's best-known works are the comic *Whisky Galore* (1947), set on the Catholic Isle of Barra (where he lived from 1933), and *Monarch of the Glen* (1941), many of Mackenzie's other works reflect his desire to promote his twin passions, political nationalism and Catholicism, and his desire to prove Scotland as a Celtic, Catholic nation. As noted earlier, Mackenzie had converted in 1914 while on the island of Capri. His *Parson's Progress* trilogy details the conversion of the Anglican protagonist Mark Lidderdale over forty years, with him finally accepting the Church of Rome in the final instalment, *The Heavenly Ladder* (1924). But Mackenzie's passionately polemical, at times troublingly anti-Protestant, history *Catholicism and Scotland* (1936), published in Routledge's *Voice of Scotland* series (which also produced Muir's *Scottish Journey*), is of most relevance here.

Catholicism and Scotland is concerned to highlight Protestant interpretations of the country's history and culture which have (mistakenly) served to bolster the conception of Scotland as a Presbyterian nation. In common with much literary criticism of the time, Mackenzie reviles the Reformation and denigrates 'the crimes of the Reformers against beauty and decency'.[81] John Knox is Mackenzie's bitter target, and he is a figure of intolerable vanity, cowardice and hatefulness in this history. Mackenzie suggests that 'he spent his last days in the November of 1573, alternating between expressions of devotion to God and savage denunciations of his enemies', and he suggests, rather astonishingly, that Knox is now in hell.[82] By the end of his book, Mackenzie engenders the concerns that Colm Tóibín expresses sixty years later, writing: '[t]he Irish who settled in Scotland settled in a country which seemed to them to have surrendered what they had never surrendered – nationhood'.[83] Scotland is a poor and cowardly Celtic cousin to Ireland, then, and Mackenzie is depressed to report that 'the whole National Party of Scotland [is] believed by many to be no better than a sinister agent of Popery'.[84] Nonetheless, he ultimately concludes that it is more important for Scotland's vilified Catholics to remain true to their faith than to promote nationalist politics:

> Fortunately for his peace of mind, the Scottish Catholic knows that he can do his country no richer service than to devote all his energy, all his emotion, all his eloquence to upholding and spreading what he believes to be the only Truth that can guide man safely towards his

immortal destiny. The Real Presence of God upon her altars will be more precious to Scotland than the real presence of a Parliament in Edinburgh. The Scottish Catholic can afford to forget Bannockburn, will repine no more at Flodden or Pinkie Cleugh, and may count even Culloden well lost, if he reminds himself that no country's independence is worth winning unless it be won for the greater glory of God.[85]

The message here (familiar to us through Muir's work, though he was no nationalist) is that the scourge of English empire-building and industrialism has almost irreparably damaged Scotland. Mackenzie's solution – a reawakening of the nation's ancient, Celtic Catholicism – is shared by many of his contemporaries, including the converts Tom MacDonald (1906–75) and George Scott-Moncrieff (1910–74).

MacDonald's work was published under the *nom de plume* Fionn Mac Colla. He was raised in the evangelical Plymouth Brethren and, after undertaking missionary work in Palestine for the United Church of Scotland for three years, he converted to Catholicism in 1935. MacDonald felt strongly that the Presbyterian Kirk had betrayed Gaelic culture and removed the connection between Catholicism and nation-state that still existed in Ireland. He writes similarly anti-Protestant rhetoric to Mackenzie and, like Mackenzie, learned Gaelic, and moved to the Isle of Barra in 1946. In the introduction to his first novel, *The Albannach* (1932), he claims that 'Reformation Protestantism was not Christianity, or even a form of Christianity, but its almost complete antithesis'.[86] MacDonald notes that the novel's Catholic priest, Father O'Reilly, is based on a real-life clergyman whose photograph can be found in the seventh volume of Compton Mackenzie's autobiography, *My Life and Times*. Father O'Reilly, writes MacDonald, 'was the typical Catholic priest, his spirit unclouded by Jansenist or any other negations, the keynote of whose personality was joy and affirmation'.[87] It is clear then that MacDonald, the eager convert, is keen to stress Scottish and Irish Catholicism's lack of puritanism (a debatable point) in contrast to Scotland's dark and savage Calvinism. MacDonald's ideas – and particularly his fury over the injustice of the Highland Clearances – were expressed vociferously in one other novel, *And the Cock Crew* (1935), his novella *Scottish Noel* (1958) and a book of philosophical and (very) polemical essays entitled *At The Sign of the Clenched Fist* (1967). Like his close friend MacDiarmid, MacDonald chose a Celtic *nom de plume*. His adoption of the pen name Fionn Mac Colla – a Gaelicised version of Fionn MacCool, Celtic hero of the Fenian Cycle – also contained within it a reference to Alasdair Mac Colla Chiotaigh Mac Dhòmhnaill, the Catholic Highland warrior of the seventeenth century. It is no surprise then to learn that in his work the fiery Catholic prophet MacDonald zealously promoted Scottish Gaelic language and culture, Scottish nationalism and a return to Scotland's ancient Catholic faith.

With George Scott-Moncrieff, the author of another revisionist history of

Scotland from a convert's perspective (*The Mirror and the Cross: Scotland and the Catholic Faith,* published in 1960), the story of Catholicism and nationalism is related to that of Mackenzie and MacDonald, but it is rather more complex in timbre. Scott-Moncrieff came from a thoroughly Protestant background, but he was received into the Church in 1940 through the influence of his Orcadian wife Ann, née Shearer. In *The Mirror and the Cross,* Scott-Moncrieff recalls the anti-Catholic riots of 1930s Edinburgh and describes them vividly:

> I remember bitterly the horror of seeing human beings, largely adolescents and women of a disappointed mien, possessed beyond the reach of reason, screaming and rushing, ready for murder, upon the car in which Archbishop Andrew Joseph MacDonald drove up to the city chambers. Veneration of John Knox had once again inspired emulation of his tactics. This was 'protest' and as such it was the genesis of Protestantism. [. . .] it seemed to me then to exist only in distinction only as a negation, a protest against something that it did not appear even to wish to understand [. . .]
>
> I was not the only Protestant witness of those ugly scenes in the summer of 1935 who within a few years found himself no longer Protestant, having progressively discovered how much of the stock picture of my country's history was mere myth.[88]

Like Mackenzie, Scott-Moncrieff reacts against readings of Scottish culture and history which ratify its Protestant identity, and like MacDonald he sees something essentially life-denying and violently negative in Protestantism. Alongside Mackenzie, MacDonald and MacDiarmid, he also threw himself into nationalist politics, acting as election agent for the novelist Eric Linklater in his unsuccessful National Party of Scotland candidacy in the East Fife by-election of 1933. He was editor of the nationalist-leaning *New Alliance* magazine from 1939 to 1941.

In his writings – and especially in his remarkable novel *Death's Bright Shadow* (1949) – Scott-Moncrieff engages in intertextual Catholic literary borrowing in a rather more sophisticated way than, for example, MacDonald. *Death's Bright Shadow* is particularly notable for adapting the conventions of the French Catholic novel to a Scottish setting. As such, it is a curious mixture of the tropes used by Scott-Moncrieff's French co-religionists and predecessors with very late Scottish literary modernism (though the novel was published in 1949, it is set in the inter-war period, uses a good deal of Scots vocabulary and contains a Scots glossary). Moreover, it might not be too far of a stretch to suggest this novel's plot is based heavily on Scott-Moncrieff's own experience of grief after the death of his young wife, aged twenty-nine, in 1943. Ann Scott-Moncrieff was also a convert, a talented writer of children's books, and is remembered by her fellow Orcadian Edwin Muir as being something like Emily Brontë in terms of her literary skill and tragically early death. 'You are this unsettling star /

That shines unchanged in my eye', writes Muir in his poetic elegy for her.[89] Both Muir's poem and Scott-Moncrieff's novel look back fondly on their heroine laughing in the sunshine of Edinburgh's Princes Street.

Death's Bright Shadow details the spiritual progress towards conversion of its aristocratic protagonist, Robert Nisbet, who has fallen in love with a young Highland woman, Mairi MacSween. Before Robert is able to declare his love, he discovers that Mairi has died. News of her death reaches Robert via Ewan MacNish, a bohemian writer and the son of a distinguished Edinburgh judge. Ewan reveals that he too had been in love with Mairi, and that they had lived together during a tumultuous relationship. Mairi became pregnant, and at one point had an adulterous affair with a young lecturer at Edinburgh University. She suffered a miscarriage before her death, but not before resolving to return to her childhood faith, Catholicism. This decision filled Mairi with happiness, catalysing a kind of religious mysticism in her, and eventually it led Ewan to conversion. After hearing all of this, Robert Nisbet becomes increasingly fascinated by the faith of this young Catholic woman, and eventually he too is drawn to reception into the Catholic Church.

Scott-Moncrieff's novel recalls the preoccupation with sin, sex, adultery and faith in the works of Mauriac, Bloy et al., and, in fact, Mairi is just the kind of Catholic literary type to be found in their works. Not only does she dramatise the French Catholic theme of 'mystical substitution' – where a character is seen to be giving up their life, and even their salvation, for another – but she also embodies the 'woman as cross' archetype of much French Catholic fiction. Theodore P. Fraser notes that, '[a]s vessel of sin and salvation, the female is at the very heart of the drama of salvation presented in the fiction universe of these Catholic novelists. Woman thus combines the roles of seductress [. . .] and spiritual mother, whose capacity for suffering and redemption raises up all sinful creatures.'[90] This is a formula that can also be found in Greene's slightly later novel, *The End of the Affair* (1951). Indeed, while Greene's engagement with the ideas of the French Catholic Literary Revival has been discussed extensively in critical writings, it is certainly possible that he read Scott-Moncrieff's novel of Mairi, the adulterous but saintly female protagonist, before writing his own tale of Sarah Miles, the tragic, saintly heroine who is loved both by her husband, Henry, and her lover, Maurice Bendrix.

Scott-Moncrieff is surely also inspired by Waugh's *Brideshead Revisited* (1945). Waugh's characters are landed gentry, while Scott Moncrieff's are aristocratic Edinburgh lords and ladies – he even borrows Waugh's well-known phrase in describing the Scottish capital's 'bright young things' and their decadent, riotous behaviour. While in Waugh's novel, Lady Julia Flyte and the narrator, Charles Ryder, cannot be married because Julia realises that their mixed marriage (after her divorce) would be sinful, in *Death's Bright Shadow* Mairi initially refuses to marry Ewan because he is not a Catholic. Like Charles Ryder, Ewan and Robert's earthly love for a woman leads them to divine love of God, and by the end of the novel they are both converts. But this novel is not simply a derivative work where newly religious men are prevented from loving the women they desire. While *Death's Bright Shadow* borrows the French literary recipe of sin, sex and conversion, it is also a distinctive snapshot of the Scottish political climate in 1930s Edinburgh. Robert's upper-class friends meet in their club, a 'hotbed of nationalism', and discuss Communism, Calvinism and the nature of Scotland's religious history.[91] For once, there is some discussion of Calvinism that verges on the respectful, where Dr Ron Brown, a lecturer in English Literature, remarks: '"It's easy enough for people to attack Calvinism now: no doubt the Calvinist beliefs were absurd. But there were guts to them. [. . .] There was something robust and uncompromising about it."'[92] Unfortunately, by the end of the novel Ron has become an incoherent, murderous villain. But Scott-Moncrieff at least allows for some religious dialogue in the text, which is more than can be said for many of his contemporaries.

The most interesting part of *Death's Bright Shadow* for this study is its depiction of a specifically Highland Catholicism. It is certainly possible that this mirrors something of Scott-Moncrieff's own experience. After the death of Ann Scott-Moncrieff, in 1945 he moved with their three children to the Isle of Eigg, one of the small isles of Scotland with a Catholic population dating back to before the Reformation. In Scott-Moncrieff's novel, Robert goes to Mass in an old Highland chapel and finds that,

> Inside, it was very different from St Peter's in Edinburgh. The woodwork was unstained, the pews worn until the knots rose above the grain. Now there seemed too few of a congregation to wear them further. The walls were decorated with damp, and the oil-print Stations of the Cross were curled in their frames. The sanctuary was hung with faded reds and greens. Only the crucifix and the candlesticks gleamed with any freshness. Yet to Robert the whole occasion was tremendously impressive: the people kneeling throughout Mass, infinitely still and recollected. Mostly they were old, with fine lines to their faces, their dark thick clothes hanging from their shoulders, posed like draperies, and beads between the gnarled fingers of the hands before them. The priest was white-haired. He preached in Gaelic, his eyes gently resting on the remaining handful of his congregation, patiently, quietly exhorting them, to what end Robert could not tell, but he felt it was all true – it was bound to be true. And he thought, 'I never heard a sermon with which I agreed more deeply!'[93]

This small scene, depicting a native and almost painterly, 'exotic' Catholicism of the Gàidhealtachd, has much to tell us about Scott-Moncrieff's romantic vision of Scotland's ancient religion. In many ways tapping into the romantic nostalgia and vision of things lost that Waugh employs, here the scene is localised to the north of Scotland. The worshippers are old and the chapel is worn by formidable decay, but at the heart of this is a still-thriving, deeply felt devotion. Scott-Moncrieff focuses the form of worship in this Highland chapel through the lens of an outsider, in turn educating a non-Catholic, Scottish readership, whose services would be conducted in relatively una-dorned churches, their walls bare of images, with no stained-glass windows, no altars and no crucifixes. In fact, the colourfulness of Catholic worship and the mysteriousness of the Mass for the uninitiated are frequent motifs of Catholic fiction; Richard Griffiths notes that depictions of Catholic liturgy from this period often provide 'dramatic moments', which illustrate 'the heroism of the days of persecution' and evoke 'the eternal truths of a faith lasting from century to century. Explanations of the form that the Mass took could be used to contrast it with Protestant practices.'[94] Of course, another curious and alien feature of this religious celebration for Robert is the unfamiliarity of the language in which it is conducted. While the Mass itself would have been conducted in Latin – this being a scene of Tridentine worship before the Second Vatican Council (1962–5) heralded Mass in the vernacular – the sermon is read in Gaelic. And though Robert cannot commit to an intellectual conversion experience here, his imagina-tion is fired and his heart is touched. Even though this section of the novel comes long before Robert formally commits to his new faith, we see him experience a powerful spiritual conversion in the small Highland chapel.

Despite the undoubted romance of this scene, the tawdriness of the chapel's decoration also gestures to wider issues of class in Scott-Moncrieff's novel, and in English Catholic writing especially. Griffiths notes that 'tacky aesthetics' are a predominant feature of novels designed to explain the faith to non-Catholics in this period, and this led to a stress on 'the "bad taste" of popular objects of devotion'.[95] However, 'British Catholic novelists also took delight in pointing to the aristocratic nature of the Catholic reli-gion, as opposed to "middle-class" Anglicanism'.[96] Although the discussion of class is not much to be found in Scottish Catholic fictions of the time, it is certainly a feature of *Death's Bright Shadow*, with Robert's 'more English than Scots' Anglican stepmother complaining to him, '"You must admit, Fr Reilly is very vulgar. I know all priests are not like him. But in our Church you know where you are: and parsons are nearly always gentlemen.'[97] Scott-Moncrieff's convert, Robert, delights in his rather scandalous decision to become a Catholic. The 'garish church' which he attends in Edinburgh is filled with 'a posse of highly coloured statuettes', while '[t]he tabernacle bulged beneath sheeny flounces' and '[t]he Stations of the Cross were executed in almost unbearably high relief, richly coloured'.[98] This is no site of soaring Renaissance art, nor is it one of detailed medieval illumination. The gaudy aesthetics of Scottish popular devotion give Robert's well-bred, puritan eyes a thrill, while, at the same time, he is slightly disappointed by the un-mystical, down-to-earth priest from whom he receives instruction: '"Like a grocer", Robert thought.'[99]

Readers could be forgiven for thinking that Scottish Catholic fiction in the early decades of the twentieth century was made up entirely of polemical and newly zealous converts, who trashed Calvinism and gazed towards the Church of Rome with totally uncritical eyes. But this is not quite the full picture. With A. J. Cronin (1896–1981) and Bruce Marshall (1899–1987) we find two Catholic novelists who are more concerned with depicting the lives of everyday Catholics than they are with portraying the conversion experience, or re-evaluating Scottish religious history.

An alumnus of both St Aloysius College in Glasgow and the University of Glasgow (where he studied medicine), the cradle Catholic Cronin is largely forgotten now. If he is remembered at all, it is because he is the author of the Dr Finlay stories, which became the hugely popular, long-running BBC radio and television series *Dr Finlay's Casebook* (1962–71). The Catholicism of the Dr Finlay stories was largely written out of the television series, but in his novels Cronin often explores themes of faith, conscience and morality.

The problem of sectarianism – which Cronin experienced after marrying Agnes Gibson, whose family were Plymouth Brethren – can be found in his novel *The Keys of the Kingdom* (1942). This novel, which was filmed in Hollywood in 1944 and starred Gregory Peck, details the struggle of a Catholic priest, Father Francis Chisholm, to establish a mission in China. Like Cronin, Francis Chisholm is the child of a mixed marriage, and he suffers the effects of brutal religious bigotry in childhood. Early in the novel, the young Francis reflects:

> A hundred years before the Ettal moors had blossomed with the blood of Covenanters; and now the pendulum of oppression had relentlessly swung back. Under the leadership of the new Provost a furious religious persecution had recently arisen. Conventicles were formed, mass gatherings held in the Square, popular feelings whipped to a frenzy. When the violence of the mob broke loose, the few Catholics in the town were hounded from their homes, while all others in the district received solemn warnings not to show themselves upon the Ettal streets. [. . .] Francis flinched at his own thoughts and his small fists clenched violently. Why could not people let each other be? His father and his mother had not the same belief; yet they lived together, respecting each other, in perfect peace. [. . .] Like a blade thrust into the warmth of his life came a dread, a shrinking from that word 'religion', a chill bewilderment that men could hate each other for worshipping the same God with different words.[100]

His father is beaten to death by an anti-Catholic mob, and, while trying to lead him to safety, both he and Francis' mother die in a bridge collapse. Eventually Francis joins a seminary and goes to a mission in China. The novel looks on the mission systems critically, and takes a refreshingly generous view of both the atheist and Protestant characters who play a role in shaping Francis, who, as can be seen in the quotation above, displays clear-thinking compassion and a total lack of religious bigotry from an early age.

There is no blunt and unthinking praise of Cronin's Holy Mother Church in this novel; indeed, the message is ultimately one of a Christian open-mindedness, with respect for free thinking and tolerance. As he looks over his own life, Father Francis Chisholm finds himself grateful for the 'undue liberality' he has inherited from his Protestant grandfather. He ruminates on Catholicism, which, he thinks, 'has led [him] unfailingly to the source of all joy, of everlasting sweetness', and he ultimately concludes:

> My outlook has simplified, clarified with my advancing years. I've tied up, and neatly tucked away, all the complex, pettifogging little quirks of doctrine. Frankly, I can't believe that any of God's creatures will grill for all Eternity because of eating a mutton chop on Friday. If we have the fundamentals – love for God and our neighbour – surely we're all right. And isn't it time for the churches of the world to cease hating one another . . . and unite?[101]

In the midst of some of the more violently anti-Protestant writings of the early twentieth century in Scotland, this simple if somewhat sentimental plea is a refreshing one.

The novels of Bruce Marshall demonstrate another kind of Catholic writing again. Like Cronin, he was hugely prolific, writing more than forty books over a career which spanned seventy years. A convert to Catholicism in 1917, his comic novel *Father Malachy's Miracle: A Heavenly Story with an Earthly Meaning* (1931) is one of his best. The scant attention this satirical work has received has not been hugely positive; Griffiths calls it 'a strange mixture of sentimentality and silliness [. . .] twee and rather quaint', while Reilly calls it 'a disconcerting union of comic exuberance and dismissive contempt, the gusto consorting oddly with a biting mockery of human folly'.[102] But this is to miss the point. In his precise and even-handed swipes at different Christian traditions, narrow-minded notions of Scottish and British identity, and other novels – both Catholic and secular – Marshall displays a keen sense of *contemptus mundi* which anticipates the work of David Lodge.

Marshall's Father Malachy is a very different clergyman to Cronin's heroic, spirited Father Francis; there is little chance that Gregory Peck would play the part of Marshall's 'little old clergyman in a shabby black coat'.[103] In the novel, the Benedictine monk Father Malachy is sent to a parish in Edinburgh to instruct its parishioners and priest on the use of Gregorian chant. Father Malachy's Edinburgh parish is a world away from the thrilling, often-tropical and seedy terrain of 'Greeneland', with its themes of pursuit, betrayal, sin, grace and damnation, while Scott-Moncrieff's servant-owning baronets and ladies inhabit another Edinburgh entirely. As he sits on a train, Father Malachy muses on his new parishioners, and the experience of everyday Catholics, with all their mistakes, transgressions and misunderstandings:

He knew, and knew with gentle pity, all their follies: all their silly lust-ings in secret places, all their silly jazz and broadcastings and speed trials which made them think the Trinity such poor fun, all their silly interpretations of all the silly scientists which made them think the Trinity such poor geology, all their prideful belchings of opinion, all their imaginings that comfort was civilisation and sin a mediaeval name for taking away for a week-end an actress to whom you were not married, all their petty conceits, all their superstitious rationalisms.[104]

Father Malachy is troubled by the notion that people have become so involved with the petty trivialities of the everyday that they have forgotten to attend to the spiritual dimension of reality. He worries especially that people have become blind to the truly miraculous. However, Marshall's humble, comical little priest has his prayers for a miracle answered when a dance hall named the Garden of Eden is supernaturally transported from opposite his church to the Bass Rock in the Firth of Forth, making it Scotland's answer to the Holy House of Loreto. But unlike many of his fellow clergy, Malachy is not offended by this dance hall's 'indecency'. He is far more concerned to convert unbelievers and restore faith where it is lacking than to punish the Garden of Eden's clientele. Malachy's prayers are answered because of the grace granted for his unconditional faith. His devotion to God is neither dryly academic like the Rev. Humphrey Hamilton's, nor is his outlook rigidly judgemental like the Canon Collins'. His forgiving, artistic point of view leads him to see revelation as 'a beauti-ful poem which was, by the grace of God, true'.[105]

However, the miracle fails to truly evangelise Malachy's parishioners. It provokes cynical responses from those who 'wore a mental kilt and were all for Rabbie Burns whom they had never read and for the Church of Scotland which they never attended' that are similar to the blinkered reactions of the Catholic clergy.[106] Indeed, Malachy's clerical colleagues are often the target of this author's satire. When the Rev. Hamilton is seen reading a racy novel by the scandalous author Elinor Glyn, the Canon Collins and Fathers Neary and O'Flaherty, 'to whom any novel in which men and women made love competently was *anathema maranatha*, looked very grave'.[107] Marshall then skilfully redirects his satire at the authors of popular and sentimental Catholic Victorian piety, as both priests 'made a silent resolution to preach at the earliest opportunity on the folly of reading any book in which the characters did not all become Catholics on the last page'.[108] This little section is made funnier still by the knowledge, in retrospect, that in the works of possibly the most famous of Catholic novelists, Greene, characters make love frequently and more than competently. And in Waugh's *Brideshead Revisited*, one of the gold standards of Catholic fiction, Charles Ryder's genuflection on the last page signals his profound final capitulation to Christ, the 'Hound of Heaven'. Marshall good-naturedly satirises popular novels of

Victorian piety, but also anticipates future works of Catholic fiction in his non-partisan mockery.

Clearly, this history of Catholic writing in Scotland is male-dominated. It is true that women writers have been marginalised especially in early studies of the twentieth-century Scottish 'Renaissance' movement, though this has changed in recent years, as a fuller picture of the contribution of writers like Nan Shepherd and Willa Muir has begun to emerge. Alexander Moffat's painting *Poet's Pub* (1980), which includes MacDiarmid and George Mackay Brown, is a fitting exemplar of the apparently wholly male contribution to poetry during the first half of the century. But in the canon of Scottish Catholic writing, one figure towers above the rest in terms of the number and critical success of her faithful fictions, and this is Dame Muriel Spark (1918–2006).

Although Reilly includes converts in his account of Scottish literary Catholicism from 1878 to 1978, like Tóibín he does not allow Spark a place, arguing that she does not qualify for '"historical involvement", the writer's relevance to the experience of being a Scottish Catholic'. For Reilly, Spark simply does not dwell enough on 'the Scottish Catholic situation'.[109] Spark is frequently seen as problematic in discussions of Scottish literature and culture. Gerard Carruthers has noted the writer Robin Jenkins' attempts to categorise Spark as a 'cosmopolitan misfit'; he argues that Jenkins speaks as 'one entrapped by a predominant impulse in twentieth-century Scottish literature' – a 'vigorous nativism in expression', cultural nationalism, and prioritising of Scottish subject matter.[110] The intense scrutiny of Scotland's religious past, and the consequent use of Scottish settings, characters and political backdrops, has meant that the cosmopolitan Spark has been denied access to the male-centred Scottish literary canon of the first half of the twentieth century. Her work has instead been subsumed into a wider canon of Catholic fictions, and fruitful comparisons have been made between her novels and the writings of both Alice Thomas Ellis and Flannery O'Connor, both of whom share Spark's interest in questions of mortal sin and the operation of grace.

While Spark's work is mostly set in locations outside Scotland, her writing also displays a more complex engagement with Scottish literary traditions than essentialist critical notions of Scottishness would accept. In perhaps her most 'Scottish' novel, *The Prime of Miss Jean Brodie* (1961), Spark gleefully maps disrupted teleology against failed attempts at predestination by her titular heroine, who 'thinks she is Providence [. . .] she thinks she is the God of Calvin, she sees the beginning and the end'.[111] Still her best-known work, this comic but chilling novel uses prolepsis strikingly, to sabotage its own presentation of a coherent fictional world and thus demonstrate that God is the one great author. *The Prime of Miss Jean Brodie* tells us that our feeble attempts to predetermine our own paths do not allow for the (often unsettling) gift of supernatural grace.

Apart from its sustained theological critique of the limits of Calvinist predestination in 'dark heavy Edinburgh', the novel also subtly reflects on anti-Irishness in Scotland's capital in the 1930s.[112] As Liam McIlvanney points out, the text's (arguable) villain, Sandy Stranger, is struck by the poverty of the Old Town as she marches alongside her teacher and class-mates. McIlvanney writes:

> The streets which Spark names – The Canongate, The Grassmarket, The Lawnmarket – do not only betoken a 'misty region of crime and desperation': these are also the streets of Edinburgh's Irish ghetto. So when Sandy feels that she is in a 'foreign country', to some extent she is – she is in an Irish enclave.[113]

Sandy's powerful imagination – one nourished by the plethora of fictions created by her artful teacher – is hungry for religious *difference*. This small scene is not considered pivotal to Sandy's own conversion experience in critical writings, but it is part of the process of gradual conversion that Sandy undergoes. Sandy thirsts for religious rebellion against Calvinism early on, but because of her English mother's Anglicanism, 'nobody in her life, at home or at school, had ever spoken about Calvinism except as a joke that had once been taken seriously'.[114] Yet, 'it was the religion of Calvin of which Sandy felt deprived [. . .] She desired this birthright; something definite to reject.'[115] Over time, Sandy's imagination is fed by Miss Brodie on images as various as the *Mona Lisa*, the Lady of Shalott, Dante and Beatrice, and Botticelli's *Primavera*. The girl, who has a predisposition towards sto-rytelling and 'making patterns with facts', gradually adopts a religion of statues and images, stained glass and incense, and extracts the Catholicism of Brodie's one-time lover Teddy Lloyd 'as a pith from a husk', while at the same time rejecting Miss Brodie, the novel's justified sinner.[116] The child-hood walk through the Irish ghetto situates Spark's characters in a realistic 1930s Edinburgh, but it also helps to nurture the seed of rebellion in Sandy early on. She is not single-minded enough at this point to break free from the groupthink of Miss Brodie's *fascisti*, but – perhaps slightly thrilled – she trembles at the sight of the Irish in Scotland's historical capital. Like Scott-Moncrieff's convert Robert McNish, who also has an Anglican mother, Sandy adopts the religion of the Irish, delighting in her counter-cultural new faith. Sandy is a fitting example of literary conversion in early twenti-eth-century Scotland. The title of her own psychological religious treatise, *The Transfiguration of the Commonplace*, is an apt description of the Catholic literary imagination.

One final Scottish Catholic writer deserves consideration here, before this book turns to a fuller discussion of George Mackay Brown and the wide dimensions of his own Catholic imagination. This writer is George Friel (1910–75), who – with Brown and Spark – is one of Scotland's three great-est writers of short fiction in the modern period. Friel is a hugely neglected writer. He has received no place in mainstream studies of Catholic fiction, and receives barely a mention in general histories of Scottish literature.

But he is a wise, humane, funny author whose works reflect both life's potential for greyness and defeat, and the possibility for salvation and redemption. Brought up in a room-and-kitchen tenement flat in Glasgow's Maryhill Road, Friel was the fourth of seven children. His father came to Glasgow from Donegal in 1879, and Friel's works often contain characters of Irish extraction who live in the cramped surroundings of the Maryhill tenements. Friel was a great admirer of James Joyce and, as Gordon Jarvie observes, his manuscript drafts and notes outline his hopes for 'publishing a *Dubliners*-type collection of his own short stories of the 1930s'.[117] The Joycean influence can be seen in Friel's delight in wordplay in his novels *The Boy Who Wanted Peace* (1964), *Grace and Miss Partridge* (1969) and *Mr Alfred M.A.* (1972), as well as in his short stories, where Glasgow's dialect, violence, gossip, humour and petty criminality coalesce.

Like A. J. Cronin, Friel was a cradle Catholic, and his writing is not uncritical of both Church and clergy, particularly when compassion and sensitivity are necessary in the midst of bleak and squalid surroundings. His short stories 'A Marriage' and 'Father Twomey's Friday Night Dance' both reflect on poverty and an inflexible clergy's reaction to human weakness. But 'A Couple of Old Bigots' might be considered one of Friel's finest works. It focuses not on clerical failures, but on the failure and capacity of people to love one another. This short story is focalised mostly through the perspective of Geddes, 'a quarrelsome atheist', and his best friend Rooney, 'a practicing Catholic'.[118] Both are miners, and spend the years working together, and arguing (fairly) good-naturedly about their different theological positions. Rooney is not quite as waspishly shrewd as his free-thinking friend, but he is helped to reply with a zesty comeback on occasion by his little daughter, who, we are told, 'looked up perkily from her secondary school homework [. . .] and gave him advice'.[119] Rooney's daughter nicely illustrates the movement into the professional classes of Scottish Catholics with the sea change heralded by the 1918 Education Act, which brought Catholic education under free, comprehensive state control: we find out later in the story that the girl becomes a teacher, as Friel did.

However, the men become horribly estranged in their old age, as Geddes, 'with a good drink on him [. . .] dragged in the Virgin Mary and spoke of her with a coarseness he had never used before'.[120] For Rooney, this is hard to forgive. After denouncing Geddes' 'wicked blasphemy', he announces, '"You've went too far this time. You're just an old bigot, so you are. I'm finished wi' ye!'[121] Rooney dies in his sleep a week later, and his old friend is left to mourn silently, his macho terseness masking the deep grief he feels. When the Rooney family invite him to the funeral, Geddes finds the rites difficult to comprehend:

> He stood beside the grave while a chubby priest, talking Latin with a Donegal accent, said a lot of prayers he couldn't follow [. . .] Stuck on the edge of the dismal pit, he felt he was a white man taking part in the

rites of a black tribe. On the other side of the grave four of Rooney's unknown brothers, big men with heavy coats and dull faces, huddled together and their lips moved knowingly to the priest's last prayer.[122]

Far from the romance of Scott-Moncrieff's Highland Mass with its Gaelic sermon, this scene of mourning takes on a completely unfamiliar, ethno-religious dimension under Geddes' perspective. It is so different from Scottish Protestantism that Geddes finds the service alienating and awkward. But his love for Rooney prevails. Determined to fit in and grieve properly for his friend, Geddes makes the sign of the cross with the other men and, after remembering a phrase that Rooney had often used, 'he repeated it deliberately in a willing suspension of his disbelief. "God rest him," he mumbled.'[123] The story's final sentence is at once a realistic counterpoint to the potential Celtic romance of Catholicism in Scottish literature, and also a hint that grace has been bestowed on an old, recalcitrant man. Friel writes: 'The wind across the cemetery crested his white hair, slapped at the tails of his coat and chilled his old bones.'[124] Though Geddes leaves the graveside alone and lonely, there is a redemptive ending to this short story. Geddes' show of love is looked on with fondness by his creator, the architect of love itself.

What can this navigation through a swathe of faithful fictions tell us about Scottish Catholic writing? First, it is important to note that this trajectory has been far from exhaustive. The texts examined here are only a small selection from a much bigger corpus of writing. It is also important to state that this is a survey of a tradition that is far from homogenous. In drawing together the warp and weft of devotional literature in Scotland over the centuries, I have included Episcopalian and Jacobite writings, and works that could be called anti-Calvinist before they are considered Catholic. But a more inclusive view of Scotland's faithful fictions is necessary if we are to extend and reshape the discourse around the Catholic spirit of writing in Scottish literature. The cultivation of a more expansive understanding of Catholic writing in Scotland must draw together several literary voices who sometimes critique the Church of Rome, but often react against the dominant cultural (and sometimes anti-Catholic) attitudes of Presbyterianism and the Enlightenment.

However, a major theme that emerges when considering these texts is that their relationship with an overwhelmingly Protestant culture does not constrain them artistically. The writers discussed here have been energised, imaginatively stimulated and provoked by Reformed Christianity, for good or for ill. And, until some of the more aggressive forms of nativism in the early decades of the twentieth century, Scottish Catholic writing has borrowed, translated and augmented the ideas of religious writing from far beyond Scotland, making this a truly magpie fiction of emulation, engagement and exchange. The most obvious theme to emerge here has been the strength of the faith to survive Scotland's tempestuous history; this is something writers return to frequently across the centuries. Catholicism has been a storehouse of images for eyes eager for the ornate, decorative and colourful in Scotland. Medievalism and nostalgia are recurring motifs, as are reactions against modernity, secularism and notions of progress. But perhaps this is not surprising. Donat O'Donnell defines Catholic writers as 'time foreigners' who 'have a sense of exile, a feeling for being astray in modernity', while Marion Crowe writes:

> [e]ven if an attachment to an earlier period is not evident, some readers sense that the Catholic writer is judging the modern world in a medieval tribunal and failing to see it clearly. These tendencies often earn Catholic writers the epithet of *romantic* or *reactionary*. Sonnenfeld asserts that the distaste for their own period leads 'Catholic romantics to idealize the asceticism and self-mortification of the medieval monks' and believes that it was 'possibly perverse and reactionary nostalgia which made the Catholic Novel possible.'[125]

Of course, these epithets have been earned most frequently by Scotland's by now best-known (but little-understood) Catholic writer of the modern period, George Mackay Brown. To date, Brown has not been firmly situated within an international canon of Catholic writers who share these interests, but, alongside Sigrid Undset, Evelyn Waugh and J. R. R. Tolkien, his depictions of a historical Orkney mean that assessments of his work as backwards-looking, and his Catholicism as part of a rich historical – if parochial – backdrop are missing the point. It is rarely noted within the Scottish critical canon that Brown's concerns situate him very clearly within a wider twentieth-century tradition of Catholic apologetics and creative fiction, written especially by converts. Brown's use of the 1930s as (more or less) his most recent chronological setting and his frequent railing against the 'new religion, Progress, in which we all devoutly believe' (*OT*, 28) may lead his reader to the conclusion that he is a deeply conservative writer. His sources, 'the old stories, the old scrolls, the gathered legends, and the individual earth-rooted imagination' (*OT*, 30), are certainly not the stuff of new and experimental contemporary developments. But again, Brown is not alone in this regard, and in light of his unease with modernity, he can be viewed less as the solitary antiquarian of Orkney, and (more appropriately) as one of many writers who converted to Catholicism in the twentieth century, in Scotland, Britain and beyond. But before going on to explore the religious territory of Brown's imaginative world in Orkney, this chapter will offer a more cohesive idea of the terminology used to describe it. What is a 'Catholic imagination'?

IV. The Catholic Imagination in Literature: Some Definitions, with Reference to the Land and Seascapes of George Mackay Brown

In an interview with Isobel Murray in 1985, Brown's contemporary, the novelist Robin Jenkins (1912–2005), notes that the Jenkins family were 'pagans'. He then qualifies this claim by stating: 'Oh yes, we were Protestants! And I'm telling you they would have fought bitterly to get Protestant in front of that word pagan, which is astonishing.'[126] Published some eight years previously, Jenkins' novel *A Would-Be Saint* (1978) draws heavily on his own boyhood in the central belt of Depression-era Scotland, where the titular hero, Gavin Hamilton, is raised by 'protestant pagans' in the mould of Jenkins' own family. In his case, paganism does not indicate interest in nature religions (as it appears to when applied to Brown by his critics), but rather the absence of any formal and regular Christian worship. Nonetheless, Jenkins is eager to point out the family's keenness to be considered 'Protestant' pagans, or specifically (we might infer) non-Catholics. Notably, when the professed atheist Jenkins is asked about whether he ever investigated Catholicism alongside other denominations during his childhood, he replies, 'I never tried the Catholics. No, I did not! Because the Catholics were a breed apart ...'[127] For this author, like the later self-avowed 'Protestant atheist' James Kelman (who has inherited much from Jenkins as a writer of a modern Protestant sensibility), the world of Catholicism is profoundly other.

In Jenkins' *A Would-Be Saint*, the local minister, Mr Rutherford, ponders young Hamilton's intentions to join the clergy, and considers him to be

> a Christian, an over-zealous one at that, but like other ambitious young men entering the Church of Scotland ministry nowadays he had no patience with impossibilities like the Resurrection, the Virgin Birth, and other miracles. He saw Jesus Christ as a Great Example, which seemed to Mr Rutherford as rational an attitude as any.[128]

Hamilton, a 'lad o' pairts' familiar to readers of nineteenth-century Scottish 'Kailyard' fiction, is a Protestant success story – a clever boy of humble origins who, through hard work and determination, will receive a university education and deliver much back to the Presbyterian community which nurtured him. But Hamilton is also a 'would-be saint', and it is in his depiction of Hamilton's attempts at sanctity that his author reveals his own Protestant understanding of Sainthood. Hamilton is a believer, and though we are never allowed any insight into his religious devotion (we never witness him praying and there are no scenes of churchgoing or Bible-reading in the novel) we do know that he sees Christ as a 'Great Example', and that he views his vocation to ministry as a kind of useful social work. Jenkins' view of sanctity is shaped by the post-Reformation view of the saints as role models and good examples of faithfulness and virtue. For this reason, Jenkins avowed that the saints must surely have 'a tremendous amount of pride'.[129] It is in his ever-increasing pride that Hamilton becomes more saintly, and gradually set apart from his community in Jenkins' novel.

Hamilton could not be more different to the saints depicted in the fiction and poetry of George Mackay Brown. For Brown, the saints are far more than role models; they are God's holy intercessors, who can be approached for supernatural assistance as intermediaries to the divine. Indeed, in an article written late in life and defending the Catholic conception of sainthood, Brown describes the martyrdom of the Orcadian St Magnus as 'a poem', which 'went like a flame through all the northern parts of Europe'.[130] Sainthood for Brown is a sacramental activity – a creative act which makes the divine present – and a world away from the sensible behaviour of Jenkins' self-conscious do-gooder, Gavin Hamilton. Indeed, Hamilton is very similar to the modern ministers who Brown often gently satirises in his short fiction. Like Brown's couthily pragmatic 'Rev. Garry Waters', who believes miracles to be 'the exercise of a supreme common sense', and Christ to be 'the best organiser, the best planner who ever lived' (*TK*, 66), Jenkins' Gavin Hamilton is rational, ambitious, but ultimately rather unimaginative. While Jenkins does not understand his protagonist's solid commitment to his faith (noting, 'it's a wee bit difficult for me to see just what the fellow was after'), he still grudgingly admires it.[131] The narrative perspective in Brown's work would find Hamilton's religious perspective tragically lacking in mystery, and in poetry.

Brown's gently ironical view of this type of character versus Jenkins' puzzled respect for him begins to illustrate the dissimilarities in the religious sensibilities of these two Scottish contemporaries. Jenkins avowed, 'God has shown great signs to me that he doesn't give one damn about fellow man.'[132] But for a writer so keen to stress his lack of belief, his work is drenched in the language of faith – albeit a faith that differs in significant ways from his Catholic counterpart, Brown. Jenkins remained absolutely bellicose in his criticism of religion:

> If you're going to exasperate me, you'll bring forward some instance where God has involved people in some dreadful predicament, and then has released them from it. I immediately say, who the hell put them into it in the first place? Therefore I think God has got nothing whatsoever to do with love of humanity, and we are on our own as regards that, and we have to look at humanity's manifold crimes, which are far greater, as far as I can see, than its manifold kindnesses, and are far more dangerous. We are now in a situation where we can and I do think that we will destroy ourselves. I do think that deeply.[133]

Yet this avowal of disbelief still takes God seriously. While the God here is a Gnostic-sounding deity, who abandons his creations to suffering and sin (or 'crimes'), Jenkins' apocalyptic language betrays something of his formation as a God-fearing Protestant in the most traditional sense. His answers in this interview, and the landscape of fallen humanity seen in his work more generally, are indicative of a writer who cannot escape the biblical religion of his youth. Jenkins is not a writer imaginatively stunted by Scottish Calvinism; on the contrary, it allows him to creatively explore morality in the territory of a deceptive, fallen world.

Brown's imaginative territory (no better because it is Catholic) is quite simply different to Jenkins'. His work might be said to follow Flannery O'Connor's advice to the Catholic writer: to 'cherish the world at the same time you struggle to endure it'.[134] Brown's Orkney is no idyllic rural retreat from the harshness of Jenkins' post-war realist fictions. Many of his works linger on themes of alcoholism, bereavement, suffering and violence. And yet, the geography of Brown's fictional universe is far more hopeful than Jenkins'. Where Jenkins only ever reluctantly commits himself to the possibility of 'some kind of grace' (the name, incidentally, of his 1960 novel), Brown crafts a landscape of grace where redemption is always possible and encounters with the divine are not just conceivable, but frequent.

In his now definitive study, *The Analogical Imagination* (1981), the theologian David Tracy illuminates the differences between these two kinds of religious imagination. Tracy argues for two forms of religious expression – 'proclamation' and 'manifestation'. 'Proclamation' is a dialectical form of expression, which stresses the fallenness of the material world. Tracy finds that 'radical nonparticipation dominates' in biblical or Protestant proclamation theologies where the divine is radically other or separate to the world (as seen in the work of Robin Jenkins).[135] Conversely, in the more analogical expression of 'manifestation', 'a radical sense of participation predominates', and this understanding of the world, argues Tracy, is rooted in 'the exaltation of a fundamental trust, a wonder at the giftedness of life itself, a radical, universal, and finally incomprehensible grace, a pervasive sense of a God of love who is never an "inference" but an always-present reality to each and to all'.[136] In this kind of religious imagination – one in which creation contains and discloses something about the nature of God – the divine is close at hand.

Tracy's work is a rich source for the study of Catholic (and Protestant) literature, and it has been foundational for a number of cultural commentators – most notably the sociologist Andrew Greeley, who traces the analogical 'Catholic imagination' in film, architecture and fine art. His study *The Catholic Imagination* makes a statistical argument for the difference in work made by Catholic artists working in predominantly Protestant cultures, and in it he summarises the differences in Catholic and Protestant imaginations pithily:

> Catholic writers stress the nearness of God to His creation, the Protestant writers the distance between God and His creation; the Protestants emphasize the risk of superstition and idolatry, the Catholics the dangers of a creation in which God is only marginally present. Or, to put the matter in different terms, Catholics tend to accentuate the immanence of God, Protestants the transcendence of God.[137]

This concise definition nicely illuminates the fundamental difference between writers like Jenkins and Brown. It is the immanence of God that Brown remarks on so often in his letters to Sr Margaret Tournour. Even in the depths of a harsh Orkney winter, Brown reminds her: 'Soon the world will be full of light [. . .] soon there'll be a kind of Transfiguration.'[138] Tracy's (and Greeley's) understanding of Catholic artistic production does not confine this work to a narrow set of themes, plots or structures. Rather, their view of the analogical Catholic imagination – which can also appropriately be called sacramental in that it outwardly reveals the potential to bestow an inward grace – broadens the lens with which we can view Brown's work. Rather than a strange, Scottish 'pagan pape', Brown can be read as a Catholic writer who shares much in common with other artists whose imaginations are shaped by sacramental theology.

There has been a good deal of debate over the defining features of Catholic fiction in recent decades. Griffiths suggests that a Catholic novelist is one whose fiction 'could not be understood by a reader who had no knowledge of Catholicism and the particular obligations it entailed for its adherents'.[139] But this does not help to explain the sustained popularity of authors like Graham Greene, Evelyn Waugh and Muriel Spark. Marion Crowe justly criticises Albert Sonnenfeld's narrow definition, which makes salvation or damnation of the protagonist the decisive issue. She also notes Gene Kellog's claim, that the 'mainspring of dramatic action depends upon Roman Catholic theology', does not allow for more subtle and allusive ways of depicting a Catholic universe.[140] However, J. C. Whitehouse argues that '[t]he Catholic writer need not necessarily write about, except in the very widest sense, Catholic subject-matter or create Catholic characters [. . .] It is the underlying stance and imaginative viewpoint which is decisive here.'[141] This inclusive classification gestures most obviously towards Tracy's fruitful understanding of a 'Catholic imagination' – a guiding principle that the current book follows.

In Brown's work, celebrations of ritual and communal myth are access points to the reality of a world suffused with divine love, but these things are not the only routes to the numinous. God is made present by analogy far and wide in Brown's prose and poetry. For Brown, the world is a 'God-ordained web of creation', in which 'rhythms and images and legends are everywhere. To utter a name or a word is to set the whole web trembling.'[142] Consequently, in Brown's poetry his reader is faced – bombarded, even – with constant analogy: three bright daffodils 'shawled in radiance' become the three Marys, a 'triangle of grief' weeping at the foot of the cross (*CP*, 36). A crofter labouring in the fields becomes an Orcadian Christ, re-enacting the Stations of the Cross (*CP*, 178–9). And the poor parishioners in a pre-Reformation chapel are reminded by their priest that their immortal soul, 'a rich jewel indeed', links them to all creation, which 'rejoices in the marriage of Christ and His Church, animals, fish, plants, yea, the water, the wind, the earth, the fire, stars, the very smallest grains of dust that blow about your cornfields and your Kirkyards' (*TK*, 74–5). The Orkney historian Ernest Marwick noticed early on, without articulating the idea explicitly, that Brown's imagination was analogical. 'He discovered in the quiet countryside behind the town the wonder of grass and green corn almost as if it were a sacrament', writes Marwick.[143] Brown's work is permeated by a sacramental understanding of the universe; one that is utterly saturated in 'the Grandeur of God', and which contains Him, as David Tracy suggests.

This is perhaps no surprise to readers who know that Brown's creative imagination was fired by the poetry of Gerard Manley Hopkins throughout his life. Brown writes in his autobiography that Hopkins was 'the strange shy passionate tormented poet that I devoted myself to for two years at Edinburgh University' (*FI*, 156). And while the connection between their poetic outputs has been treated extensively elsewhere, it is worth remembering that it is the idea of art as sacrament which binds these two convert writers together most closely in artistic terms.[144] Brown writes:

> Where does it come from, that streams forever through the firmament and the world of nature with its endless variety of creatures, and maintains them and keeps them in their courses, and has a keeping of them always, beginning to end?
>
> It comes from God; the marvellous bounty comes from God and belongs to the glory of God: 'Glory be to God for dappled things ...'. Thus Hopkins and his shouts of joy. (*FI*, 152)

Like Hopkins, Brown's appreciation of and affection for the natural world borders on rapture, and, like his poetic predecessor, he finds that the 'dearest freshness deep-down things' reveal something about their maker.[145] In 1992, Brown writes to Sr Margaret Tournour: 'snowdrops, tulips, daffodils: their beauty stirs the dead spirit. And even now they are waiting under the storm-beaten earth.'[146] Like the corn that Brown observed growing and being cut down, before miraculously becoming 'resurrected' as bread for hungry folk, Orkney's spring flowers allude to the life, death and resurrection of Christ. And if the world can disclose something about God through simple flowers and the harvesting of crops, so can literature.

In his explanation of the creation-centred approach of Catholic artists, Greeley is keen to stress that under their perspective all things can confer grace. God's creativity is not something confined to the pages of Genesis – it is in the here and now:

> The Catholic imagination in all its many manifestations [. . .] tends to emphasize the metaphorical nature of creation. The objects, events, and persons of ordinary existence hint at the nature of God and indeed make God in some fashion present to us. God is sufficiently like creation that creation not only tells us something about God but, by so doing, also makes God present among us. Everything in creation, from the exploding cosmos to the whirling, dancing, and utterly mysterious quantum particles, discloses something about God and, in so doing, brings God among us.[147]

Brown's appreciation of the spiritual dimension of his surroundings, and his belief in the power of writing to make God present in the heart of the believer, illustrate Greeley's point well. Brown's land and seascapes reveal what he believes are the spiritual truths of grace, redemption and resurrection. This does not make Brown a pantheist or a pagan, but a writer powerfully expressing a profoundly Catholic trust in material reality. The same could well be said of Tom Tweedale, the factor in Brown's children's novel, *Pictures in the Cave* (1977). When faced with the gloomy parishioners who troop sullenly during sunny days to listen to the hellfire and brimstone sermons of their minister, Tweedale reprimands them: '"Look at the free clouds up there. Look at the sun and the huge blue sea. They're God's handiworks and he wants us to enjoy them. That's what I'm going to do anyway – I'll worship out here in "greenfields kirk".'[148] In this scene, Brown's narrative method can be compared very fruitfully with his contemporary, Muriel Spark. Ruth Whittaker points out that frequently Spark's characters 'either refuse to accept that everyday reality has a divine dimension, or they concentrate on isolating the spiritual, rejecting callously the material aspects of God's creation'.[149] But for Tweedale, as for his author Brown, and for Spark, grace is everywhere, and can be accessed through objects, materials and matter.

Nonetheless, as affirmative as examples of Catholic writing by Hopkins, Brown and Spark may be, there is no escaping the fact that overtly pious, sentimental and didactic works have been hallmarks of Catholic fiction from the late nineteenth century onwards, and that many readers feel as one reviewer for *The Month* did in 1874: '[a] bad novel is a bad novel . . . Trash is trash, in whatever form it presents itself, and Catholic trash is worst of all.'[150] Flannery O'Connor's admission that '[e]ver since there have been such things as novels, the world has been flooded with bad fiction for which the religious impulse has been responsible' is difficult to dispute, and this, combined with sophisticated secular (and religious) readerships has resulted in many authors avoiding religious themes or topics altogether.[151] Several Catholic writers of the twentieth century have faced the problem of appearing to proselytise, including Spark ('Mrs Spark returns again and again to thematic deceptions and conversions as she tries to deceive and convert us')[152] – and most famously Graham Greene, who ultimately rejected the label of 'Catholic writer', remarking: 'I would not claim to be a Catholic writer, but a writer who in four or five books took characters with Catholic ideas for his material.'[153] The desire for Catholic writers to avoid the charge of religious didacticism is then a common one, and their audience is sometimes hostile from the offset, as David Lodge explains:

In seeking to convey to his non-Catholic audience a technical and emotional understanding of Catholic experience, the Catholic novelist risks arousing in this audience whatever extraliterary objections and suspicions it entertains about the Catholic Church as an active, proselytizing institution; while on his own part he has to grapple with the problem of retaining his artistic integrity while belonging to a Church which has never accepted the individual's right to pursue intellectual and artistic truth in absolute freedom.[154]

These 'extraliterary suspicions' are notable in criticism of Brown regarding his depictions of pre-Reformation faith communities and individual belief. His writing process reflects his own anxiety over possible reactions to his Catholicism by critics, readers, the Church and the community in which he lived. Brown embeds Catholic material in a significant number of his unpublished writings and manuscript drafts, before softening this or removing it entirely in subsequent drafts and published versions of texts.[155] This is not surprising given criticism such as that of Berthold Schoene, who writes: '[Brown] surprises, if not startles, his readership with what initially looks like his one and only solution to all our problems: Catholicism.'[156] Alongside Brown's worry (which increased as he aged) about offending his readership, it is highly likely that this kind of criticism was a major factor in his creative process. It is also probable that Brown was aware of reviews, such as one of Nancy Brysson Morrison, which criticised her 'overt Christianity, [which], like Mackay Brown's [. . .] becomes intrusive and at odds with the real aesthetic shape of her work'.[157] But the fact that Brown was a Catholic writer should surely first indicate the nature of his religious belief, and not notions of his writing's aesthetic worth. Brown's admission in the last year of his life, that writing 'requires, sometimes, a little courage; especially at a time when it is not fashionable to mention the divine in connection with art', recognises that his critical climate was not always an understanding or friendly one for a writer of the Catholic imagination.[158]

The following chapters offer a re-evaluation of Brown and his Catholic literary sources that dispenses with the notion of the Catholic artist solely as propagandist. A fresh approach is necessary in order to offer a sustained biographical and literary-critical commentary on this Scottish author's constantly evolving body of prose, poetry and theatrical work, written over several decades. In order to offer a newly 'religious' perspective on this work, and to retrieve elements of its meaning within a larger Scottish aesthetic and religious design, this book navigates a route through selected texts in pursuit of highly defined Catholic influences and themes. This study takes in the entire scope of Brown's writing and is not committed to any single literary mode or genre in his corpus: novels, short stories and poetry will all be discussed. Manuscripts and correspondence are referenced throughout, to shed light on the place of Scottish Catholicism and a network of Scottish convert writers in Brown's writing process. The book also makes use of a 'ladder of love' structure, in that it begins by discussing the sacramentality of the word, or literature, with its hold over the creative imagination of Brown the Scottish Catholic artist, before moving to consider the intercessory powers of Mary the Mother of God, St Magnus the martyr and, finally, Christ, 'the Word' himself.

Notes

1. Ian Bell describes Brown as 'a monk at his devotions' in 'Breaking the Silence', p. 14. Letter of Brown to Sr Margaret Tournour, 17 July 1994, MFA. Sr Tournour was born in 1921, the same year as Brown. She was received into the Catholic Church in 1943 and became a novice in 1951, at Woldingham, in the Society of the Sacred Heart. See David Burnett, *Sister Margaret Tournour*.
2. Letters of Brown to Sr Margaret Tournour, 23 March 1995 and 5 November 1995, MFA.
3. See Maggie Fergusson, *George Mackay Brown: The Life*.
4. Schoene, Review of *Interrogation of Silence*, p. 131.
5. Brown, quoted in an undated essay by Ernest Walker Marwick, OLA D31/30/4.
6. Muir taught Brown at Newbattle Abbey College in Dalkeith from 1951 to 1952.
7. Gifford, 'Scottish Fiction Since 1945', p. 15.
8. Woodman, *Faithful Fictions*, p. xii.
9. Griffiths, *The Pen and the Cross*, p. 5.
10. Whitehouse, 'Catholic Writing: Some Basic Notions, Some Criticisms, and a Tentative Reply', p. 247. Sherry, 'The End of the Catholic Novel?', pp. 166, 173.
11. Muir, 'Scotland 1941', in *Collected Poems*, p. 97.
12. Schoene, *The Making of Orcadia*, p. 211.
13. Gifford, 'Renaissance and Revival', p. 2.
14. Moffat and Riach, *Arts of Resistance*, p. 100.
15. Dunn, 'The Poetry: "Finished Fragrance"', p. 38.
16. MacDiarmid, *The Raucle Tongue*, p. 55.
17. Muir, *John Knox: Portrait of a Calvinist*, pp. 307–8.
18. Ibid.
19. Ibid., p. 309.
20. Letter of Brown to Renée Simm, 24 September 1980, MFA.
21. Muir, 'Mrs Grundy in Scotland', in *Imagined Selves*, pp. 75–6.
22. Muir, 'Scotland 1941', in *Collected Poems*, p. 97. Scott, 'Calvinist Sang', in *The Edinburgh Book of Twentieth-Century Scottish Poetry*, p. 309.
23. Scott, 'Introduction', *The Penguin Book of Scottish Verse*, p. 42.
24. Thomson, 'The Scarecrow', in *The Edinburgh Book of Twentieth-Century Scottish Poetry*, p. 336.
25. Lindsay, 'John Knox', in *The Enemies of Love: Poems 1941–1945*, p. 14.
26. Lindsay, *History of Scottish Literature*, p. 71.
27. Farrow, *John Knox: Reformation Rhetoric and the Traditions of Scots Prose, 1490–1570*, p. 9.
28. For more on anti-Irish and anti-Calvinist attitudes in Scottish Literature, see McIlvanney, 'The Scottish Literary Renaissance and the Irish Invasion: Literary Attitudes to Irishness in Inter-War Scotland', pp. 77–89.
29. Rev. John Maclagan of Glasgow, quoted in Brown, '"Outside the Covenant": The Scottish Presbyterian Churches and Irish Immigration, 1922-1938', p. 19.
30. Rev. Duncan Cameron of Kilsyth, quoted in ibid., p. 20.

31. MacDiarmid, *Albyn*, p. 3, p. 4, p. 12.

32. Ibid., p. 4.

33. Letter of Brown to Ernest Marwick, 6 December 1960, OLA D31/30/4.

34. Walker, *Scottish Literature Since 1707*, p. 173.

35. MacDougall, *Writing Scotland*, p. 130.

36. Ibid, p. 148.

37. MacMillan, 'Scotland's Shame', p. 14.

38. Available at <http://www.heraldscotland.com/news/12508472. In_1999_Jam es_MacMillan_launched_a_furious_attack_on_anti_Catholic_bigotry_He_ha s_not_talked_to_the_Scottish_press_since_2000_Now_as_his_latest_work_pr emieres_in_New_York_the_composer_is_ready_to_speak_out_once_again/> (last accessed 24 February 2016).

39. Dunnigan, 'The Return of the Repressed', pp. 111–31.

40. Gribben and Mullan (eds), *Literature and the Scottish Reformation*, p. 2.

41. Ibid., pp. 4, 5.

42. C. R. A. Gribben, 'The Literary Cultures of the Scottish Reformation', p. 81.

43. Bold, *George Mackay Brown*, p. 11.

44. Reilly, 'Catholics and Scottish Literature 1878–1978', p. 184.

45. Tóibín, *The Sign of the Cross*, p. 134.

46. Ibid., p. 138.

47. Stannard, *Muriel Spark: The Biography*, p. xv.

48. Tóibín, *The Sign of The Cross*, p. 138.

49. Foremost among the poets and writers who contributed to the *Glasgow Observer* are John Luby of Bridgeton and James Lynch of Coatbridge, but many others – including Tom Burns, Thomas McMillan and Francis Joseph – write popular poetry for the Irish Catholic diaspora in the west coast of Scotland at the time. Their work reveals a preoccupation with social change, the religious life and tribulations of Catholic migrant communities, and Irish politics. Copies of the *Glasgow Observer* are held on microfilm by the Mitchell Library, Glasgow.

50. Deane, 'Extremes', pp. 12–14.

51. Reilly, 'Catholics and Scottish Literature 1878–1978', p. 183.

52. For more on the crosscurrents between Ireland and Scottish literature in the twentieth century, see McGonigal, O'Rourke and Whyte (eds), *Across the Water: Irishness in Modern Scottish Writing*.

53. Woodman, *Faithful Fictions*, p. xi.

54. Petrina, 'The Medieval Period', in *The Cambridge Companion to Scottish Literature*, edited by Carruthers and McIlvanney, p. 33.

55. MacDiarmid, *Albyn*, p. 29.

56. Dunnigan, 'Reformation and Renaissance', in *The Cambridge Companion to Scottish Literature*, edited by Carruthers and McIlvanney, p. 45.

57. Ibid.

58. Ibid., pp. 45, 48.

59. Davies, 'The Aftermath of Union', in *The Cambridge Companion to Scottish Literature*, edited by Carruthers and McIlvanney, p. 59.

60. Carruthers, *Scottish Literature*, p. 55.

61. Newman, *Essays Critical and Historical*, p. 267.

62. Brown, 'Scotland and the Oxford Movement', p. 56.

63. Quoted in Ibid.

64. Ibid., pp. 57, 63.
65. Mackenzie's conversion trilogy is made up of *The Altar Steps* (1922), *The Parson's Progress* (1923) and *The Heavenly Ladder* (1924).
66. Woodman, *Faithful Fictions*, p. 14.
67. Ibid.
68. Griffiths, *The Pen and the Cross*, p. 90.
69. Bosco, *Graham Greene's Catholic Imagination*, p. 7.
70. Lodge, Introduction to Mauriac's *The Viper's Tangle*, quoted in Fraser, *The Modern Catholic Novel in Europe*, p. xiv.
71. Bosco, *Graham Greene's Catholic Imagination*, p. 8.
72. Woodman, *Faithful Fictions*, p. xiii.
73. Ibid.
74. Grieve, 'Five Sonnets Illustrative of Neo-Catholic Tendencies in Contemporary Scottish Literature', pp. 74–6.
75. Muir, *Scottish Journey*, p. 170.
76. Ibid., p. 9.
77. Ibid., pp. 102, 164.
78. Crowe, *Aiming at Heaven, Getting the Earth*, p. 39.
79. Tóibín, *The Sign of the Cross*, p. 138.
80. Kidd, 'Scottish Independence: Literature and Nationalism'.
81. Mackenzie, *Catholicism and Scotland*, p. 44.
82. Ibid., p. 86.
83. Ibid., p. 185.
84. Ibid., p. 186.
85. Ibid., p. 188.
86. Mac Colla, *The Albannach*, p. iii.
87. Ibid., pp. vi–vii.
88. Scott-Moncrieff, *The Mirror and the Cross*, pp. 153–4.
89. Muir, 'For Ann Scott-Moncrieff (1914–1943)', in *Collected Poems*, p. 156.
90. Fraser, *The Modern Catholic Novel in Europe*, p. xviii.
91. Scott-Moncrieff, *Death's Bright Shadow*, p. 16.
92. Ibid., pp. 34–5.
93. Ibid., pp. 112–13.
94. Griffiths, *The Pen and the Cross*, p. 113.
95. Ibid., p. 102.
96. Ibid.
97. Scott-Moncrieff, *Death's Bright Shadow*, pp. 251–2.
98. Ibid., p. 234.
99. Ibid., p. 235.
100. Cronin, *The Keys of the Kingdom*, pp. 18–19.
101. Ibid., p. 275.
102. Griffiths, *The Pen and the Cross*, p. 76; Reilly, 'Catholics and Scottish Literature 1878–1978', p. 197.
103. Marshall, *Father Malachy's Miracle*, p. 1.
104. Ibid., p. 4.
105. Ibid., p. 36.
106. Ibid., p. 51.
107. Ibid., p. 106.
108. Ibid. Authors of such works in England include Emily Agnew, whose novel

Rome and the Abbey: A Tale of Conscience (1849) contains a number of Catholic teachings, delivered in rather saccharine style.

109. Reilly, 'Catholics and Scottish Literature 1878–1978', p. 183.
110. Carruthers, '"Fully to savour her position": Muriel Spark and Scottish Identity', pp. 488, 487.
111. Spark, *The Prime of Miss Jean Brodie*, p. 120.
112. Ibid., p. 111.
113. McIlvanney, 'The Scottish Literary Renaissance and the Irish Invasion: Literary Attitudes to Irishness in Inter-War Scotland', p. 77.
114. Spark, *The Prime of Miss Jean Brodie*, p. 108.
115. Ibid.
116. Ibid., pp. 72, 123.
117. Jarvie, Introduction to Friel, *A Friend of Humanity*, [n.p.].
118. Friel, 'A Couple of Old Bigots', in *A Friend of Humanity*, p. 191.
119. Ibid., p. 194.
120. Ibid., p. 195.
121. Ibid., p. 196.
122. Ibid., p. 198.
123. Ibid.
124. Ibid.
125. O'Donnell, *Maria Cross: Imaginative Patterns in a Group of Modern Catholic Writers*, p. 231; Crowe, *Aiming at Heaven, Getting the* Earth, pp. 17–18.
126. Murray, 'Robin Jenkins', p. 140.
127. Ibid., p. 105.
128. Jenkins, *A Would-Be Saint*, p. 159.
129. Murray, 'Robin Jenkins', p. 120.
130. Brown, 'The Magnus Miracles were Manifold', p. 14.
131. Murray, 'Robin Jenkins', pp. 120–1.
132. Ibid., p. 120.
133. Ibid.
134. O'Connor, *The Habit of Being*, p. 90.
135. Tracy, *The Analogical Imagination*, p. 203. Angela Alaimo O'Donnell has also written convincingly of the Calvinism of Emily Dickinson, which is not dissimilar to the angle of religious vision seen in Jenkins' work. O'Donnell notes that 'God's indifference to the world and the suffering of its creatures [. . .] is typical of the Puritan vision' seen in Dickinson's poetry. O'Donnell, 'Seeing Catholicly: Poetry and the Catholic Imagination', p. 331.
136. Tracy, *The Analogical Imagination*, pp. 203, 311.
137. Greeley, *The Catholic Imagination*, p. 5.
138. Letter of Brown to Sr Margaret Tournour, 7 March 1996, MFA.
139. Griffiths, *The Pen and the Cross*, p. 6.
140. Crowe, *Aiming at Heaven, Getting the Earth*, p. 24.
141. Whitehouse, 'Catholic Writing: Some Basic Notions, Some Criticisms, and a Tentative Reply', p. 243.
142. Brown, 'Writer's Shop', p. 23.
143. Marwick, *North* 7, p. 7, OLA D31/30/1.
144. For an extensive evaluation of the relationship between Brown's and Hopkins' work, see Schmid, *'Keeping the Sources Pure': The Making of George Mackay Brown*, pp. 121–215. Brown was not dedicated enough to produce a doctoral thesis

on the subject of inscape in Hopkins' poetry. He writes in his autobiography, 'Somewhere in a cupboard upstairs my Hopkins essays still lie in manuscript, unread for years, sheathed in cobwebs' (*FI*, 157–8), but these are not available in archives and, so far, appear to be lost.

145. Hopkins, 'God's Grandeur', in *The Major Works*, p. 128.
146. Letter of Brown to Sr Margaret Tournour, 5 January 1992, MFA.
147. Greeley, *The Catholic Imagination*, pp. 6–7.
148. Brown, *Pictures in the Cave*, p. 64.
149. Whittaker, *The Faith and Fiction of Muriel Spark*, p. 60.
150. Quoted in Griffiths, *The Pen and the Cross*, p. 26.
151. O'Connor, 'Novelist and Believer', in *Mystery and Manners*, p. 163.
152. Malin, 'The Deceptions of Muriel Spark', in *The Vision Obscured: Perceptions of Some Twentieth-Century Catholic Novelists*, edited by Friedman, p. 107.
153. Greene, quoted in Whitehouse, 'Catholic Writing: Some Basic Notions, Some Criticisms, and a Tentative Reply', p. 243.
154. Lodge, *The Novelist at the Crossroads and Other Essays on Fiction and Criticism*, pp. 88–9.
155. For a more detailed discussion of Brown's editing of Catholic material in the manuscript of his short story 'Celia', see Bicket, 'George Mackay Brown's "Celia": The Creative Conversion of a Catholic Heroine', pp. 167–82.
156. Schoene, *The Making of Orcadia*, p. 151.
157. Gifford, 'Scottish Fiction Since 1945', p. 17.
158. Brown, 'Tablet Essay' (1996), ms [n.p.], OLA D124/2/3/11.

CHAPTER 2

A Biography of Faith

In 2004, Berthold Schoene noted the 'scholarly neglect and even impending erasure' that threatened George Mackay Brown's critical reception.[1] It is remarkable that just over a decade later, Brown has come to be regarded as one of the great Scottish writers of the modern era. As already noted, Brown's place in the canon has been firmly established by a number of recent biographical studies, many of which deal with his personal relationships, struggles with alcohol and depression, and influence on other religious people, and so this book will not linger on these subjects in a detailed way. But a number of Brown's writings which display little-known aspects of his faith and its connection to his literary craft remain to be explored. In Brown's letters this connection can be seen best; in these, his maturation from critical young man to a mature and contemplative writer is revealed. The seapinks and stars that are scattered across Orkney's fields and skies are noted as signs of divine presence by Brown, while the hypocrisy and injustice he sees in human nature is, for him, evidence of the Fall. Brown's autobiography is another literary medium entirely, that constitutes defence, construction and literary mode suited to religious expression. After imbibing influence from figures as diverse as Newman, Francis Thompson and Lytton Strachey, the idea of fiction and poetry as 'a sacramental, a vehicle of grace for those disposed to receive it', results in Brown's own fresh interpretations of the faith, so that he too becomes a creator-figure, giving glory to God through his imaginatively created universe, and contributing to the process of evangelisation.[2]

This chapter will concentrate on three major biographical strands in order to obtain a clearer idea of Brown's literary Catholicism. It will focus particularly on his correspondence, left in archives and privately owned by his biographer. It will also discuss his autobiography, which we might call the 'authorised version' of his religious life, and it will look more broadly at spiritual autobiography written by Brown's contemporaries, to see how his own conversion narratives interact with theirs.

I. Childhood, Conversion and Lifelong Faith

In his study of Edwin Muir, George Marshall writes that despite Muir's mother's 'deep respect for religion', and his father's 'spontaneous piety', '[t]he family appear to have kept themselves slightly aloof from full commitment to church membership'.[3] Marshall notes that the United

Presbyterian Church in which Muir was reared on the Orkney island of Wyre 'cannot be characterised as oppressive either in faith or discipline'.[4] Four decades later, in the Brown household on Orkney's mainland, religious attitudes and family worship were not hugely different. Brown's mother, Mhairi Sheena (Mary-Jane) Mackay, overcame her qualms at working on the Sabbath when she left Sutherland for a job in the Stromness Hotel in her mid-teens. She had been raised in the Calvinism of the Free Presbyterian Church, but after marrying John Brown in 1910 their family worshipped in the Victoria Street church in Stromness. This was one of the town's three Presbyterian churches, which was founded in the United Presbyterian Church and then merged to become part of the United Free Church tradition.

Brown recalls in his autobiography that one of his father's great heroes was the founder of the Salvation Army, William Booth, but that 'he had no regard, in general, for minister or elders' (*FI*, 18). Brown has claimed, elsewhere, that although he languished during the weekly 'dreadful sermons' that 'seemed endless, eternity', his parents did not become members of their church, and, he said, 'my father didn't believe in christening or anything like that'.[5] Nonetheless, John Brown 'sang the hymns and psalms, full-throated, from the very back seat of the gallery', while Brown's mother passed her children a paper bag of sweets (*FI*, 18–19). It was into this environment, where Presbyterianism was observed but not adhered to devotedly, that Brown was raised. In his mid-teens he began to question why there should be so many divisions among churchgoers, and so many branches of faith, asking: '[w]hy were the followers of Christ so divided?' (*FI*, 50). As his interest in poetry developed in his teens, Brown soon became fascinated by Francis Thompson's poem 'The Hound of Heaven', in which Christ, the hound, pursued a Catholic – 'a very sad and weak and fallible one' (*FI*, 50). Soon, Brown began to worship in Stromness' Episcopal church, where he was put in charge of lighting candles.[6]

It has long been noted that Brown was reticent to discuss matters of faith publicly as his fame grew, and he confirms this in a late letter to Sr Margaret Tournour, writing, 'it's too much of a strain, being interviewed: especially on a delicate subject like belief.'[7] However, his early journalism is not nearly as self-censorial as his later 'Under Brinkie's Bray' and 'Letters from Hamnavoe' columns, which contain far gentler and less polemical reflections on life in Orkney. Brown's 'Islandman' columns and correspondence from the 1940s and '50s confirm that religious belief often occupied his thoughts. He wrote about religion frequently, and in rather more opinionated terms than in his later, mature correspondence.

Letters from Brown to Ernest Marwick from 1947 express his growing interest in Catholicism in less than sober terms; indeed, this correspondence is often more than a little irreverent, humorous and rascally. Brown writes on 11 May that he is reading Acts of the Apostles and notes, 'Saint Paul rather gets up my back, though he was a brave little soul.'[8] Referring

to an essay (that is presumably to be read aloud in public), he instructs
Marwick:

> I should like you to substitute 'Christ' for 'Our Lord', as it is very pos-
> sible that the audience will not be a devout one, and might regard the
> latter designation as a piece of insufferable presumption. I will risk
> letting them think that the whole thing is a religious tract.[9]

As this passage indicates, there is a definite feeling of Brown's separation
from the Protestant Kirk in these early letters. He is often playful and
even haughty in his rejection of the community's religious worship. In an
undated letter to Marwick, he encloses a description, which he calls 'very
sharp and satirical', of the village of Dounby:

> Now has agricultural ugliness found its deadest expression, in this
> flat village. Flat fields, flat souls, flat houses. From the three parishes
> flock here all the deniers of life, the humbugs, the money-grubbers.
> [. . .] An ugly flat kirk is their latest marvel, where ugly flat hymns are
> flatly and hideously sung and ugly flat sermons preached by a money-
> grubbing and life-denying doctor. Flat and ugly as paddocks they are.
> Flat earth, flat sky. O Lord, one might pray, make them round, fecund,
> jolly! Even the beer is flat.[10]

This satirical passage, though more than a little insulting, was clearly
intended to amuse Marwick in private. But Brown was controversial in print
too, and his journalistic style is frequently combative and cantankerous in
this period. A reader of his *Orkney Herald* column castigates Brown in 1955
for his insensitive response to a newspaper strike. Brown's response is not
at all repentant; he later admitted that he was surprised by his '"peculiar
and perverse gift [. . .] of being able to sneer at people"' in his column.[11]
But hidden among Brown's peevish response, in which he claims he 'is
not really sorry' for his insensitivity, there is an interesting nod towards his
growing interest in Catholic worship. Brown writes: 'As for the newspapers
being sanctuaries, I wonder whereabouts in the "Daily Mirror" or the "Daily
Express" they keep their stained glass windows, their altars and their holy
water. I prefer to do my worshipping in other places.'[12] Indeed, Brown's
'Island Diary' column often hints at his interest in Catholic rite and aesthetics, as well as broader religious matters. Throughout the 1950s there are
references in this column to religious discussions with Jehovah's Witnesses
(he calls their religion a 'mild and inoffensive one compared to some of
the tooth-and-claw sects that write Love in letters of blood'), and a note that
Brown has attended Mass in a Catholic church during a visit to Armadale.[13]
Brown discusses the evangelical preacher Billy Graham's upcoming trip
to Scotland more than once, but decides ultimately that he 'mistrusts' this
'mass emotionalist'.[14]

Brown's growing antipathy to Calvinism (and something of the literary
sneer mentioned above) takes on a comical timbre again in one of his

earliest, unpublished poems. The poem is entitled 'Kirk Elder'. It is dated
March 1943 – meaning that Brown was twenty-one years old:

> Observe him on his way to church –
> The pious plainness of his dress;
> A haloed bowler on his head;
> His face alive with holiness.
>
> He worships at the shrine of love,
> Whose shrunken soul is mean with hate:
> Opens his wallet with an air
> And slaps a pound note in the plate.
>
> O demons of the judgement day
> Hedge him and guard him well,
> This puissant prince, and flag him through
> The shouting gates of Hell.[15]

Bombastically anti-Calvinist and certainly less than subtle, it is clear that
this is an early attempt at poetry by the young Brown, who inserts himself
into a long-established Scottish poetic tradition of religious satire in his
youthful and bitter swipe at the Orcadian Holy Willie. While certainly not
one of his best, this poem reflects Brown's dislike of the pious and sanctimonious members of a small Presbyterian community. Brown was intensely
self-conscious about his own scoundrel status at this point in his life. The
tuberculosis which prevented him from entering the army in the Second
World War, and which kept him at home in his mother's care, meant that he
became highly sensitive to community disapproval. This was not helped by
his frequent drinking bouts (funded by National Assistance money) in the
bars of Stromness. These often led to Brown being taken to his doorstep, or,
he wrote, 'dumped inside like a sack of potatoes'. When on one occasion
he was taken home in a police van, his mother was incensed by the ensuing
local gossip, commenting, 'They'll say anything but their prayers' (*FI*, 68).

However paranoid and subsequently disparaging about Calvinist judgement he was privately in his early poetry, though, Brown had no difficulty
in remaining great friends with people of deep Calvinistic faith. One of
these was Peter Esson, the Stromness tailor and librarian. A Free Kirk elder,
Esson revered his Church 'with a deep devotion', and in his writing Brown
tenderly acknowledges the 'earnestness and veneration' of Esson's faith.[16]
Clearly, Esson was a very different kind of Kirk elder to the man in Brown's
early poem of the same name. In the 1959 collection *Loaves and Fishes*, a
sonnet celebrates the life of Esson in the wake of his death. This later poem
shows the evolution from scorn to a very real respect regarding Calvinism
in Brown's work:

> The Free Kirk cleaves gray houses – Peter's ark
> Freighted for heaven, galeblown with psalm and prayer.

The predestined needle quivered on the mark.
The wheel spun true. The seventieth rock was near.

Peter, I mourned. Early on Monday last
There came a wave and stood above your mast. (*CP*, 18)

As in much of Brown's poetry, in this poem the image of a Church is transformed into a great ship, sailing throughout time. Peter Esson's ark is one
that will meet a predestined end and it shares its imagery with the kirk in
Brown's most anthologised poem, 'Hamnavoe', which is also 'freighted for
heaven' (*CP*, 25). The movement from parody to respectful memorialisa-
tion is clear here.

Along with Peter Esson, Brown became friends with Robert Rendall
(1898–1967), the Orkney dialect poet who belonged to Ernest Marwick's
circle of friends. Brown referred to him in his autobiography as 'a theologian of that strict Evangelical sect called Plymouth Brethren' (*FI*, 75).
He committed a chapter of *An Orkney Tapestry* (1969) to a description
of Rendall, whom he very much admired, despite his reservations over
Rendall's religious convictions. In 1954, Brown writes to Ernest Marwick
that there has been some difficulty in the collation of poems for his first
poetry collection, *The Storm*, and that Robert Rendall objects to one poem
in particular 'about the orra-man who was "saved"'. In his letter, he writes:

> More than once [Rendall] has earnestly entreated me to modify it, or
> better still omit it all together: neither of which things I am prepared
> to do, seeing that I have lately improved it and tightened it and made
> a presentable poem of it.
>   Originally it began like this:
> When Peter, orraman at Quoys
> Joined the Pentecostals
> They dipped him in the sea ...

[Rendall] objected to the second line. On reflection I did too, but for
quite a different reason, and I changed it to this:

> Was 'saved' by hell-fire evangelists.

Up came RR, from the Herald office, waving a proof sheet in the air,
and saying it would never do; if anything, it was worse than before.

> I suppose the whole thing is really trivial and amusing. I don't want
> to hurt Robert's feelings, but then one must make a stand somewhere,
> and I don't feel disposed to weaken the structure of my poem merely
> to save the feelings of a group of life-denying schismatics. What will I
> do? I would welcome your views on this matter.[17]

Ultimately Brown compromised, as the published poem's second line
was changed, becoming: 'Was "saved" by Pentecostals' (*CP*, 13), meaning
that the line retains a sense of scepticism regarding evangelicalism, while

eschewing the potentially unflattering 'hell-fire' description. As with 'Kirk Elder', a poem that may well have upset Peter Esson had it seen the light of publication, this poem is modified in light of Rendall's religious objections. While Brown could reject certain religious ideologies and satirise them harshly in print, he could not do the same to his friends, and his work and writing process reflect this conflict.

As he recovered from a bout of tuberculosis in Eastbank Sanatorium in 1953, Brown had plenty of time to think carefully about different Christian traditions. He was certainly catered for in pastoral terms during his fifteen months of convalescence, and would have had time to discuss religion with the clergymen who visited the wards. The hospital setting also provided him with a good deal of material for later short stories, and seems to have been a rich source for his creative imagination. He wrote to a variety of friends during his stay at the sanatorium. One of these was Flora MacArthur, who had been secretary at Newbattle Abbey College when Brown studied there under Edwin Muir. Brown writes to her affectionately, signing one letter: 'Here endeth today's sermon by Father George Brown'. In his letters, he describes the hospital's grim daily routine of injections, medications and examinations, but also its religious life:

> There's a great lot of religion in this hospital. Every week a Presbyterian minister comes round and talks a lot of mealy-mouthed platitudes. Occasionally the Episcopalian minister comes, with an eternal grin of delight on his face (a nice man though). The priest comes frequently, and smokes and talks about T. S. Eliot. Some days we get the Salvation Army on the veranda, storming the gates of paradise with brazen clamour and nearly bursting my ear-drums in the process.[18]

This reference to the priest may appear casual, but he is given the highest accolade possible at this stage in Brown's life – an interest in Eliot's poetry. This early experience of a visiting clergyman interested in one of Brown's literary idols would have delighted Brown in his isolation, and would perhaps have appealed to his early sense of the Catholic imagination as intimately connected to the arts. Indeed, the experience of different Christian traditions and the differences in their pastors may well have fed into the later 'A Treading of the Grapes', from *A Time to Keep* (1969). In this story, the narrator meditates on the ruins of a pre-Reformation church in Orkney. He subsequently discovers the records of three very different sermons preached on the theme of the wedding at Cana, given by a present-day, rather couthy Church of Scotland minister, an eighteenth-century Calvinist preacher, and a mystical-sounding pre-Reformation priest, who makes full use of his sacramental imagination in his words to the faithful at Mass.

As 'A Treading of the Grapes' indicates, Brown was still able to use the experience of listening to spiritually uninspiring, 'mealy-mouthed platitudes' creatively. Similarly, evangelical Christianity seems to have allowed Brown to take part in the hospital's religious life, and it provided another wellspring of imagery, characters and plots. Brown writes to Marwick from the sanatorium, '[t]here was a Salvation Army lass up preaching to us today [. . .] It was quite simple and sincere. I gave my bad lung some much-needed exercise bawling rag-time hymns.'[19] This vignette can also be traced in 'The Eye of the Hurricane', another short story from *A Time to Keep*. Here, Barclay – a Catholic writer – is fascinated by Miriam, a young woman who is a member of the Salvation Army. Despite her distrust of Catholicism, she is ultimately the only truly altruistic and devout character of the story, and tells Barclay: "You should come to our Joy Hour some Thursday evening. There's choruses and readings from the Good Book, and O, everybody's so happy!" Her eyes drifted uneasily over the crucifix and the Virgin' (*TK*, 154). 'The Eye of the Hurricane' ends with a view of Miriam, filled with the grace granted for her unconditional faith in God and for her acts of Christian charity: '"*Will your anchor hold in the storms of life?*" the songsters chanted. Miriam rattled her tambourine among the shining trumpets. The big drum thudded at her side. Her face was radiant under the street lamps' (*TK*, 181). This short story, along with Brown's writing about friends like Peter Esson and Robert Rendall, reflects his admiration for religious conviction that was genuine, sincere and life-embracing. And, along with a number of other works, this text demonstrates the care with which Brown hoarded the scant creative treasures he was given during long periods of recuperation.

Brown was eventually discharged from Eastbank in 1954. During his time at the University of Edinburgh (1956–60), he was still hesitant to commit entirely to conversion, but, nonetheless, he began to go to Mass every week at the Catholic chaplaincy in George Square. Fergusson notes that Brown 'also had regular meetings with Father Barrett, a Jesuit, in Lauriston Place, though whether he was receiving formal instruction is not clear'.[20] However, by June 1960, Brown's thinking had clarified, and he announced the news of his conversion in letters to friends. He writes to Ian MacArthur, 'I'm receiving instruction [. . .] with a view to being received into the true original kirk of Scotland. Poor Scotland! All her woes began when she forsook the light.'[21] He expresses this rather more tactfully in a letter to Marwick, whose wife Brown describes in his autobiography as 'a devout Anglican' (*FI*, 76), and notes, 'Best wishes to Janette. Tell her I've gone to a priest at last, and am receiving instruction.'[22] Although Brown's life appeared to change very little after his reception into the Catholic Church on Christmas Eve 1961, he felt that aspects of it were enriched and renewed. In 1964, he writes to Stella Cartwright, 'Dear Stella, I'm always thinking about you and praying too. [. . .] If only you were a Catholic! At least it would give you firm ground under your feet. At best it would show you a great many things shot through with a new beauty.'[23]

From the evidence of Brown's correspondence throughout the 1970s, however, his newly adopted faith was not all affirmation and strength. Brown was pessimistic about the state of Scotland in the months before the failed Scottish devolution referendum and general election of 1979. He writes despondently to his friend Renée Simm, 'I hope you are well and happy in this cold time. Cold not only weatherwise, but politically and industrially: a cold bitter greed devouring the nation's spirit.'[24] Brown's gloominess about his own spiritual state is often palpable in this correspondence. He reveals: 'I am very much off colour, both physically and mentally (and spiritually, too, if it comes to that)' and 'to a large extent my faith has evaporated too …'[25] Brown occasionally consoles himself by uniting his suffering with others in the world – a gesture which points to the ancient devotional practice of entering into Christ's suffering as a gift to God. He writes, during a period of illness:

> My 'lung fluid' is long in drying up: added to which there are black depressions, during which life seems utterly drained of beauty and wisdom and delight. To experience these things is to participate in humanity: to take a share of the world's suffering on one's shoulders.[26]

But physical frailty, ill-health and depression were not the only difficulties that Brown faced as his fame grew and he became an increasingly successful author during the 1970s and '80s. Often, during these years, Brown laments his status as a kind of Orcadian tourist product, and he writes in 1981: '[o]ne begins to feel like a peepshow'.[27] He was visited constantly by tourists and aspiring young writers, and mentions a desire to live a more contemplative life like a monk in Pluscarden Abbey with striking frequency in letters to various friends.[28]

Nonetheless, from the evidence of his correspondence from the late 1980s, Brown's outlook began to improve. He unburdened himself about his depression in letters to a GP in London, Dr Michael Curtis, and this relationship seems to have provided Brown with an outlet for some of his more morbid and frightening feelings of guilt and despair. There was no pressure on Brown to discuss his health with Dr Curtis face to face, and so the highly confidential, almost anonymous nature of this correspondence is likely to have provided him with comfort, security and friendship.[29] It was in 1986 that Brown met the young artist Kenna Crawford, and this relationship – though platonic and conducted mostly by letter – seems to have utterly reinvigorated Brown. He often writes to Crawford in these years to thank her for providing him with inspiration, happiness and creative encouragement.[30]

Most significantly, the 'feeble flicker' of Brown's faith was stoked considerably during the last decade of his life. His letters to Sr Margaret Tournour clearly indicate an intimate, cherished correspondence, in which Brown sounds far less weary than he did in previous years. Like Sr Tournour, Brown found that creativity helped him to bear physical pain and depression: he writes, 'The main release is writing. I put down some good words on paper, as if to compensate for the malfunctions of the flesh. So the imagination fights her battles.'[31] In a letter written to Sr Tournour in

February 1993, there is a real sense of Brown's caution and frailty in old age, but this is touched by affection for the natural world that borders on rapture:

> Yesterday was such a lovely afternoon, though the north wind was cold, that I ventured along the street: a thing I rarely do. A few people were complaining about the wintry weather: something seems to have gone wrong with some people's aesthetic sense, for it was a day to rejoice the heart, with blue sky and clean cold air . . . There are 3 swans on the sea just below me; they've been there for weeks; they drift along the waterfront getting bread and scraps here and there.[32]

Brown's focus in his late letters is still fixed on his Orcadian surroundings, but rather than the bitter or satirical swipes of his youthful observances, here there is a clear-eyed and compassionate view of the world. His writing is infused with a sense of the spiritual value of the changing seasons and shifting weather. Grace is not only conferred through the intervention of a priest during the Mass, but by interaction with all of creation, which has a sacramental potential. People, birds, winds, flurries of snow, night skies and the patterns of agriculture fascinate Brown in his old age. His illnesses trouble him and he is still harassed during summer months by tourists and ambitious young writers, but he retains a more developed sacramental perspective than was in evidence during his youth, and he delights in it. On Maundy Thursday 1992, Brown is pleased that 'the daffodils dance and the birds are at their songs', while a few months later, in July, he tells Sr Tournour that he has recently finished a novel – possibly *Vinland* (1992), or *Beside the Ocean of Time* (1994). He adds that he is 'always giving forth a song or two like a bird – alas, not with such joy and purity'. But, Brown notes, 'truly, I love writing, and would have much the poorer life if I couldn't do it'.[33] There are also a great number of references to Brown's prayer life in these late letters to Sr Tournour. He writes about the changing seasons frequently, musing: '[June] is most beautiful. One feels the stirrings of a Gloria – the darkness is only a few shadows round about midnight.'[34] He mentions frequently that he can hardly believe that he has lived so long and that he is grateful for his creativity.

Brown had come a long way from the cynical young man who was disgusted by religious life in Orkney. These late letters show an acute awareness of sacramentality, of the divine in the ordinary, and of the wholly graceful in the everyday. Brown's faith was not always steady and sure-footed, and perhaps this was part of the reason that he avoided becoming embroiled in theological debate, declaring 'the way of argument and reason were not for me' in his posthumously published autobiography (*FI*, 55). But his letters offer a hugely valuable, intimate glimpse of his unique personality and lifelong trajectory of religious opinion. Conversely, the 'authorised version' of conversion that Brown offers in his autobiography presents quite another side to his literary Catholicism

– one that is far more rhetorical and crafted for consumption by his reading public.

II. Spiritual Autobiography: Writing the Self and Statements of Belief

In an interview with Isobel Murray and Bob Tait in 1984, Murray asks Brown if he has ever thought of writing anything autobiographical. He answers, 'No, no fear. Oh no', and then laughs.[35] Murray betrays, perhaps, her instinct that Brown's life may not have been particularly eventful or interesting in Orkney, where she ventures, 'I don't think one has to have a particularly varied or exciting life to write a fine autobiography.'[36] Brown answers:

> GMB: No certainly not [. . .] But I don't know, I think a lot of autobi-
> ographies are very distorted, they're all concerned to put themselves
> in a good light, and I think they nearly all must be distorted unless
> they're a good artist like [Edwin] Muir, you know, who can see himself
> objectively.
> [. . .]
> IM: So you're fairly determined to keep your own self as tucked away
> as the ballad maker or the skald, or whatever.
> GMB: Yes, I won't be writing any autobiographies.[37]

In fact, Brown's answers in this interview concealed the fact that he had been considering writing an autobiography for decades, and his interest in this creative endeavour was growing. As early as 1966, Brown writes to Charles Senior, 'I'm trying my hand at a light-hearted autobiography. If the first few fragments go alright I'll continue with it.'[38] In 1993, he writes to Sr Margaret Tournour: '[l]ast Saturday I picked up the MS of an autobiogra-phy I wrote for fun ten years ago. it [sic] was so very badly written I bundled it away for a while. (it won't be published, anyway, in my lifetime.)'[39] There is no archival evidence of this first, very early attempt at autobiography by Brown from the 1960s, but the manuscript that he mentions to Sr Margaret undoubtedly forms the basis for the posthumously published *For the Islands I Sing* (1997), which Brown claims in the text's appendix was written in 1985, making its date of composition one year after the interview with Murray and Tait.

Structurally, *For the Islands I Sing* draws together Orkney's geography and history; the marriage of Brown's parents; his childhood and later life in Orkney; and adulthood in Dalkeith, Edinburgh, and Orkney again. It concludes with Brown's final corrections and revisions, signalled by an appendix that is added and dated November 1993. This autobiographical bricolage demonstrates that 'the process of selection and interpretation, especially in autobiography, where narrative design and historical truth very soon come into conflict, necessarily involves "the unconscious polem-ics of memory"'.[40] Brown's interpretation of Orkney's history is just that

– his own interpretation – while the recounting of his parents' courtship and marriage has a distinctly literary flavour and cannot possibly be the recounting of memory, as he was born several years later. The depiction of Brown's childhood, too, depends on his recollection of his mother's memories, and the time Brown spent studying at Newbattle Abbey College in Dalkeith under Edwin Muir takes the form of an 'impressionistic essay'.

Brian and Rowena Murray describe *For the Islands I Sing* as 'a treasury of information and stimulus whose poetic treatment of themes is illustrated by the excellent acrostic poems that break up the prose ...'[41] But this could well be an evaluation of semi-fictional works like *An Orkney Tapestry* (1969), *Portrait of Orkney* (1988) or *Northern Lights: A Poet's Sources* (1999), and seems a strange summation of autobiography. Should a *life* include a 'poetic treatment of themes' or creative work that disrupts the recounting of events and memories? Tellingly, the Murrays also write that the autobiography 'fills in some of the gaps of our knowledge of Brown, but his reticence will raise new questions for some readers'.[42] It is probable that most, if not all, readers will be left with questions after the conclusion of *For the Islands I Sing*. Although it includes a section on conversion, there is no mention of how this was received in Orkney by Brown's family or by the community at large. Moreover, Brown's caginess extends, at times, to plain untruths. He writes, 'I never fell in love with anybody, and no woman ever fell in love with me' (*FI*, 79).[43] Brown's deep discretion in this work draws attention to the construction and rhetorical underpinning of autobiography as a literary mode, and in particular as a place of constructing the self and the subject's relationship with God.

This is not to suggest that readers always take autobiography to be a literal transcription of events. As Avrom Fleishman notes, autobiography today 'welcomes displays of fictionality, artfulness, and even tailoring of the facts in behalf of skilled performance in an autobiographical role'.[44] William Spengemann identifies that the genre has moved from a historical mode in the Middle Ages and Enlightenment, to a philosophical mode in the late eighteenth and early nineteenth centuries, culminating finally in a 'poetic' form in the nineteenth century onwards, in which 'the self is seen to depend for its existence upon the "verbal action" which therefore describes its own poetic creation'.[45] Brown's readers are thus complicit in his construction of autobiographical artifice, particularly regarding the text's conversion narrative, which is an expanded version of a well-documented essay by the writer, and which also echoes in some of his short fiction.

Augustine's *Confessions* is still regarded as the original model for autobiography in the West. He is often called the first spiritual autobiographer, despite his utilisation of earlier traditions and sources, including the letters of St Paul, the psalms, the philosophical meditations of Marcus Aurelius, and Christian hagiography.[46] The *Confessions* relies upon 'intertextuality [. . .] upon other texts and upon literary conventions', while the story of Augustine's conversion 'involves a complex chain of conversion-narratives'.[47] In the same way, Newman's spiritual autobiography *Apologia pro vita sua* (1864) is indebted to Augustine's *Confessions*, while evangelical self-writing (and Newman's *Apologia*) of the mid-nineteenth century is indebted to John Bunyan's Calvinist text *Grace Abounding to the Chief of Sinners* (1666). Bunyan's text is itself informed by St Paul's Acts of the Apostles and Letters to the Romans.

Brown's autobiography and the conversion narrative at its heart can be read and made sense of in light of this tradition of intertextuality. It is striking to see just how carefully Brown uses intertextual narrative technique in his own autobiographical writing. This is no mere emulation, however. In his conversion texts, Brown inserts himself into the tradition of spiritual autobiography as a Catholic convert who justifies his new-found devotion to an ancient faith by means of a distinctively Orcadian voice and perspective.

III. 'The way of literature': The Authorised Version of Conversion

Simon Hall writes: 'As a practising Roman Catholic from the early fifties until his death in 1996, Brown was by no means typically Orcadian in his religion.'[48] Hall notes that 'the islands are predominantly Church of Scotland in their denomination' and that the majority of Catholics in Orkney today are those who have moved to the islands from the West of Scotland and Ireland, 'usually during the last half century'.[49] Hall's work confirms that Brown's decision to enter the Church in 1961 would have meant that he was only one of a small number of Catholics in Orkney, while Maggie Fergusson has noted that Brown was one of only three people to convert to Catholicism in the whole of the twentieth century.[50] While not singular in his convert status, then, Brown was certainly deeply unusual for having become a Catholic.

Brown did not write a brand-new account of his conversion for *For the Islands I Sing*, but instead reproduced an already published essay, 'The way of literature: *An apologia by George Mackay Brown*', which first appeared in *The Tablet* in 1982 and was advertised by the magazine as 'a Scot's testimony'.[51] The title Brown chose for this essay is significant in two ways. First, this piece indicates Brown's borrowing of the 'apologia' mode, derived from the Classical Greek system of apologetics, where the very earliest Christian writers including Aristides and Tertullian composed 'reasoned defence and recommendation of their faith to outsiders'.[52] In writing this piece, it is likely that Brown hoped he would have publicly explained his conversion and would be asked no more about it. This title is also important, however, because it echoes John Henry Newman's *Apologia pro vita sua* (1864), a text cited within the article as a 'cause for wonder' and a milestone on Brown's path to conversion. Newman's *Apologia* was also written as a defence – in his case against the novelist and historian Charles Kingsley's perceived attack on Catholic doctrine and clergy. Newman's *Apologia* 'is very much a fiction, a literary construct, a product of intertextuality', and Wright notes that 'like a true Romantic, Newman quotes mainly from his own work, citing numerous excerpts from his earlier letters and articles'.[53]

In *For the Islands I Sing* Brown writes, rather testily, '... a few years ago I wrote an essay for *The Tablet* about my conversion. The following, based on *The Tablet* article, tells all there is to say' (*FI*, 48). In the style of Newman, he then reproduces the article virtually verbatim with minor structural changes and a list of literary quotations, or 'a few fragments of truth and beauty' that appealed to his developing Catholic imagination early on. However, Brown neglects to mention that *The Tablet* article and the later, almost identical, autobiographical conversion narrative are themselves based on another, fictional, text. 'The Tarn and the Rosary', a short story from Brown's 1974 collection *Hawkfall*, is the direct ancestor of these conversion narratives. Isobel Murray notes the story's autobiographical basis in her interview with Brown in 1984 but he denies this, saying 'it's by no means a self-portrait; it's just one or two facets that are the same [...] I'm quite different from the man in that story.'[54] However, this text is striking not just for its deep biographical resonances, but, more importantly, considering the development of Brown's own conversion narrative, for its structural similarity with the adapted *Tablet* article in his autobiography. Short story, essay and autobiography set out the terms of their argument, or the reasons for conversion to Catholicism, before going on to list quotations from other texts that illustrate the beauty and power of art inspired by Catholic devotion. Thus, Brown's conversion first appears as short fiction in 1974, before becoming adapted as an essay of apologetics in 1982 and as a section in his autobiography, initially drafted in 1985 and published posthumously. Brown's conversion is explained first through art, and later through 'real life' accounts.

While it is unwise to read every detail of Brown's 'The Tarn and the Rosary' as neatly autobiographical, much of it is certainly taken from life. His fictional doppelgänger, the convert Colm Sinclair, can express Brown's feelings in (thinly disguised) fiction more openly than he may have felt possible in the 1970s. Early in this short story, which is set on the fictional island of Norday, young Colm overhears a discussion about Catholicism in the town's smithy. This scene echoes Brown's early experiences of sitting at his father's and Peter Esson's feet as they worked in the tailor shop. It includes a long dialogue, filled with ironic misinterpretations of Catholicism, between various island men. Their remarks range from the simply curious (Colm's father asks why the date of Easter changes every year) to the prejudiced. William Smith the general merchant – a 'money-grubber' worthy of Brown's earliest and most satirical writing – announces authoritatively that '[t]he Irish people are very poor [...] Very poor and very oppressed. You'll find, if you study the matter, that all Roman Catholic countries are very backward' (*H*, 182). Meanwhile, the blacksmith's wife, Bella Simison, reports her scandalised reaction to the sensationalist, anti-Catholic book

Awful Disclosures of Maria Monk, or, The Hidden Secrets of a Nun's Life in a Convent Exposed (1836), crying, 'You can't tell me anything I don't know about Roman Catholics' (*H*, 184).

What emerges most clearly from this conversation between the islanders is that Catholicism is seen as notably foreign and decidedly un-Scottish. The men chuckle at Smith the merchant's impression of the aristocratic Miss Siegfried, who orders flowers for her Maundy Thursday celebration in a 'loud posh English accent'. '"Of course, they're Episcopalians up at The Hall"', says Smith, dismissively (*H*, 181). The gothic horror of Bella Simison's book about infanticide and sexual abuse in a Montreal convent seeps into the douce, Protestant environs of the smithy, and as he hears about the Virgin Mary, priests in black 'accepting money from strangers' and rosary beads, 'Colm shivered with supernatural dread' (*H*, 183). The dimly lit surroundings, illuminated faintly by the glowing forge, contribute to Colm's idea of Catholicism as a sinister foreign creed, and he looks forward to being home by his bed, 'where he would soon kneel and say his one simple good Presbyterian prayer' (*H*, 185). Orkney's Catholic past means nothing to the little boy, who clings to the familiarity of his Protestant upbringing in the face of Catholicism, described to him in lurid terms as 'the Scarlet Woman spoken of in the Bible [. . .] the Whore of Babylon [. . .] the abomination of desolation' (*H*, 185). In Brown's much later autobiography he recalls only one incident of outright sectarian bigotry, and this occurs in Edinburgh. But he also reveals to his reader that as a child in Orkney there 'was something sinister in the very word Catholic'. Ethnoreligious tension was clearly not a feature of Brown's boyhood, because of the near homogeneity of religious worship in the islands. But Colm's experience in the smithy certainly recalls Brown's autobiographical declaration that when he was a boy: 'I can't remember that we were ever instructed to hate Catholicism or Catholics; it was just that Catholicism and its mysteries lay outside our pale, and it was better so' (*FI*, 49).

In the final section of 'The Tarn and the Rosary' we find that years have passed and the adult Colm now lives in digs in Edinburgh, where he has converted to Catholicism. The autobiographical details of this short story are neat enough to include a description of Colm's painfully recurrent asthma that mirrors Brown's own tuberculosis. Colm attends Mass '[i]n a beautiful square a quarter of a mile from his lodgings [which] looked like an ordinary Georgian house' (*H*, 191). This sounds very like the Chaplaincy in George Square, where Brown may have received instruction while living in Marchmont. More importantly, this final section of the text becomes Colm's effective *apologia*, which Brown later reprinted in 'The way of literature' and in his autobiography as his own conversion account. Colm writes a letter to Jock Skaill, Norday's scandalous atheist, who has been his best friend since childhood, and in his letter he cites six quotations from texts that have shown him the beauty and truth of Catholicism. These are from Dante's *Paradiso*, Chaucer's *The Second Nun's Tale*, Hopkins' *The Wreck of the*

Deutschland, Herbert's 'Love', and the anonymous medieval ballad 'I Sing of a Maiden that is Makeles'. Brown's later essay 'The way of literature' and autobiography also use these same quotations, alongside others.

The major theme of this short story, and of Brown's subsequent conversion accounts, is the 'unfolding sequence of images', or 'stations', which bring faith alive (*H,* 187). As this allusion to Christ's way of sorrows indicates, conversion is not necessarily an easy process. Colm hears an anti-Catholic discussion in childhood, and shivers with supernatural dread. Soon, he discovers another kind of fear – a mingling of awe and religious reverence when confronted by the powerful beauty of Norday's desolate interior landscape. As he scrambles over the hills and finds himself staring at Loch Tumilshun, 'a small shiver went over Colm's skin', and he experiences the sublime. Colm finds that the hills, 'silent presences [. . .] were frightening too', but soon he 'felt a kinship with that high austere landscape, a first fugitive love' (*H,* 174). The boy's fear of the landscape sounds like fear of the Lord where Colm realises that his own small voice in the midst of such awe-inspiring surroundings sounds 'like blasphemy' (*H,* 171).

Colm is a Wordsworthian creation as well as being drawn from autobiography. His deep, Romantic connection with the Orcadian landscape fires his imagination and creative powers, so that, like Brown, he is soon writing the best compositions in the schoolroom. Romanticism is so deeply embedded in the text that Loch Tumilshun becomes Colm's Lake District-esque 'tarn', and the connection of this tarn with the 'rosary' of the title marries together an intense awareness of Orcadian landscape with a new, eventually Catholic, form of devotion. Indeed, the title of this story takes its name from Wordsworth's 'Fidelity', a poem which the young Colm must memorise for school, and it is surely no coincidence that 'Fidelity' is also quoted in Brown's autobiography, where he describes his early education, and also in 'Writer's Shop', another autobiographical essay.[55]

In his discussion of the parallels joining Romantic literature and the Oxford movement, Michael H. Bright argues that

> . . . in the field of literature the role of the poet becomes exalted, even elitist, since it is only he, with the special gift of a powerful imagination, who can perceive and commune with the supernatural; secondly, the means by which the poet communicates his extraordinary insights and experiences is through symbolism since literalism is inadequate to comprehend and express the ineffable.[56]

Under this lens, Colm is the text's poet (he later becomes a novelist) with 'the special gift of a powerful imagination' that has been steadily growing since childhood. It is Colm who perceives the supernatural lurking in creation, and it is Colm who begins to communicate his experiences through the sacramental symbolism of the Catholic Church. In his own *apologia* later in the story, the now adult Colm cites evidence of God in a way that directly prefigures Brown's own apologetics of conversion. Colm considers God's gift of grace – Himself – in the Eucharist:

> The most awesome and marvellous proof for me is the way he chose to go on nourishing his people after his ascension, in the form of bread. So the brutish life of man is continually possessed, broken, transfigured by the majesty of God. (*H*, 189–90)

Like Brown, Colm is introduced to Romantic poetry as a boy, and he finds that it explains his own feelings of awe and wonder about the landscape around him, which cannot be fully articulated through his Presbyterian environment. As he reads Wordsworth's poem, Colm is struck by the thought that '[t]his poet must have seen Tumilshun too, or else some loch very like it. He had felt the same things' (*H*, 174). Soon, the boy's Romantic view of nature is charged with a spiritual dimension. And eventually, Colm's 'mystical and imaginative apprehension of the supernatural' becomes more focused, so that agriculture speaks in a definite symbolic way about the life of Christ: the crop of corn is cut down, or 'crucified', only to be 'resurrected', harvested, and turned into soon-to-be-consecrated bread.[57] Moreover, this process has a sanctifying effect: man's 'brutish' existence is 'transfigured' by grace. The adult Colm now understands his boyhood fear and awe of the land, because it mirrors the 'terror and exaltation' the first ploughman must have felt, 'to put wounds on the great dark mother', the earth (*H*, 188). But that agricultural process brought forth ripeness, barley, bread and Eucharist. Colm's imagination has moved from the Romantic to the Catholic: reality is seen as revelation of the presence and saving power of God.

For Colm and for his author, an initially Romantic view of the world sees, indistinctly, the world's spiritual design: in the later *Tablet* article Brown notes, 'The elements of earth and sea, that we thought so dull and ordinary, held a bounteousness and a mystery not of this world.'[58] Under this lens, Catholicism is not something utterly foreign: it is locally and culturally appropriate. The Orkney land and seascapes, the fishermen with their apostolic professions, and the island's agricultural processes become, ultimately, a means of grace and not simply prompts for feelings of the sublime: Brown argues, 'That the toil of the earth-worker should become, in the Mass, Corpus Christi, was a wonder beyond words, and still is.'[59] There are discernible textures of John Henry Newman's writing in this work. Newman, who Brown called 'a true child of the Romantic movement who wrote moreover an exact and luminous prose' (*FI*, 50–1), and whose own spiritual autobiography astonished him, wrote that '[t]he heart is commonly reached not through reason, but through the imagination, by means of direct impressions'.[60] Nonetheless, Newman's warning that spiritual feeling by itself is not 'worth a straw, or rather it is pernicious, if it does not lead to *practice*' is deeply embedded in Brown's Romantic and sacramental account of conversion.[61] Perhaps Brown, like Newman, forever remained 'deeply suspicious of his own Romantic sensibility', making sure that his swooning descriptions of the natural world were underpinned by commitment to the Catholic faith.[62] Brown is not worshipping nature itself in this writing. Colm, his fictional creation and effective 'I' or self, receives the grace of a Christian God through, but not from, the land. For Wordsworth, nature was 'an organic part of God, a physical expression of his "personality"', and it is this personality that communicates with and bestows the free gift of faith on Brown's protagonist, who reads Romantic poetry.[63]

Indeed, a key idea in 'The Tarn and the Rosary' is the sacramental power of words. In this text, Colm writes: 'I have for my share of the earth-wisdom a patch of the imagination that I must cultivate to the best of my skill' (*H*, 189). Colm's threshing-place is the imagination. He does not work the land but his mind brings forth the fruits of faith in the literature of praise. Colm's status as a novelist is fundamental to understanding Brown's conversion narratives in all their forms. In 'The way of literature' Brown recalls the meaning he found in Christ's parables of agriculture that were so relevant and appropriate to his rural environment, noting, 'Those words were a delight and a revelation, when first I understood them.'[64] For Brown, literature is the entry point into religious experience and literature itself has a sacramental function. Like his fictional doppelgänger, Colm, he finds that '[a]ll my life, I suppose, a vocation as a writer had been forming in me'.[65] Colm finds this when Wordsworth's poetry transforms Norday into a place touched by the finger of God. He is transformed by poetry which reveals with divine intervention in the world, and realises that 'the poem had worked the change' (*H*, 174). Both Brown and his fictional self, Colm, have received poetry as a sacrament. Both go on to become Catholic writers.

Brown notes in his *Tablet* essay, 'The mystery and the beauty increased, as I read more widely', and he discusses how deeply impressed he was with Greene's *The Power and the Glory* when he first encountered the novel.[66] He continues: 'In the end it was literature that broke down my last defences. There are many ways of entering a fold; it was the beauty of words that opened the door to me.'[67] In Brown's last account of his conversion, *For the Islands I Sing*, he illustrates this power and beauty with nine literary quotations that speak to him spiritually, extending the six quotations listed in 'The Tarn and the Rosary' and in 'The way of literature' with additional verse from Hilaire Belloc, Dylan Thomas and the anonymous 'Lyke-Wake Dirge' (and replacing Dante with Thomas Traherne). Brown's faith was deeply indebted to literature, so much that it was first catalysed through interest in other spiritual writing, and then sustained and explained via this medium. Indeed, G. K. Chesterton's maxim in *Orthodoxy* might as well have been written by Brown: '... this world of ours has some purpose; and if there is a purpose, there is a person. I had always felt life first as a story: and if there is a story there is a story-teller.'[68] For these two writers of the Catholic imagination, text and faith are inextricably intertwined.

IV. A 'God-ordained web of creation': The Rhetoric of Conversion in Muir, Brown, Spark and Newman

What can examples of spiritual autobiography contemporaneous with Brown's contribute to the unfolding story of his own conversion and the experiences of other Scottish convert writers in the mid-twentieth century? First, the idea of 'spiritual autobiography' requires some unpicking. Peter A. Dorsey identifies that, for some, the term 'spiritual autobiography' can 'be used to describe any self portrait that describes the conditions of the "inner life." For others, spiritual autobiography is a purely religious narrative that describes the relationship between an individual and God.'[69] Many of the spiritual autobiographies that interact with Brown's *For the Islands I Sing* fall into a curious middle ground between these two definitions. The autobiographies of the converts Brown, Muriel Spark and John Henry Newman all touch on religious conversion, but tantalisingly withhold information about the emotional import of conversion on their own and their families' lives.

Reticence is, in fact, a curious feature of spiritual autobiography that is common to twentieth-century Scottish convert writers. Edwin Muir's autobiography is often considered to be spiritual, but despite his focus on the theme of the Fall and his early evangelical conversions, he hesitates to commit fully to conversion to Catholicism in later life, 'preferring [instead] the articles of his private faith'.[70] Similarly, after reading *Godspells*, Brown admitted to Sr Tournour: 'it is maybe too much soaked in "the spiritual" where I find it difficult to breathe freely, longing always to keep one foot at least on the earth'.[71] This religious restraint also pervades Spark's autobiography, *Curriculum Vitae* (1992), which commits no more than two hundred words to her decision to become a Catholic. As Benilde Montgomery notes, '[a]lthough not so speculative and defensive as [Newman's] *Apologia*, *Curriculum Vitae* ends like it: with its subject's conversion to Catholicism but with no mention of the latter tensions that conversion to Catholicism necessarily includes.'[72] And this is true too of Brown's *For the Islands I Sing*, which – as we have seen – does not include any reference to the Orcadian response to Brown's conversion, nor to the vagaries and trials that a religious change of heart might bring. Yet, this text ends on a crescendo of prayer, with Brown acknowledging a 'shaping divinity' in human lives, and beseeching Orkney's patron saint: '"Saint Magnus, pray for us ..."' (*FI*, 187).

Jean Starobinski writes that internal transformation is often the catalyst for life writing. She notes that '[o]ne would hardly have sufficient motive to write an autobiography had not some radical change occurred in his life – conversion, entry into a new life, the operation of Grace'.[73] Muir's *An Autobiography* (1954) concludes by confirming Starobinski's theory that recognition of the operation of grace is the motivation for compiling the events of one's life into a coherent narrative. Muir states that 'in St Andrews

I discovered that I had been a Christian [for years] without knowing it'
after an intense religious experience in which he meditates on the mean-
ings generated by the words of the Lord's Prayer in an act of spontaneous
lectio divina.[74] As his autobiography closes, Muir realises:

> ... in the infinite web of things and events chance must be something
> different from what we think it to be. To comprehend that is to rec-
> ognize a mystery, and to acknowledge the necessity of faith. As I look
> back on my own life, my own fable, what I am most aware of is that
> we receive more than we can ever give; we receive it from the past, on
> which we draw with every breath, but also – and this is a point of faith
> – from the Source of the mystery itself, by the means which religious
> people call Grace.[75]

An Autobiography may seem, at first glance, to adhere to Dorsey's first definition of spiritual autobiography, in that it concentrates heavily on the
'inner life' without fully committing to a religious viewpoint or ideology.
However, Muir's autobiography concludes with the acknowledgement of
a freely given and unmerited gift from a divine source, and this realisation
can be said to colour the whole text in retrospect, particularly for a reader
alert to the text's crypto-Catholic themes of prelapsarian childhood and
the Fall.

It is no coincidence that this autobiographical writing sounds very like
Brown's. While Muir concludes his autobiography by noting the 'infinite
web of things and events', his Orcadian successor ends *For the Islands I Sing*
by reflecting: 'We are all one, saint and sinner. Everything we do sets the
whole web of creation trembling, with light or with darkness' (*FI*, 186).
Indeed, in his work Brown often mentions 'the sacred web of creation
– that cosmic harmony of god and beast and man and star and plant'
(*H*, 131). Brown frequently acknowledged the creative debt he owed to
Muir's *An Autobiography*, and critics including Sabine Schmid, Peter Butter
and Simon Hall have impressively explored the echoes and resonances of
this text in Brown's work. Hall identifies the connection between Muir's
archetypal 'story and the fable' dichotomy and Brown's writing, in which
Brown 'extends the philosophy to articulate it more closely with his Roman
Catholicism'.[76] He notes that Muir's descriptions of the landscape and
agricultural patterns seen in the Orkney of his childhood are celebratory, 'without investing quite the same enhanced level of significance' that
Brown sees.[77] It is no surprise then to find that at the close of his autobiography the convert Brown sacralises Muir's rather vague, earthly 'web of
things', so that it becomes 'sacred', and, elsewhere, 'God-ordained' (*TRC*,
212).

Furthermore, while it was undoubtedly the peaceful, Edenic childhood
of Muir's autobiography that affected Brown the most, the savagery of farm
life depicted by Muir is often to be found in the necessary agricultural violence of Brown's poetic and literary landscape. When a neighbour comes

to 'stick the pig', Muir decides that '[t]here was a necessity in the copulation and the killing which took away the sin, or at least, by the ritual act, transformed it into a sad, sanctioned duty'.[78] In Brown's *Magnus* (1973), an unnamed narrator interrupts the plot to speak at length about the spiritual value of suffering and death. He traces salvation history from the earliest times, and concentrates especially on the ritual sacrifices of animals and men which prefigure the ultimate sacrifice on Golgotha. Instead of Muir's 'sad, sanctioned duty', Brown notes that slaughtered animals honour God with 'broken flesh and spilled blood' and 'a solemn sacred ritual'. Where Muir describes the 'ritual act' which 'took away the sin', Brown notes a tribe 'ritually washed clean [. . .] The earth flames with blood – the sin is consumed – the heart is purified' (*M*, 154–65). Although the influence of Muir on Brown's poetry is sometimes critically over-stated, it is certainly the case that Muir's life writing was a rich creative well for Brown, and the younger writer drew from it deeply. Not only does Brown borrow Muir's narrative transplantation of biblical themes into an Orkney setting, he engages so deeply with his predecessor's autobiographical writing that he echoes its very rhythms and cadences in his own creative work.

Muir's *Autobiography* also resonates tangibly in Brown's account of his conversion, and becomes part of its textual heredity. In *An Autobiography* Muir writes about his friend John Holms, whom he met very often after he and Willa Muir moved to London in 1919. Muir describes the first day that he met Holms. They walked together in the countryside, while Holms recited poetry:

> Perhaps it was this that recalled to Holms Traherne's 'orient and immortal wheat, which never should be reaped, nor was ever sown,' for he began to recite the passage, which moved me more deeply than Donne. He held Traherne's and Vaughan's and Wordsworth's theory of childhood, which was bound up with his belief in immortality; in time he converted me to it, or rather made me realize that my own belief was the same as his.[79]

This passage is key to the intertextual relationship between Muir and Brown's autobiographies, and it speaks to the web of literary allusions and influences that can be seen more broadly in conversion narratives. Muir describes Holms' belief in the 'theory of childhood' – the belief that children are especially in tune with their immortal souls and have particularly keen awareness of the divine in nature – that he was also then 'converted' to. Traherne, largely unknown and unpublished until the twentieth century, writes in his *Centuries of Meditations* that the city of Hereford had 'seemed to stand in Eden', a description that Muir very possibly seized upon and appropriated for the famously prelapsarian depiction of Orkney in his autobiography.[80] The line 'orient and immortal wheat' is also quoted in Brown's autobiography: it appears alongside other verse quotations which illustrate Brown's attraction to Catholicism.

In fact, this intertextual web of quotation and allusion, which took in Traherne, Vaughan and Wordsworth, had been working on Brown's imagination since his early tutelage by Muir at Newbattle Abbey. In 1952, Brown wrote enthusiastically to Ernest Marwick, 'Edwin is lecturing these days on the 17th century poets. The other morning we got a brilliant talk from him on Thomas Traherne, he who wrote about the corn being "orient and immortal wheat" – according to Edwin one of the happiest and most innocent souls who ever lived.'[81] Decades later, as he drafted his autobiography, Brown drew on the connections between Muir, Traherne and Wordsworth once more. He describes his formative experiences of literature:

> I read the autobiography of Edwin Muir, *The Story and the Fable*. He grew up in the small fertile island of Wyre, on his father's farm. The early chapter of that book, about his childhood, is a very beautiful piece of writing, and reminds one again and again of the accounts of infancy written by Vaughan and Traherne, Wordsworth and Dylan Thomas . . . (*FI*, 63–4)

These poets and their themes of a prelapsarian childhood are intensely bound up with one another. For Brown, the works of Vaughan, Traherne and Wordsworth became a major resource for writing about infancy, childhood and conversion. Brown's conversion narrative, first written in 'The Tarn and the Rosary' as the story of Colm Sinclair, is steeped in the Romantic notion that the child is closer to God than the adult, whose ability to comprehend the divine slowly atrophies with age. The Romantic idea of the child as spiritually insightful, and of nature as the best and most insightful teacher of children, is one that is powerfully present in Brown's writing. In his work, children like Colm often recognise spiritual truths that adults fail to see, and go through formative experiences where grace is bestowed on them.[82] This idea was learned from Muir and the chain of other poets who ascribed to the idea of the divine child, the shining figure of Wordsworth's 'Intimations of Immortality'. This is signalled subtly in 'The Tarn and the Rosary' by Colm's reading of Wordsworth's 'Fidelity'.

The Romantic belief in children's susceptibility to supernatural experience is also notable in Muriel Spark's autobiographical writing. Ruth Whittaker notes that Spark identified with this notion, which was also present in Newman's spiritual autobiography, his *Apologia pro vita sua*:

> Like Newman, too, [Spark] retained an awareness of childhood as extraordinary. In an interview she tries to describe this strangeness: 'I had the impression of childhood itself being unusual, life being unusual [. . .]. I think children are capable of almost mystical experiences [. . .] I think that one had intimations of immortality.' Newman, writing about this childhood when he was a young man, recalls, 'I thought that life might be a dream, or I an Angel, and all this world a deception, my fellow-angels by a playful device concealing themselves from me, and deceiving me with the semblance of a material world.'[83]

Spark, Brown, Muir and Newman all live childhoods influenced to some degree by Calvinism. In their work, the seeds of grace that call them to God are sown, they think, in childhood. Perhaps Scottish converts reach for romance so often because it runs contrary to their early, overwhelmingly Presbyterian surroundings. Romantic literature is frequently the Scottish convert's first encounter with a sacralised, enchanted world, as Spark's reference to Wordsworth demonstrates. The initially Calvinist view of the fallen world as depraved, a snare, and not to be trusted, is re-enchanted by a romantic frame of mind, which sees the land as alive with goodness and an almost magical allure. The romantic re-enchantment of the Calvinist world, and the subsequent appeal of the Church of Rome, is illustrated well by Brown's 'The Tarn and the Rosary' and subsequent autobiography. And although Newman cannot be counted as a Scottish convert, his own account of conversion is intensely appealing to both Spark and Brown. It speaks to their own experience of the movement from Calvinist distrust to Catholic romance.

But Newman's writing about childhood spirituality also connects with Muir's work in important ways. Both write about the moral perceptions of the child and of the development of ideas of guilt and sin in childhood. Newman argues:

> when [the child] has done what he believes is wrong, he is conscious that he is offending One to whom he is amenable, whom he does not see, who sees him. His mind reaches forward with a strong presentiment to the thought of a Moral Governor, sovereign over him, mindful, and just.[84]

Meanwhile, Muir recognises that 'a child has also a picture of human existence peculiar to himself, which he probably never remembers after he has lost it: the original vision of the world.'[85] Muir's analysis of the development of morality in childhood has a less positive tint than Newman's, however, in that the 'mindful and just' sovereign God who broods over Newman's moral actions is, in Muir's vision, replaced by a misguided sense of guilt in later years. He argues: 'There comes a moment (the moment at which childhood passes into boyhood or girlhood) when this image is broken and contradiction enters life. It is a phase of emotional and mental strain, and it brings with it a sense of guilt.'[86] The latter assertion in particular may have affected Brown, who writes in his autobiography that he will not dwell on the years between the ages of fourteen to sixteen, since 'they were wretched years, full of shames and fears and miseries' (*FI*, 46).

The 'nameless terrors' of these years, which meant that Brown 'yearned back towards [his] childhood' (*FI*, 46), habitually affect some of the more sensitive characters in his novels and short fiction. These terrors are often explicitly connected with a yearning for the sacrament of reconciliation to ease the pain of guilt or allay fears explicitly connected with a Calvinist mind-set. Brown notes in his autobiography that '[w]hat made [his teenage years] so particularly dreadful was that there was no one I could unburden myself to' (*FI*, 46). The best and most striking example of a character haunted by Calvinism in Brown's work is Mrs McKee the minister's mother, in *Greenvoe* (1972). Mrs McKee longs to confess her past regrets and mistakes, but instead of unburdening herself through confession, her daydreams are warped into terrifying fantasies where she is interrogated by an imaginary prosecutor during a 'trial' in 'the ecclesiastic division of [a] court' (*G*, 130). Mrs McKee worries, anguished, that her niece has converted to Catholicism because of her own negligence in allowing her to enter a Catholic church as a child. The 'young clever Scottish voice' of the old woman's imaginary prosecutor torments her, and, suddenly, the speech of her tormentor moves from a poised legalese to 'sudden savagery'. The clever Scottish prosecutor's voice gives way to the sneering denunciations of an angry preacher:

> Think how the church of pre-Reformation Scotland was – to use a rather vulgar but descriptive phrase – tarted up with all manner of destructive tinsel: the statues and the stained glass, the fuming censers swung by acolytes at gilded altars, the grove of candles about the plaster feet of some saint. The wretched and the ignorant of the earth have always gone down on their knees before this mumbojumbo.
>
> I do not need to tell you that Rome still flaunts these gauds and baubles in the face of mankind. And many there are who still hanker after these things, though nominally they are members of our kirk: not only the superstitious either, but people who are supposed to be clever, artistic, cultured. I say it with sorrow; year after year we lose a flock of such people to Rome. (*G*, 107–8)

This is the closest Brown's reader gets to hearing about the reaction to his entry into the Church in 1961. Ironically, it may be that for Brown, like Mrs McKee, this prosecuting, Calvinistic voice was simply an internal one. The bitter reaction to Brown's conversion was imagined, but no less distressing for being so. Brown reflects in his autobiography:

> When one has been bred a Catholic, one can never rid oneself of the essence of it. A cradle Catholic is quite different from a convert. [T]extures of Calvinism, generations old, are still part of me and I think I will never be rid of them: ancient guilts, rebukes in the silence of thought [. . .] as if some Presbyterian ancestor from the seventeenth century was murmuring to me, and not mildly. (*FI*, 120)

This suggests that for Brown there was a tension between his new, Catholic faith and the teachings and conditioning of his childhood which could never be resolved fully. In Muriel Spark's first novel, *The Comforters* (1957), this tension is highlighted when the newly converted Caroline Rose is told, 'Converts have a lot to learn. You can always tell a convert from a cradle Catholic. There's something different.'[87]

Like Brown, Edwin Muir also experienced a 'conviction of sin' after the happy innocence of his childhood. He writes in his autobiography that while he lived in London:

> every one, like myself, was troubled by sensual desires and thoughts, by unacknowledged failures and frustrations causing self-hatred and hatred of others, by dead memories of shame and grief which had been shovelled underground long since because they could not be borne.[88]

Fleishman identifies that Muir's mental state at this time 'can readily be compared with the long-gathering crises that spiritual autobiographers have recounted'.[89] Brown's work utilises this convention, but, as noted before, he adds weight and significance to the echoes of Muir in his auto-biography by framing his thoughts in specifically religious terms. Brown is not haunted by what Muir eventually recognises as 'a realization of Original Sin' but by the legacy of the Reformation in Scotland.[90] Brown's depression is personified in a particularly religious way; the neurosis that haunts him (and Mrs McKee) takes the form of a Calvinistic ancestor. This signals something that is truly unique to the Scottish Catholic convert imagination. Brown's imaginary 'Presbyterian ancestor' rebukes and accuses him, reviling his faith, filling him with guilt, and subduing his need to unburden himself through sacramental confession. Whittaker identifies that '[t]here is perhaps a sense in which the convert can never feel as "Catholic" as a person born into that faith, and reminders of this difference can be painful'.[91] But Brown felt worse than an impostor: his imaginary prosecutor in *Greenvoe* howls warnings against the 'stark horror of [the devil] whose aim is and was and always will be to seduce us from allegiance to the faith of our fathers' (*G*, 107). Nagging feelings of isolation and disloyalty were clearly a part of the post-conversion experience for this Orcadian writer.

Nonetheless, Newman, Muir and Brown all express in their autobiographies what they see as the more positive sacramental and incarnational impulse of Catholicism, discovered as adults. Each writer makes particular reference to the Catholicism of Italy, with Muir and Newman travelling there later in life. As early as 1945, Brown reflects in his *Orkney Herald* column on Orkney's Italian Chapel, built by Italian prisoners of war. He writes:

> We who are brought up in the Calvinistic faith, a faith as austere, bracing and cold as the winds that trouble Lamb Holm from year's end to year's end, can hardly grasp the fierce nostalgic endeavour that raised this piece of Italy, of Catholicism, out of the clay and the stones [. . .] the faith that created this thing will endure to the end of the world.[92]

Brown was not alone in being moved by the Church's visible presence in the ordinary materials of 'the clay and the stones'. During his travels to Italy and Malta, while still belonging to the Anglican Communion, Newman claims in his *Apologia* that 'the sight of so many great places, venerable shrines, and noble churches, much impressed my imagination. And my heart was touched also.'[93] While in Milan, it is the sacrament reserved in the tabernacles of Catholic churches that strikes Newman the most. However, as Ian Ker points out, it is not just the reservation of the sacrament in Catholic churches that illustrates the particularly incarnational focus of Catholicism for Newman, 'but also through the whole Catholic system of sacraments and sacramentals, as well as the crucifixes and statues and pictures that surround the worshipper in a Catholic church'.[94] This could also have been written about Muir, who – like Newman – 'without participating in Roman Catholic worship [. . .] learned to have tender feelings towards the Church of Rome'.[95] It is while he is in Rome that Christ's image, Muir realises, can be seen everywhere. He sees it

> not only in churches, but on the walls of houses, at cross-roads in the suburbs, in wayside shrines in the parks, and in private rooms. [. . .] That these images should appear everywhere, reminding everyone of the Incarnation, seemed to me natural and right, just as it was right that my Italian friends should step out frankly into life.[96]

For Brown, Muir and Newman's autobiographies had a very real and lasting spiritual and not simply literary effect. Through Muir's account, Brown would have been able to connect on a local and intimate level with the descriptions of landscape, occupations and culture, particularly the heavily word-based accent of Presbyterianism, which characterised both their childhoods. But also, through both these texts Brown would have been able to travel imaginatively to Catholic cultures abroad, where religion seemed foreign, but related, to the Christianity of his own upbringing. He never travelled in Europe himself, and so could only experience foreign Catholicism through these other writers, but the frequent reference to pre-Reformation ruins in his later prose fiction signals Brown's keenness to stress that Orkney once contained the material culture seen in Catholic nations abroad. It is almost certainly Muir and Newman's accounts of intellectual, imaginative and spiritual conversion to Catholicism that led Brown to announce that he 'could live cheerfully in a Catholic country, or in pre-Reformation Orkney if that were possible', in the mid-fifties.[97]

In fact, Brown's contemporary and fellow-convert Muriel Spark did just that. In 1967, she relocated to Italy, remaining there until her death in 2006. Spark's own conversion narratives follow a strikingly similar trajectory to Brown's. Her wary *apologia* appeared first as fiction, in *The Comforters* (1957), a novel which dramatises the pressure and unwillingness that Spark felt to explain her conversion to friends and strangers. Some answers were then tentatively suggested with the publication of Spark's autobiographical essay, 'My Conversion', in 1961 (the year of Brown's reception into the

Church), before the subject of conversion was broached again, very briefly, in Spark's autobiography, *Curriculum Vitae* (1992).

'My Conversion' makes for an interesting comparison with some aspects of Brown's own conversion narratives in its biographical details. Both writers note their Presbyterian schooling and the narrative appeal of the Bible. Spark recalls: 'I was terribly interested in the scriptures [. . .] I think I had strong religious feelings as a child which were really bound up with art and poetry, although Christ was a romantic, moving figure', while in one of Brown's autobiographical essays he too acknowledges the early artistic appeal of 'such stories from the Old Testament as Joseph and his Brothers, David and Jonathan, Samson, Jacob and the Angel' alongside the border ballads, fairy tales and the Sagas.[98] But most striking is the incentive to write that Brown and Spark share after their conversion experience. In 'My Conversion', Spark writes, 'I became a Catholic in 1954. I think there is a connection between my writing and my conversion, but I don't want to be too dogmatic about it. Certainly all my best work has come since then.'[99] In Brown's 'The way of literature', he too suggests that Catholicism and other Catholic fictions provided a stimulus to his writing. However, this may not be surprising, because as Helena Tomko suggests, 'it is not uncommon for conversions to be accompanied by an outpouring of creative or intellectual enthusiasm [. . .] A turning towards God presupposes God's turning towards man; this prompts a desire to speak out in praise and thanks.'[100] Tomko cites St Paul's transformation after conversion on the road to Damascus, and writes: 'Accordingly, in Catholic thinking, what converts receive upon entry into communion with the Church in her sacraments is a new way to perceive.'[101] In this way, and in many others, Brown and Spark's conversion narratives speak to one another. It is likely that Spark's 'My Conversion' was read by Brown in the year of his conversion, and certainly possible that it informed some of his own conversion narrative, published in *The Tablet* twenty-one years later.

In *Curriculum Vitae*, Spark dedicates less than two hundred words (one paragraph) to her reception into the Church on 1 May 1954. Like Brown, Spark attributes her conversion to the influence of the writings of John Henry Newman, and, like Newman, Spark recognises the impossibility of summarising conversion in a few sentences, concluding: 'the existential quality of a religious experience cannot be simply summed up in general terms'.[102] Spark also emulates something of Newman's intertextual autobiographical style in this work, and, Montgomery notes, 'Letters are reprinted, critical reviews are recalled and corrected, poems are reproduced, all in Newman's words, "to prevent misconception" [. . .] and in Spark's, "to put the record straight".'[103] However, it was not Newman's rhetorical panache or theology which drew Spark to his spiritual autobiography. Spark notes: 'My own conversion was really an instinctive rather than an intellectual experience. I suppose it was conditioned by the God-building atmosphere – with its very indefinite location – of my childhood. Newman helped me to find a definite location.'[104] Spark's insistence on conversion as a process of intuition and feeling for the emotion, rather than the theology of Christianity, is very similar to Brown's own insistence that, 'A few fragments of such truth and beauty, like treasures long lost, were sufficient; the way of argument and reason were not for me.'[105]

Sheridan Gilley confirms that Newman's *Apologia* so strongly conveys the force of his personality that it provides 'an enchantment to the literary-minded like no other'.[106] He writes:

> The *Apologia* shows the inner life as a work of divine grace, but so binds natural gracefulness as to seem to make the life a work of art. This is partly why its influence has been strongest among converts with a literary calling or vocation like Miss Spark, who have come to Newman with an ear for his verbal music, and partly why the Catholic revival has been so much a literary affair, with a greater impact upon writers than among scientists or businessmen who have no such notable Catholic convert model.[107]

Newman's writing was so influential that he took on heroic qualities for both Spark and Brown, and for Brown especially he was a seminal Catholic literary influence. He writes to Ernest Marwick in 1947: 'Have you ever read John Henry Newman's "Apologia Pro Vita Sua"? I've just finished it and, as always, it has shaken me to the core. There is magnificent devastating logic in it. Tell Mrs Marwick she might see me a priest someday yet.'[108] It was to be another fourteen years before Brown was formally received into the Church, and he acknowledges: 'I lingered for years in this state of acknowledging Catholicism, while doing nothing about it' (*FI*, 53), a statement which resonates strongly with one of Newman's, in an essay about sudden conversions: 'When men change their religious opinions really and truly, it is not merely their opinions that they change, but their hearts; and this evidently is not done in a moment – it is slow work.'[109] Just as Brown praises his 'magnificent devastating logic', Spark writes that '[h]is reasoning is so pure that it is revolutionary in form', confirming Gilley's assertion that 'it is in his stern unbending call to sincerity and seriousness that Newman is master of the convert mind'.[110] And although Newman tempered the Romantic impulse of his work with rallying cries to be guided by reason and not mere imagination, both Spark and Brown were beguiled by the beauty of his writing. Late in her life, Spark insisted: 'I felt he wrote like an angel', and in her foreword to a selection of his sermons, she writes:

> I have noticed that to those who have been attracted by Newman his personality remains very much alive. It is one of his gifts. [. . .] It was by way of Newman that I turned Roman Catholic. Not all the beheaded martyrs of Christendom, the ecstatic nuns of Europe, the five proofs of Aquinas, or the pamphlets of my Catholic acquaintance, provided anything like the answers that Newman did.[111]

For Brown, too, Newman's writing contained a spiritual value beyond price, and he confesses in his autobiography that while most of the *Apologia* bored him, he was nonetheless inspired artistically and spiritually by 'those passages, all exquisite and soaring as violin music, that rise clear above his own dilemmas and difficulties' (*FI*, 51). It is remarkable how often Newman's thought connects Brown, Spark and Muir. He occupies a place in the minds and hearts of convert writers that is unparalleled by any other literary figure, churchman or theologian. Newman's literary depiction of lifelong conversion beguiled Brown and Spark as creative artists, and his sharp and overwhelming way of thinking confirmed them in their initial attraction to the faith.

Peter Dorsey argues that all conversion narratives are reliant on other texts and that spiritual autobiographies are intertextual by their very nature:

> The communal context of the spiritual autobiography was frequently acknowledged (and sometimes celebrated) in many narratives as authors embedded the accounts of others who have undergone similar experiences into their own texts. In many such cases 'conversion' is actually triggered by reading or hearing the narratives of others.[112]

One assertion of Brown's in *For the Islands I Sing* demonstrates Dorsey's point particularly well. Brown writes that the Bloomsbury critic Lytton Strachey's essay on Cardinal Manning in his *Eminent Victorians* (1918) 'gave me one of the great thrills I have got out of literature', despite Strachey's obvious disdain for the Catholic Church. He continues:

> The phrase in some book that finally, for Newman, led from Anglicanism to Catholicism [. . .] made me catch my breath, and not in derision either, as Strachey had intended. It was the same kind of astonishment as Newman had felt; though much diluted of course. (*FI*, 51)

Brown is referring here to the phrase '*Securus judicat orbis terrarum*', or 'the whole world judges securely'.[113] This Augustinian phrase was printed in the *Dublin Review* in 1839. A friend of Newman's pointed these words out to him, and they affected Newman powerfully:

> He repeated those words again and again, and, when he was gone, they kept ringing in my ears. 'Securus judicat orbis terrarium;' [. . .] Who can account for the impressions which are made on him? For a mere sentence, the words of St Augustine, struck me with a power which I never had felt from any words before. [. . .] they were like the 'Tolle, lege, - Tolle, lege,' of the child, which converted St Augustine himself.[114]

T. R. Wright argues that this particular moment of intertextuality 'links the *Apologia* with Augustine and the whole tradition of religious autobiography'.[115] He adds that 'Newman's conversion-narrative, at this point at least, is modelled upon Augustine's just as Augustine's was modelled on earlier narratives of a divine calling'.[116] We can now add Brown's autobiography to this textual heredity. Brown inserts himself into this tradition by becoming the latest of a long chain of literary converts affected spiritually by the sacramental power of words.

As the autobiographies of Muir, Brown, Spark and Newman show, they are profoundly related in a number of ways, and Brown's own conversion narrative clearly compliments them. Brown's autobiographical writing on conversion is overflowing with literary reference – it is almost oversaturated in allusion, echo, quotation and reference to other converts and their new songs of divine love. And yet, the literary references in Brown's conversion narratives are more than simple echo and allusion. He delves deep into the textual weave of spiritual self-writing, and unpicks and reclaims literary influences, before threading these into the very fabric of his autobiographical self-construction. Brown's conversion is deeply textually driven and sustained; it upholds Geoffrey Galt Harpham's claim that 'spiritual "conversion" might simply be a strong form of reading'.[117] Brown (and Spark's) reception into the Roman Catholic Church is more than an intuitive, imaginative or intellectual experience; it is intimately bound up with a vocational sense of, and commitment to, the creative process.

Most interesting for his status as a Scottish Catholic writer is Brown's visible debt to his (albeit lightly) Calvinist formation. He rebels against this at first by reaching for the Romantics and their vision of an enchanted world – one that is full of the visible signs of God's goodness and Christ's redemptive sacrifice. But eventually he writes his own conversion narratives, and inserts himself into the tradition of spiritual autobiography as 'semimystical exercise [. . .] in intertextuality'.[118] Dorsey claims that 'the very conformity found in spiritual autobiographies illustrates the way conversion rhetoric was a means by which Christians recorded their particular relationship to a larger culture'.[119] Alongside other Scottish literary converts, Brown's relationship with his larger Presbyterian culture is guarded and careful at times. As with Spark and Muir, he is keen to murmur religious declarations only in the confessional, in prayer, in private letters or embedded in fiction and poetry. It is this creative work that reveals Brown's conversion experience most fully. But as it grew, and took on an increasing cast of saints, sinners, redeemers and tempters, Brown's creative oeuvre was to open up new possibilities for Scottish Catholic writing and for Scottish literature itself.

Notes

1. Schoene, Review of *Interrogation of Silence*, p. 131.
2. Reichardt, *Exploring Catholic Literature: A Companion and Resource Guide*, p. 6.
3. Marshall, *In a Distant Isle: The Orkney Background of Edwin Muir*, pp. 103–4.
4. Ibid., p. 107.

5. Murray, 'A Sequence of Images: George Mackay Brown', pp. 12–13.
6. Fergusson, *George Mackay Brown: The Life*, p. 40.
7. Letter of Brown to Sr Margaret Tournour, 5 January 1992, MFA.
8. Letter of Brown to E. W. Marwick, 11 May (year undated but likely to be written in 1947), OLA D31/30/4.
9. Ibid., 15 February 1947.
10. Ibid. This letter is undated but is likely to be written in the mid-1950s.
11. Quoted in Fergusson, *George Mackay Brown: The Life*, p. 78.
12. Letter of R. Johnson to the editor of *The Orkney Herald* in response to Brown's 'Island Diary', *Orkney Herald*, 3 May 1955, [n.p.], OLA D31/30/1.
13. Brown, 'Island Diary', 13 December 1955 and 12 June 1956, [n.p.], OLA D31/30/1.
14. Brown, 'Island Diary', 1 February 1955 [n.p.], OLA D31/30/1.
15. Brown, 'Kirk Elder' typescript dated March 1943, OLA D31/30/2.
16. Brown, *The First Wash of Spring*, pp. 216–17.
17. Letter of Brown to E. W. Marwick, 25 February 1954, OLA D31/30/4.
18. Letter of Brown to Flora MacArthur, 2 May 1953, MFA.
19. Letter of Brown to E. W. Marwick, 14 February 1954, OLA D31/30/4.
20. Fergusson, *George Mackay Brown: The Life*, p. 142.
21. Letter of Brown to Ian MacArthur, 1 June 1960, MFA.
22. Brown to E. W. Marwick, 27 June 1960, OLA D31/30/4.
23. Letter of Brown to Stella Cartwright, 27 November 1964, EUL MS 3117.1. For a more detailed account of Brown and Stella Cartwright's relationship, see Fergusson's *George Mackay Brown: The Life* pp. 149–61, Brown's *For the Islands I Sing* pp. 136–41 and Green, 'Muse to the Makars', p. 9.
24. Letter of Brown to Renée Simm, 8 February 1979, MFA.
25. Ibid., 21 March 1979 and 10 April 1979.
26. Ibid., 16 March 1981.
27. Ibid., 28 May 1981.
28. In letters to Renée Simm 1978–93, Brown notes his desire to flee to Pluscarden Abbey three times. He writes, anguished, in June 1981, 'The number of visitors tends to overwhelm me. It becomes a burden, when all one's body and mind are crying out "Rest! – let me rest".' Letters of Brown to Renée Simm, MFA.
29. Letters of Brown to Dr Michael Curtis, 1977–85, MFA.
30. Letters of Brown to Kenna Crawford, 1986–94, MFA.
31. Letter of Brown to Renée Simm, 10 March 1981, MFA.
32. Letter of Brown to Sr Margaret Tournour, 27 February 1993, MFA.
33. Ibid., Maundy Thursday 1992; 7 July 1992.
34. Ibid., 19 June 1991.
35. Murray, 'A Sequence of Images: George Mackay Brown', p. 10.
36. Ibid., pp. 10–11.
37. Ibid., p. 11.
38. Letter of Brown to Charles Senior, 10 March 1966, MFA.
39. Letter of Brown to Sr Margaret Tournour, 27 February 1993, MFA.
40. Wright, *Theology and Literature*, p. 93.
41. Murrays, *Interrogation of Silence: The Writings of George Mackay Brown*, p. 267.
42. Ibid., p. 266.
43. Fergusson's *George Mackay Brown: The Life* reveals that this claim is simply not

true, and that Brown was involved in a number of romantic relationships, most notably with Stella Cartwright.

44. Fleishman, *Figures of Autobiography*, pp. 18–19.
45. Spengemann, *The Forms of Autobiography: Episodes in the History of a Literary Genre*, p. xvi.
46. Wright, *Theology and Literature*, p. 95.
47. Ibid.
48. Hall, *The History of Orkney Literature*, p. 145.
49. Ibid.
50. Fergusson, 'Up vistaed hopes he sped', p. 9.
51. Brown, 'The way of literature: *An apologia by George Mackay Brown*', pp. 584–5.
52. Livingstone, *The Concise Oxford Dictionary of the Christian Church*, p. 29.
53. Wright, *Theology and Literature*, p. 109.
54. Murray, 'A Sequence of Images: George Mackay Brown', p. 11.
55. Brown, 'Writer's Shop', p. 22.
56. Bright, 'English Literary Romanticism and the Oxford Movement', p. 386.
57. Ibid., p. 386.
58. Brown, 'The way of literature', p. 585.
59. Ibid.
60. Newman, *An Essay in Aid of A Grammar of Assent*, p. 65.
61. Newman, *The Letters and Diaries of John Henry Newman*, III, p. 292.
62. Wright, 'Newman on Literature: "Thinking Out Into Language"', p. 185.
63. Wright, *Theology and Literature*, p. 147.
64. Brown, 'The way of literature', p. 585.
65. Ibid.
66. Ibid., p. 585.
67. Ibid.
68. Chesterton, *Orthodoxy*, p. 53.
69. Dorsey, *Sacred Estrangement*, p. 3.
70. Fleishman, *Figures of Autobiography*, p. 285.
71. Letter of Brown to Sr Margaret Tournour, Maundy Thursday 1992, MFA. *Godspells* (1992) is a text by John Prickett, which Sr Tournour illustrated.
72. Montgomery, 'Spark and Newman: Jean Brodie Reconsidered', p. 96.
73. Starobinski, 'The Style of Autobiography', p. 78.
74. Muir, *An Autobiography*, p. 276.
75. Ibid., p. 277.
76. Hall, *The History of Orkney Literature*, p. 70.
77. Ibid., p. 71.
78. Muir, *An Autobiography*, p. 26.
79. Ibid., p. 173.
80. Traherne, *Centuries of Meditations*, p. 153.
81. Letter of Brown to E. W. Marwick, 30 April 1952, OLA D31/30/4.
82. Brown's supernatural tales, published in annual ghost story anthologies and collections, also highlight the special spiritual awareness that children possess.
83. Whittaker, *The Faith and Fiction of Muriel Spark*, p. 43.
84. Newman, *An Essay in Aid of a Grammar of Assent*, pp. 77–8.
85. Muir, *An Autobiography*, p. 23.
86. Ibid., p. 24.
87. Spark, *The Comforters*, p. 31.

88. Muir, *An Autobiography*, p. 151.
89. Fleishman, *Figures of Autobiography*, p. 375.
90. Muir, *An Autobiography*, p. 152.
91. Whittaker, *The Faith and Fiction of Muriel Spark*, p. 43.
92. Brown, *Orkney Herald*, 21 August 1945, quoted in Fergusson, *George Mackay Brown: The Life*, p. 84.
93. Newman, *Apologia pro vita sua: Being a History of his Religious Opinions*, pp. 53–4.
94. Ker, *Newman and Conversion*, p. 45.
95. Dulles, 'Newman: The Anatomy of a Conversion', in Ibid., p. 30.
96. Muir, *An Autobiography*, p. 274.
97. Letter of Brown to E. W. Marwick, undated but likely to be written in the mid-1950s. OLA D31/30/4.
98. Spark, 'My Conversion', p. 24; Brown, 'Writer's Shop', p. 22.
99. Spark, 'My Conversion', p. 25. See also pp. 26–7.
100. Tomko, *Sacramental Realism*, pp. 22–3.
101. Ibid., p. 23.
102. Spark, *Curriculum Vitae*, p. 202.
103. Montgomery, 'Spark and Newman: Jean Brodie Reconsidered', p. 96.
104. Spark, 'My Conversion', p. 25.
105. In her interview with Hosmer, Spark contradicts this statement and claims to have been greatly aided in her conversion by theological studies, so slippery are the facts she let slip regarding her private life: Hosmer, 'An Interview with Dame Muriel Spark'. Brown, 'The way of literature', p. 585.
106. Gilley, 'Newman and the Convert Mind', in Ker, *Newman and Conversion*, pp. 5–6.
107. Ibid., p. 7.
108. Letter of Brown to E. W. Marwick, undated but likely to be written in 1947, OLA D31/30/4.
109. Newman, *Parochial and Plain Sermons*, VIII, p. 225.
110. Spark, quoted in Litvack, 'The Road to Rome: Muriel Spark, Newman and the "Nevertheless Principle"', p. 31; Gilley, 'Newman and the Convert Mind', in Ker, *Newman and Conversion*, p. 18.
111. Spark, in Litvack, 'The Road to Rome: Muriel Spark, Newman and the "Nevertheless Principle"', pp. 31–2.
112. Dorsey, *Sacred Estrangement*, p. 9.
113. This phrase suggests that if the majority of Christians worship in the Catholic Church and recognise her sacraments, then this must mean that their judgement is sound.
114. Newman, *Apologia pro vita sua*, pp. 116–17.
115. Wright, *Theology and Literature*, p. 109.
116. Ibid., p. 110.
117. Geoffrey Galt Harpham, quoted in Dorsey, *Sacred Estrangement*, p. 5.
118. Dorsey, *Sacred Estrangement*, p. 22.
119. Ibid., p. 42.

CHAPTER 3

Mary

In *Greenvoe*, Mrs McKee sits, wracked with guilt and fear. She remembers a family holiday to the west coast of Scotland, where, during a sudden onslaught of rain, she pulls her young niece into an open doorway and turns to speak to her:

> But Winnie wasn't there.
>
> Mrs McKee peered into the gloom, and her heart nearly missed a beat, for it was a Roman Catholic church. There were two plaster statues, one against each side wall, and at the feet of the larger one – probably the Virgin Mary – three candles were lighted. A little red flame shone like a ruby at the side of the altar. Along three of the walls ran a sequence of paintings showing the Lord on his way to Calvary. It was all very lurid, Mrs McKee thought, a bit distasteful, like a sideshow at a fair. (*G*, 143–4)

The seeds for Winnie's future faith are sown in this moment. The girl later becomes a Scottish literary convert – the author of a historical novel named *The Stag at Bay*, in which the Young Pretender, Charles Edward Stuart, takes refuge one evening in a similarly important, half-ruined chapel. Winnie's conversion scene in *Greenvoe* closely parallels the experience of Robert McNish in George Scott-Moncrieff's novel *Death's Bright Shadow*, where Robert is deeply affected by Mass in a faded and worn Highland chapel. But though both Brown and Scott-Moncrieff share comparable visual imagery to illuminate the 'tacky aesthetics' of popular Catholic devotion, Brown focuses especially closely on Marian veneration in *Greenvoe*.

As the scene progresses, Winnie and her aunt watch an old, blind woman genuflect with some difficulty. The woman lights a small votive candle in front of the statue of the Virgin:

> One of the candles guttered and went out. The new flame burned steadily. The old woman sighed. The rosary slipped through warped and cunning fingers. She has seen much birth and death and love, thought Mrs McKee. That's certain. Well, if her religion was a comfort to her . . . The flame lapped a joyous intent face.
>
> Weak sunlight filtered through the north-west window of the church. (*G*, 145)

Dreamlike and exotic in its foreignness to the two observers, the elderly woman's prayer is nonetheless moving, and like Scott-Moncrieff's elderly parishioners, who clutch their rosary beads with 'gnarled fingers', the woman is suddenly deft and confident in her commitment to petitioning the Mother of God.[1] The action takes place outside of Mrs McKee's native industrial Edinburgh and is pastoral in its gentleness. The sea is nearby, the rain falls, and 'weak sunlight' (we are encouraged to believe) is the Virgin's recognition of the devotion addressed to her. Winnie's heart is captured by the Hound of Heaven as she gazes at this unrecognisable form of piety.

The 'plaster statues' and Rosary that Mrs McKee observes are indicative of an ancient legacy of devotion to the Virgin Mary in Scotland, and yet, to date, there has been no critical engagement with Mariology in Brown's work. This is not because there is very little mention of Mary in his writing. Mary appears often in Brown's opus, if sometimes fleetingly, but this mirrors her own part in the Gospels, where in fact she plays an almost marginal role.[2] However, despite the small amount of scriptural information about Mary, her cult has flourished over centuries, inspiring startlingly beautiful prayers, poems, paintings, icons, statues and shrines. Within the huge world corpus of Marian art, a large number of Mary's titles and much of her iconography is unbiblical. These are derived from tradition but also apocrypha – non-canonical writings (most famously the second-century *Protoevangelium of James*) to 'fill in the gaps' of Mary's life for Christian believers.

A great deal of Brown's writing on the subject of the Virgin might also be called 'apocryphal'. There is a wealth of manuscript work by Brown in which Mary is a central figure, but which remains unpublished and 'non-canonical' within his opus. Conceivably, the critical attention given to St Magnus in Brown's work has meant that his Mariology has been marginalised, or perhaps the Scots' own complicated relationship with figures that still remain objects of Catholic devotion makes matters more difficult. However, Mary is a subject with whom Brown was fascinated, and she forms an essential part of his own religious life and oeuvre.

This chapter investigates Brown's engagement with Mariology in three ways: first, it discusses Brown's creative use of Mary's various iconographical depictions and cults, in order to restore her image to Orkney's landscape; then, it appraises the ways that Brown's 'apocryphal' texts reveal that he was more politically engaged than is often thought. Last, the chapter provides a new reading of enculturation in *Time in a Red Coat* (1984), a novel that has never before been understood as the high point of Brown's Marian corpus.

I. Iconography

Mark A. Hall writes that prior to the Reformation, 'Marian devotion seems to have been as popular [in Scotland] as throughout Europe. Its local uniqueness comes in its particular physical and religious setting and encompassed both genders and probably all social classes.'[3] This is an important entry point into discussion of Brown's iconographical depictions of a distinctively Orcadian Virgin Mary, who reflects the idea that, due to her incomplete biography, Mary 'has been pressed into a variety of cultural schema'.[4] While she has been seen variously as a Roman virgin queen, a sorrowing *mater dolorosa*, a tender peasant mother and a beautiful child, she has also been fashioned in ways that are specific to local cultures.

In her discussion of Orkney's ecclesiastical history, Jocelyn Rendall notes that 'by the time of the twelfth-century building boom, by far the most popular dedication was to the Virgin Mary. There are thirty-three parish kirks and chapels dedicated in her name in Orkney.'[5] The widespread popularity of Marian devotion in pre-Reformation Orkney is reflected in Ernest Marwick's *Anthology of Orkney Verse* (1949). This is one of the collections in which Brown's poetry first appeared, and Marwick was keen to reproduce early Orcadian folk poetry within its pages. 'New Year Song' is a folk song of fifty stanzas, several of which seem to have once belonged to a ballad about Henry II and his mistress, Rosamund. The song displays Marian roots, and references to Mary become the constant refrain in the second and fourth lines:

> Guid be tae this buirdly bigging!
> We're a' St Mary's men,
> Fae the steethe stane tae the rigging,
> 'Fore wur Lady.[6]

While Marwick notes that the song 'is not, in any strict sense, an indigenous work', he makes a point of stressing that 'the first singers of this quaint old rhyme were doubtless good Catholics.'[7]

The Catholic roots of 'New Year Song' worked on Brown's imagination over many years. In *An Orkney Tapestry*, published twenty years after Marwick's anthology, Brown reproduces several verses of this song to illustrate the ways in which pagan customs and Christian traditions have developed and intermingled in Orkney. He claims that '[s]ecular and holy link hands' in the song, and '[t]he Virgin Mary, Our Lady, Queen of heaven, is also invited to be present' through the refrain (*OT*, 130). Brown's Orcadian folk narrator tells us:

> In the eye of Our Lady of Heaven, who presides over the song, the good man and the good-wife are as worthy as King Henry and Rosamund [. . .] it is hard to tell what Lady is being praised – Rosamund or Mary crowned with stars – so mixed are secular and divine. (*OT*, 131–2)

Here we see Mary as the 'Maria Regina' of the fifth and sixth centuries, whom Maurice Vloberg points out, 'evolved at the very centre of the faith and was especially favoured by popes', due to her expression of 'their faith and authority'.[8] Mary is a glittering, crowned queen in this description. She conforms to depictions of the regal Mother of God in the early and high Middle Ages.

However, elsewhere in *An Orkney Tapestry*, we see a very different type of Mary. In the 'Rackwick' section of the text, Brown depicts early Norse-inflected iconography of the Virgin in the valley of Rackwick on Hoy:

> Frik, who was the best stoneworker of the valley, found a long blue stone in the ebb. He squared one end of the stone so that it stood upright. He carved with chisel and hammer dove eyes in the stone. He carried Our Lady of Rackwick into the chapel. That night the statue of Our Lady stood in a corner of the chapel, her feet dappled with seven candle flames. Next morning she was placed in the open air, on the hill, between fields and sea; it seemed her dove eyes kept watch over the labours of fishermen and ploughmen, Our Lady of Furrows. (*OT*, 35)

Mary is explicitly connected with the Orcadian agricultural realm in this passage. She is assumed into a fishing and ploughing community and becomes the guardian of the very ordinary workaday world of 'furrows'. Brown's images of Mary in these descriptions are hewn from stone, making iconography in the Orcadian context something intimately connected with organic, natural materials. Mary's stone image fulfils the role of the icon – a sacred object marking the liminal space between the human and the divine – and in a way that is local to Orcadian landscape and culture.

Brown then heaps up the Virgin's imagery in the form of short verses of poetry that punctuate the narrative. These take on the quality of a litany, listing the agricultural titles of the Virgin's cults, or her personifications, before asking for her intercession:

> Our Lady of Cornstalks
> Our Lady of the Flail
> Our Lady of Winnowing
> Our Lady of Quernstones
> Our Lady of the Oven
> Blue Tabernacle
> Our Lady of the Five Loaves
>   Take the ploughmen home from
>   the ale-house sober. (*OT*, 38)

An Orkney Tapestry contains three of these verses, which were later reproduced and augmented under the title 'The Statue in the Hills' in Brown's fifth poetry collection, *Fishermen with Ploughs* (1971), along with four other verses which connect the Virgin with mourners, washer women, tinkers, spouses, crofters and fishermen. Brown's islanders are closely in tune with the Mother of God: his depictions of Mary mean that she enters 'into dialogue with the time, space, culture, problems and actual people who relate to her' in the text, rather being a coldly abstract Goddess-figure.[9] Instead of the dazzling Queen of Heaven, Mary is patroness of all the estates of Orkney, and guardian of their labours, endeavours and relationships. Brown's imaginatively re-created pre-Reformation landscape, in which all the inhabitants of the valley of Rackwick are united by devotion to the Virgin, ties in with Mark A. Hall's observation of Marian devotion as a unifying force in medieval society. This unity played on Brown's imagination so much that he created several of these short litanies to Mary, many of which did not make the final draft of 'The Statue in the Hills' and survive only as manuscript drafts.[10] In these verses, Mary's titles range from the ethereally beautiful 'Our Lady of Violets among Green and Gold' to the domestic 'Our Lady of Kirn and Rolling Pin'.

Soon in the text, however, the iconoclasm of the Reformers takes hold. Brown writes that islanders 'could now worship God in a pure form; the Pope and his bishops had been cast down from their high Babylonish places; the idolatry of the Mass was abolished, abomination of desolation that it was ...' (*OT*, 42). The islanders' long blue statue of Mary is soon 'fallen [. . .] and woven over with heather' (*OT*, 42) and their eyes are firmly fixed on loss, gain and profit. Scapegoats are sought when farming and fishing is unsuccessful and the word 'witch' enters the community's vocabulary for the first time. Here, as elsewhere in Brown's work, we can trace echoes of the persuasive historiography of his early mentor, Muir. Brown buys into Muir's idea of the violent disabling of a homogenous national culture here, and insists upon the destruction of a harmonious socio-cultural accord by the proto-capitalist ethos of the Reformation. It is clear that Brown does not apply nearly the same scathing critique of pre-Reformation Catholicism that he does to Calvinism in this writing. The underlying theme of this section of *An Orkney Tapestry* is the Virgin's goodness, gentleness and sweetness: all of which is used as a foil to the destruction that the Reformation brings.

Brown's polemics in this text have been a major problem for Alan Bold, who is fiercely critical of what he sees as the text's overt Catholic propaganda. His critical ire is directed specifically at Brown's depictions of pre-Reformation Marian devotion, and he notes that 'Brown has neglected to show us in what way the life there was once so idyllic (unless we are expected to believe that the open worship of Our Lady is the supreme happiness).'[11] Brown is undoubtedly excessively severe in depicting an almost instant catalogue of woes in the wake of the Reformation. He insists that 'everything was utterly changed [. . .] The religion that had sweetened [the islanders'] labours and sufferings was a creed now of terror and hellfire' (*OT*, 43). But it is important to read this work in light of the tropes of Catholic literature. Reading *An Orkney Tapestry* in this way provides a more nuanced understanding of the way that Brown uses Mariology in order to insert himself into a wider tradition. Mary's image was a prominent feature of the Counter Reformation and, as Nancy De Flon points out, she has often been used (particularly during the nineteenth century, by converts such as Newman) as part of polemical verse, '[b]ecause devotion to Mary was a feature of Roman Catholicism that distinguished it from Protestantism'.[12] It may be that reading *Fishermen with Ploughs* as the sincere outpourings of Brown's devotion means that his conscious engagement with previous works is missed. Bold maintains that Brown's writing 'is carried along not by an overtly cerebral process but by intuitively experienced images and symbols'.[13] Under this lens, Brown's Marian poetry is simple whimsy, and not – as this book contends – a rather more complex response both to the cultural catastrophe that Muir depicts, and the writings of other Catholic converts.

Bold has also been critical of 'Our Lady of the Waves', the most anthologised and best-known of Brown's Marian poems, in which the monks of Eynhallow petition Mary in verses that indicate the different canonical hours of their prayer. Bold's chief complaint here is that the poem is 'ritualistic to the point of dogmatism because the reader is asked to believe that he who asks shall receive as long as he prefaces his request with a prayer to "a figure of Our Lady"'. Bold's objection to the depiction of Marian veneration is not his only grievance, however, and he adds:

> It seems to me that Brown is merely going through the motions in his dogmatic poems. They depend so much on sheer faith that the poet feels little need to actively engage the attention of the reader. He is content to offer a recitation of a supposedly heavenly situation, a litany. To create poetry – to conjure verbal magic, that is – out of verse, the words themselves have to carry conviction so far that they move the reader along with them.[14]

It is worth considering whether Bold would criticise the poetic Mariology of the medieval makar Dunbar for relying on a liturgical structure, or for depicting the veneration of a religious icon. Bold betrays a critical reflex that is typical of twentieth-century Scottish literary criticism: he distrusts Brown's portrayal of religious devotion in a secular age and decides that, as a non-Catholic reader, he is excluded from the poem's message. This criticism suggests that Brown should avoid imaginatively re-creating a vision of life in medieval Orkney in case it alienates unbelievers. There is also a clear suggestion that Brown's poetic originality leaves something to be desired when he composes texts so liturgical in form. Bold argues that the poem's readers are meant to accept that the monks' prayers will be answered. But there is no hint that they are. In this poem, Mary is a stone image: we are not to know if she will provide what the brothers seek. Critical responses such as Bold's ignore Brown's highly distinctive, Scottish Catholic literary project. His construction of an Orcadian historical and cultural backdrop and allusions to wider Mariological depictions make him markedly different to the widely imagined modern Scottish author who is supposedly haunted by the spectre of Calvin.

Although Brown contended that if ever he attempted to inform his writing with historical research, it became 'crushed under accumulated facts and figures' (*FI*, 179), his work clearly demonstrates his knowledge of pre-Reformation Orcadian history. Brown's friend and contemporary

John Mooney, author of *Eynhallow, the Holy Island of the Orkneys* (1923), believed that Eynhallow housed a monastery during the twelfth and thirteenth centuries. Archaeological evidence has yet to fully support this, but undoubtedly, Brown's reading of Mooney, as well as his knowledge of older folk traditions and orally transmitted tales about the island, was the source of his interest in the place.[15] Eynhallow's ruined monastery provided fertile imaginative ground for him in terms of his poetry and prose. In 'Our Lady of the Waves', the description of Mary's statue 'in red stone' means that it is true to the ruins left on Eynhallow, and also fits with some of the earliest surviving representations of Mary in the British Isles.

In this poem, Eynhallow's monks beseech their 'Blessed Lady' for a fine catch of fish, and chant: 'Yet the little silver brothers are afraid. / Bid them come to our net' (*CP*, 44). Perhaps it is surprising that the brothers gather together to petition Mary and not the fisherman apostle St Andrew, but once more in this poem, Brown's work displays accurate historical grounding for his representation of Marian devotion. Marina Warner explains:

> In the tenth century began the first stirrings of the adoration that transformed the Virgin from a distant queen into a gentle, merciful mother, 'Our Lady', the inspirer of love and joy, the private sweetheart of monks and sinners, and the most prominent figure of the Christian hierarchy.[16]

The brothers of Eynhallow would possibly have heard of Bernard of Clairvaux (d.1153) who ended one of his sermons, 'In Praise of the Virgin Mary', by writing:

> O man, whoever you are, understand that in this world you are tossed about in a stormy and tempestuous sea, rather than walking on solid ground; remember that if you would avoid being drowned, you must never turn your eyes from the brightness of this star, but keep them fixed on it, and call Mary. In dangers, in straits, in doubts, remember Mary, invoke Mary.[17]

Bernard's stellar and sea imagery is a major feature of Brown's poem. The brothers end 'Our Lady of the Waves' by imploring the mother of God, 'Star of the Sea, shine for us', in what is perhaps the best-known of Marian metaphors. In the Middle Ages, the Church (having subsumed astrological and planetary symbolism) began to identify Mary with the moon and stars, and Christ with the Sun. 'Ave Maris Stella', one of Mary's titles, caught hold of the popular medieval imagination, and in the eighth-century antiphon *Ave Maris Stella* 'Mary appears as the ocean's guide, the pole star, winking benignly overhead to make life's journey safe. The dancing lines evoke her also as the gate of heaven, and the light-bearer, who purifies the sinner with her gentle fires.'[18]

However, as well as displaying Brown's supple interaction with Marian metaphor, image and liturgy, 'Our Lady of the Waves' reveals something of

his latter creative process, in particular his increasing anxiety over offending those with religious beliefs. Robert Crawford's assertion that Brown's
poetry 'fell victim to a spiritual exercise regime that became repressive'
may be entirely justified in this instance.[19] The original text of the poem,
published in *The Year of the Whale* (1965), has the monks chanting:

Sweet Virgin, the woman of Garth
Is forever winking at Brother Paul.
She puts an egg in his palm.
She lays peats in his cowl.
Her neck is as long as spilt milk.
Brother Paul is a good lad.
Well he carries word and wine for the priest.
But three red midnights
His tongue has run loose among dreams. (*CP*, 45)

Unapologetically sensual, the poem recognises the difficulty that celibacy
presents to one of the brothers, particularly because of the temptation
represented by the winking 'woman of Garth'. Brown's young monk is tormented by images of ripeness and fertility in dreams of the scarlet woman,
which emerge during 'red midnights'. However, in a later version of the
text, published in *Selected Poems* (1991), Brown's Brother Paul is quite different, and the poem's sexual element is entirely absent. The result is a
Brother Paul who is a chaste and simple eunuch, committed to Godly
praise and veneration throughout the monastic year:

Sweet Virgin, the women of Garth
Bring endless gifts to Brother Paul.
They put an egg in his palm,
They lay peats in his cowl.
One neck is long as spilling milk.
Brother Paul is a good lad.
Well he brings wine and word to the priest.
At midnight he sits by a white candle.[20]

This white candle signals a broader poetic whitewash by Brown. The dust
jacket to this edition notes that the author, 'in his seventieth year [. . .] has
chosen from those books the poems he likes best, revising some of them
substantially in the process'.[21] Instead of one woman winking suggestively
and bestowing gifts on her favourite of the brothers, Brown presents his
reader with a devout young monk who is mothered by the local women.

Brown may have cringed at the interaction between sexuality and devotion in this poem in his later years, but this element of 'Our Lady of the
Waves' contributes to the convincing medieval tableau that he sets out in
his early work. Miri Rubin observes that in monastic houses of the Middle
Ages,

an awareness of sin was all-pervasive [. . .] Guibert of Nogent's first little book, on virginity, shows just how obsessed was the young monk with sin, with the struggle between body and aspiring soul. He became deeply attached to Mary, who exemplified the combination of active and contemplative life and who offered help in the struggle against sin. [. . .] The experience and witness of prayer was part of what made [monasteries] emotional communities of great intensity. Prayer was one of the most expressive genres of monastic writing, and much prayer turned towards Mary.[22]

When examined under this light, the original version of 'Our Lady of the Waves' is a communal monastic prayer to Mary, which asks for her help in one man's ongoing struggle with sexual desire. The poem shows no anxiety in asking forgiveness for this human urge; it is one of many petitions which also include prayers for milk from a cow, and Mary's protection at sea. As '[l]yrics about Mary drew on established rhetorical habits for the expression of longing' during the medieval period, and because in these lyrics of longing, 'monks were Mary's lovers, and they were also the poets of love', it was not blasphemous or highly unconventional of Brown to include expressions of desire within a poem ostensibly about Marian devotion.[23] At the poem's original date of composition, Brown would have been in his mid-forties, and seemed as untroubled by the creative interaction of the sacred and profane as many of his medieval Scottish predecessors had been. In Brown's poetry, the gifts of God (whether these were love, sex or the bounty of nature) were there to be enjoyed. But as he aged, Brown became gradually more concerned to leave a body of work that could not be accused of sensationalism. It is unfortunate that his writing became weaker for his subsequent revisions.

Another side to the Virgin can be traced in a poem of Brown's which exists only in manuscript form.[24] 'A Prayer to Our Lady for a New Child' reflects Marian devotion from the thirteenth century onwards, where Mary is seen as mother of all humankind, lavishing maternal care and attention on her children. This poem conflates Mary with a series of beautiful natural images. It is written in pen, with additions in pencil included here in square brackets:

> Thou are the [grass-] blade among
>   dead [hill] fires
> With the dew on it
>
> Thou art the washed shell
>   From a storm
> Full of small songs
>
> Thou art a piece of wool in a
>   thistle
> From the lamb's side

Thou art the star over the hill
To ox and ploughman

That this new person, this
           spirit with hands
Might have bread
And a fish
And a coat to his back
A sufficient bed
For rest, love, sickness
(The hands crossed at last,
A star frozen in the eye,
An [A guardian] angel at all the
           Five gates)

Lady, accept our small verses

And pray for this Mansie[25]

This short poem sounds like a simple lullaby in its initial, soothingly regular stanzas, and indeed it also functions as a carefully wrought and unsentimental plea for intercession that is touching in its tenderness to both Virgin and child. It is also remarkably similar to verses of supplication to Mary that appear in the folklorist Alexander Carmichael's *Carmina Gadelica*, a text which includes Marian hymns and prayers within its pages of folkloric stories, blessings and proverbs. Whether Brown was to draw upon Carmichael's (partially fabricated) collection of nineteenth-century Scottish Gaelic material, we are not to know. But Brown did insist that through his mother's Highland, 'purely Celtic blood', he had inherited 'a strong Celtic element [. . .] a mingling of mysticism and intricate image'.[26] It would not be surprising to find that Brown had looked upon *Carmina Gadelica* with interest. 'A Prayer to Our Lady for a New Child' reflects something of the structure and content of this collection's English translation of the 'Supplications of the Saints':

Thou art the garden of apples,
Thou art the lull-song of the great folks,
Thou art the fulfilment of the world's desire
           In loveliness.

Thou art the sun of the heavens.
Thou art the moon of the skies.
Thou art the star and the path
           Of the wanderers.

Since thou art the gem of the jewel,
Save me from fire and from water.

Save me from sky-hosts of evil
 And from fairy shafts.[27]

Like the petition to Mary above, Brown's poem makes use of the refrain 'thou art the'. His coda, 'And pray for this Mansie', is similar to the Supplication's imploration to save the speaker from various dangers, 'And from fairy shafts'. In Brown's poem, Mary is also surrounded by images of healing and consolation amid nature. The regal Mother of God is absent in this description: instead she is a small glimmer of hope and a promise of intercession. She is the still-green stalk of grass 'with the dew on it', while all about her hill fires rage; an image that is very much reminiscent of rosary beads, and one that Brown also uses in *An Orkney Tapestry*, where Jock the tinker promises St Magnus: '"I'll say the ten Hail Marys – beads of dew on a wild rose"' before turning to Mary, 'the sweetest statue in the Cathedral' (*OT*, 93).

It would be easy to decide that Mary is no Christian object of veneration in Brown's prayer-poem, but a nature or fertility goddess. However, this depiction is part of Brown's overarching vision of the sacramental encounter with God in his Orkney surroundings. Partly springing from his own imagination, this was also learned through literature and in particular through the poetry of Gerard Manley Hopkins. In Hopkins' 'May Magnificat', Mary emerges amid springtime bursts of joy. Nature shimmers with the refracted light of the God who made it, and the poem's speaker asks 'What is spring?' of Mary 'the mighty mother', before concluding, 'Growth in everything'. Hopkins catalogues the bounty of the natural world in May, Mary's month:

Flesh and fleece, fur and feather,
Grass and greenworld all together;
 Star-eyed strawberry breasted
 Throstle above her nested.

[. . .] All things rising, all things sizing
Mary sees, sympathising
 With that world of good,
 Nature's motherhood.[28]

Hopkins is keen to ensure in his poem that Mary is not simply being celebrated as an ideal of beauty and fertility. Her grace can be accessed by looking at and reflecting on the beauty of nature, but the real celebration is of God's perfect work in her so that she is 'blessed among women'. Although we can see that she is a mother associated with flowers, plants, birds and jubilant, animate nature, this is not 'because Mary is confused with some ancient goddess or super-creature or rival of the Lord himself, but because Mary is a symbol or image of God'.[29] Richard McBrien writes: 'It is the God who is present within her and who fills her whole being that the Catholic grasps in the act of venerating yet another "sacrament" of the divine.'[30] Accordingly, Hopkins makes sure to end on a note which stresses Christ as the ultimate redeemer:

> This ecstacy all through mothering earth
> Tells Mary her mirth till Christ's birth
>   To remember and exultation
>   In God who was her salvation.[31]

In this way the Virgin is seen as a channel to God and a means of devotion to Him. Brown makes sure of this too, with his subtle metaphor of Mary as a piece of wool in the thistle taken from a lamb's side. In his poem, Mary is the always-loving mother given to all humanity by the Lamb of God, as he died upon the cross with a wound in his side.

Another of Brown's unpublished and, until now, unseen poems that deals with Mary's motherhood and uses devotional prayer as a structural device is 'Rosary'.[32] Dated April 1965, it was written a month after 'A Prayer to Our Lady for a New Child'. This poem, which uses a type of rosary structure, is spoken by a collective voice, and not simply because of the intrusion of lines from the Ave Maria (such as 'pray for us sinners'), but because it asks 'that loaves may be on our table / And our nets full'. It speaks for an agricultural community and acknowledges the pain of Christ's crucifixion, as well as the joy of experiencing the Holy Spirit's brooding presence in the world. The original manuscript draft of this poem is almost impossible to make sense of, as it is so heavily revised by Brown. Large areas of it are scored over thickly in red pen, but in a cleaner second draft, meaning becomes clearer:

>   The angel is in the first door
>   You go, a girl, between 2 [sic] houses.
>   The ox is in the straw, Lady,
> The bairn is in the Kirk, an offering
> The Word is among lost words
>
>   Hail Mary full of grace
>
> The cup over the furrows, Lady,
> The Blood on the nets,
> A wine of black gorse,
> Five red nails,
> Then the grief, the water, the oil, Lady
>
>   The Lord is with thee
>
> The angel is in the second door
> The Word is in the Risen Psalm, Lady.
> Always now the dove is about our doors.

One door you never knocked at, the
    House of death,
Queen of Heaven.

       Pray for us sinners.

Also that loaves may be on our table
And the nets full
And our croft doors ever open to strangers.

     Pray for us now & at the hour of our death.[33]

Like the prayers that compose the Rosary, this poem presents mysteries over which to meditate and contemplate, although these are not clear-cut. The first stanza unites the Annunciation and nativity, while the second alludes in its Eucharistic imagery to the Crucifixion, and the third to Mary's Assumption. Notably, Mary is fashioned in the first stanza of this poem as an ordinary Orcadian 'girl', while her child, an equally humble 'offering', is also a 'bairn [. . .] in the Kirk'. Perhaps Brown is not so unorthodox in his recognition of what the Magi, expecting a great king and saviour, were confronted with – a modest girl with a tiny baby in perhaps a rather dirty stable. However, Brown's depiction of two of the holy family, using the Norse-derived usages 'bairn' and 'Kirk', signifies a new development in his creative ideas about a vernacular, Orcadian Mary.

In his unpublished Marian oeuvre – as in so much of his work – Brown drew on the work of Edwin Muir. Muir's experience of witnessing Catholic art and piety in Rome led him to think back to his Orkney childhood's bookish Presbyterianism, where he 'was aware of religion chiefly as the sacred Word', rather than an embodied, incarnate faith. The 'white-washed walls' of the United Presbyterian church in Orkney did not reveal 'by any outward sign that the Word had been made flesh'.[34] However, in Rome, the signs of Christ's life, death and resurrection were everywhere, and so were images of His mother. In his autobiography, Muir records that he was particularly moved by a plaque in the street which displayed Mary's angelic encounter:

An angel and a young girl, their bodies inclined towards each other, their knees bent as if they were overcome by love, 'tutto tremante,' gazed upon each other like Dante's pair; and that representation of a human love so intense that it could not reach farther seemed the perfect earthly symbol of the love that passes understanding. A religion that dared to show forth such a mystery for everyone to see would have shocked the congregations of the north, would have seemed a sort of blasphemy, perhaps even an indecency. But here it was publicly shown, as Christ showed himself on the earth.[35]

The striking illustration of love that Muir saw in this plaque is what he depicts in 'The Annunciation', where he describes the encounter between Mary and the angel in Luke's Gospel. Luke 1:29 tells us that 'she was troubled at his saying', but none of the fear that Mary initially feels in the Gospel is a feature of Muir's poem: only the angel shows signs of the intensity of the meeting, as 'Each feather tremble[s] on his wings'.[36] Muir's 'Annunciation' emphasises Mary's rootedness to the earth; she, 'the embodied', is unable to transcend time, while the angel, a pure spirit, is able to do so. The poem takes places in an 'ordinary day' where something extraordinary happens: God takes the first steps into becoming flesh and shows abundant love to humanity by offering Himself.

Brown seems to have been especially interested in Muir's startling contrast between the ordinary girl and the 'eternal spirit' who announces her maternity. He has his own poem on the subject, 'Annunciation', which was never published. It is scribbled over and is virtually illegible, but most of the first and final stanzas in this small poem can be discerned:

> The girl baked, and the girl spun a fleece all winter
> And she gutted the fish,
> She set down milk for the cats
> All that dark winter [. . .]
>
> She went for water, her broom
> Sighed on the floor.
> What brightness is this
> Man in this door?[37]

Mary is depicted in the moments before the angel greets her, 'Hail Mary, full of grace ...', as a modest peasant girl who is firmly rooted to the domestic sphere in this poem. It is difficult to imagine that she 'holds the key to eternal life and can fling open the gates of paradise' with all the grandeur of the regal Roman Virgin, or that she sorrows over humanity and prays constantly for humanity's aid, like the Madonna of the Rosary.[38] Brown's version of Mary in 'Annunciation' is very much in the mould of the Virgin mother of the Renaissance, whose 'divinity [was] diminished and her features were often coarsened'.[39] In Wilde's 'Ave Maria Gratia Plena', Mary is 'Some kneeling girl with passionless pale face', while in Rupert Brooke's 'Mary and Gabriel' she is 'young Mary', suddenly faced with 'great wings . . . showering glory', but neither of these are quite as ordinary and vernacular as the Mary of Brown's 'Annunciation'.[40] His version of the Virgin comes closest to Muir's young girl, inclined towards the angel. She also reflects something of the 'common woman of common earth' or 'maid of low degree' depicted in 'Our Lady' by Mary Coleridge.[41]

Perhaps Brown could be accused of making Mary too commonplace; her ordinariness certainly runs counter to his strong belief in the miraculous incarnation. But Andrew Greeley notes that Raphael's Madonnas are often seen to be 'too human, devoid of spirituality', and this effect was deliberate, as '[t]he real Mary and the real Jesus surely did not look particularly spiritual or mystical'.[42] Brown's creative agenda is similar. In his writing about the nurturing, motherly love of God, Brown's depictions of Mary are akin to the early Franciscans', who placed a new emphasis on the Virgin as a holy woman who 'left her starry throne to sit cross-legged on the bare earth like a peasant mother with her child'.[43] In Brown's poetry, monks, sinners, mothers, children and sailors who chart the night's sky by navigating the stars can all access the Virgin's grace. She is evident in all things and is available to all as channel to God – an egalitarian and vernacular, rather than regal, Madonna. She is a reminder of a strong tradition of Marian devotion in pre-Reformation Orkney, and insists that religious life, in Brown's eyes at least, is much diluted without her.

Brown's Marian poetry reveals a mission to restore the feminine principle of pre-Reformation religious worship back to Scottish literature in the twentieth century. Brown frees the 'chained and padlocked' word from the pulpit of the kirk, and restores the sacred feminine, with all its attendant iconography and symbolism, to his writing of Orkney's fecund land and sea.[44] This feminine principle is shaped in highly local terms, with landscapes and litanies all pointing to a Virgin Mary who has been written out of Orcadian culture and devotion, but who was once very much one of its central constituents.

II. Apocrypha

Although Brown's Marian poetry reveals his careful use of different aspects of Mary's cult, in this work she remains a speechless visual icon who does not respond when approached by devotees. But in two of Brown's 'apocryphal', or non-canonical, texts she is no stone image. In *Our Lady of the Fishing Boats* (a play) and in 'Magnificat' (a short story) Mary is of the flesh – a living, breathing woman who is placed in a recognisable and not simply historical world.

Our Lady of the Fishing Boats exists as two manuscript drafts (MS1 and MS2) that are dated December 1964. A later, clearer draft of the play (dated 1966) also survives, and is marked 'rejected' by Brown.[45] This play is a curious piece of work, and its strangeness might well explain its rejection by the publisher, but the fact that Brown kept this piece suggests his plans for possible future revision. Brown is not often read as a political commentator; his published body of work is rarely satirical and usually uses the 1950s as absolutely the last chronological setting. However, *Our Lady of the Fishing Boats* (1964), written at the height of the Cold War and one year after John F. Kennedy's assassination, is actually set in the future.[46] This makes it a huge departure from the majority of Brown's published prose.

The original manuscript draft of the play is a heavily scribbled-upon, almost illegible draft entitled *A Nativity Play for Children*, but the reasons for Brown abandoning this idea soon become apparent. In Scene One, stage directions state: 'enter Joseph and Mary', which is then changed to the more impersonal, 'the man and the young woman'. These directions note that the setting is 'the census [later changed to 'registration'] office, the year 2000AD'.[47] It becomes clear that Brown's habitual setting of Hamnavoe in the year 2000 is part of a Communist state, in which inhabitants address one another as 'comrade'. Dialogue is strangely bureaucratic, sinister and to some extent stilted, indicating either that this is an early and unsophisticated attempt at dramatic writing, or, perhaps more convincingly, that there is wider miscommunication between characters in Brown's futuristic Bethlehem. The town's 'hot gospeller' is a secret informant for the civil guard, and the innkeeper and his wife, Margit, are greedy and officious. The Magi are 'three VIPs' whose 'passes are stamped by the chief commissar in Edinburgh'.[48] The play is swathed in darkness; it is only lit, briefly, by the host of angels who appear to a simple boy at the birth of Mary's baby.

In Scene One, Brown's Orcadian nativity is set in motion. Two clerks in charge of the registration office spy Mary and Joseph, and direct them to Humphrey's, a drinking den near the seashore.[49] Mary's first words: 'I can't go further', indicate her tiredness, and soon she is offered a place to rest by Willag, the old caretaker (who is also described using the Scots usages 'ghillie' and 'orraman' in the play's first draft). Willag's garage becomes Mary's stable, and instead of kneeling beasts surrounding the holy family, there are cars and an old boat called 'Dolphin'. Soon Mary's discomfort becomes apparent:

> (The young woman turns from the light)
> MAN (going over to her) How is it now?
> WOMAN A sword through the heart
> [. . .]
> WILLAG Hush, my dear, it'll soon be over. Think how fine it'll be then, eh? ...
> (He opens the back door of the Ford) You'll be warmer in here. You can lie down. (He takes her gently by the arm.) I've got some sacks to light the fire.[50]

Despite the biblical allusion here to Luke 2:35, where Simeon tells Mary: '"Yea, a sword shall pierce thy soul also"', Brown's depiction of Mary's pregnancy is challengingly unorthodox. His very literal interpretation of Simeon's prophecy flies in the face of Francisco Suarez's declaration, that the 'troublesome weariness with which all pregnant women are burdened, [Mary] alone did not experience who alone conceived without pleasure'.[51] Arguably, in making Mary suffer both anxiety and pain, Brown somewhat diminishes the miraculous nature of Christ's conception and birth. However, it is difficult to diagnose a lack of knowledge or failure to understand Marian myth and imagery in Brown's work, when, as we have seen in his poetry, he utilises aspects of her iconography so carefully. Margaret Bruzelius acknowledges the Catholic tradition of Mary's painless childbirth, which reverses Eve's curse in Genesis, where she writes that Mary 'cannot suffer at the birth of her son, but can only mourn at his death. Her power as a speaking mother, as intercessor, is inaugurated by her tears.'[52] But in Brown's play, Mary does suffer pain and tiredness, and she speaks openly. The order of the nativity story is inverted or reversed here, so that the biblical setting is made local, but Mary's experience is universalised. Her suffering is almost a democratisation; Brown suggests that Mary was chosen (of course) because she was free from all original sin – she is the Immaculate Conception – but in his play he reinforces her ordinariness. Mary is as frightened and anxious as any Hamnavoe lass, and because she suffers like any other woman during her pregnancy she is a potent image of the divine within the familiar.

In the midst of the darker and more sinister elements of the play, Brown creates some lighter notes. There are no shepherds tending their flocks in *Our Lady of the Fishing Boats*, but fishermen, who play cards and drink Barbados rum in a shed by the seashore. Stage directions tell us that '[a] boy, Saul, is keeping the fire going; occasionally he goes to the door and looks at the night and the sea. He is a bit simple-minded.'[53] It is Saul, Brown's 'innocent', who sees the heavenly host in the sky that (in his first draft of the play) bursts into song and proclaims, 'Gloria in excelsis Deo, et Pax Hominibus Borae Voluntatis'. Saul is given special insight into the mystery of the Incarnation, where all around him there is a kind of blind uniformity and disbelief:

SAUL I just spoke to an angel down at the rock. There's six other angels on the shore, Amos.
AMOS Just keep filling the cups with rum, there's a good boy. Never mind angels. It's the snow you're seeing.
SAUL (pointing through the window) And there's another one! The brightest angel of the lot!
[Amos sends Saul to Humphrey's to buy a bottle of best Barbados rum]
SAUL But will I get past them angels? Amos, I'm feared.[54]

Typically for Brown, it is the simple and imaginative child who is open to the possibility of a host of angels, or seeing something miraculous in mists of snow. Saul's fanciful interpretation of falling snowflakes is shown to be real spiritual insight later in the play, where it corresponds to the description of the infant Christ – '[a] little white winter blossom, the King of earth and heaven' – uttered by one of the Magi.[55]

However, the play also reflects something of the intimidation and surveillance that Edwin Muir experienced in Prague after the post-war Communist coup in 1948. His autobiographical observation that under Communist Party rule 'men at last became suspicious even of their friends' is in evidence in *Our Lady of the Fishing Boats*.[56] The totalitarian regime and its severe restriction of religion in the Eastern Bloc-controlled former Czechoslovakia is built into the fabric of this play. Brown makes his arch-villain a 'hot gospeller' and secret informant, who 'speaks in a low intense voice to Civil Guards' about Amos the fisherman's nationalist leanings, while outwardly playing the part of a firebrand preacher:

> HWYE (Pointing to the Civil Guards) Look at them they're waiting for me to say something against the government. (to Civil Guards) You're wasting your time, lads. You'd be better of a jug in 'The Plough and Stars'. Or 'The Arctic Whaler' – they have a warm fire there. You'll get no bourgeois reactionary talk out of me, not tonight. The Nationalists are in the hills. I have nothing against our leader. I'm a religious speaker, strictly.
> (The four fishermen – except Saul – come in and listen for a while, then go out under the cold eyes of the Civil Guard.)[57]

Within this strange, futuristic and yet all too contemporary Cold War context, Brown situates his winter nativity play. In the last scene, Mary allows Willag to admit worshippers into his old garage to see her baby, and all kneel before the mother and child. Saul brings seven fish and one of the Magi brings a honeycomb, at which Willag exclaims: 'A honey comb? I would swear it's a bar of gold, if I didn't know better.'[58]

While the final scene therefore suggests that Christ receives all gifts, this play – as signalled by its title – is about Mary. Brown suggests then that Mary's consent at the Annunciation was the most fundamental and important stage of Christ's incarnation. His play is in accord with the Little Office of Our Lady, the medieval liturgical cycle of psalms and hymns, which states: 'Rejoice, Virgin Mary, thou alone hast destroyed all heresies in the whole world'. Furthermore, Brown uses Mary's femininity and childbearing capacity as a radical foil to the increasingly complex political situation of his own immediate context. Physicality and the material world matter deeply to Brown. In his view, it is through objects and bodies (as well as in the material accidents of the seven sacraments) that God reveals Himself, and dispenses grace. Mary's physicality is highlighted to show that both body and soul matter under Brown's Catholic perspective. Rather than imprisoning Mary, her choice to be the mother of God is stressed all the more in a play that displays a frightening and dystopian version of Brown's increasingly nuclear age. The narratives of progress and efficiency and the denial of religion that Brown saw in Communist ideology are pitted against Mary, the image of reproduction. In *Our Lady of the Fishing Boats*, Brown's heroine is paradoxically a virgin, but the mother of humankind. She is a means to grace and an antidote to the supposedly improving qualities of the myth of progress that in the twentieth century brings so much mechanised death. It is left to Brown's twentieth-century audience to decide whether being identified exclusively with reproduction, consent, modesty and meekness is constraining or heroic.

Those who would see Mary as an ideological weapon for endorsing repressive gender parameters in *Our Lady of the Fishing Boats* may well read her statement of assent, her *Magnificat*, as her ultimate constraint. Mary's song at the Annunciation announces her absolute cooperation with God, and her joyful acceptance of her maternity. She sings,

> My soul doth magnify the Lord,
> And my spirit hath rejoiced in God my Saviour.
> For he hath regarded the low estate of his handmaiden: for, behold, from henceforth all generations shall call me blessed. (Luke 1:46–8)

Mary's song underpins and gives the title to Brown's unpublished short story 'Magnificat' (1994), in which Mary plays a central role.[59] Some feminist theologians have read the *Magnificat* as a signifier of female subordination and compliance, and the precursor of oppressive Mariology – the study of Mary that Rosemary Radford Reuther calls 'the exultation of the principle of submission and receptivity, purified of any relation to sexual femaleness'.[60] The title of 'Magnificat' hints at Mary's role as a willing and obedient 'handmaiden', but it is worth investigating whether Brown conforms to or subverts notions of passive female compliance in this text.

Brown sets his 'Magnificat' in the aftermath of Christ's death. As in *Our Lady of the Fishing Boats*, Brown introduces the character of a young boy whose imagination is linked to faith: he recognises Mary's goodness before anyone else. But in the story there also lurks 'a wicked toothless old woman who had no good to say about anyone'.[61] Immediately, then, we might argue that Brown upholds a negative gender stereotype derived from early Christian thought – that Mary's 'glorious precedence prevented any analogy between herself and other women, all of whom fell short by comparison'.[62] This old woman, a Mary in negative who 'mumble[s] ominous things from her ruined wrinkled whiskery lips', may point to Brown's polarising of female types. She becomes the text's Eve, a harbinger of trouble and a cause of fear.[63]

However, in 'Magnificat' Brown does not present us with a young, beautiful Mary. She is neither a historical figure of veneration, implored by fishermen and monks for aid, nor is she a young mother who sweeps the floor and cradles her bairn. In this short story she is a poignant symbol of grief. Mary is called a 'woman of sorrows' by the text's villagers, who add,

> 'No-one has had to endure as much as that woman. Every now and again the sword enters her soul. She was there when they took her son down from the death tree. She held him in her arms, with his death wounds on him. The wonder is, she is still alive.'
> 'She is sad now because we are hungry,' said the boy.[64]

In this story Mary is no longer 'a partner in prayer', the Virgin of early medieval Europe, but instead she is 'the figure of the suffering mother – *mater dolorosa*', whose cult flourished in the late eleventh century.[65] In the description above we see the image of the *Pietà*, and Bernard of Clairvaux's description of Mary seems appropriate: 'She was more tortured than if she was suffering torture in herself, since she loved infinitely more than herself the source of her grief.'[66] In 'Magnificat' Mary's pain is a key focus, so that Christ's death is not presented as the triumphant conquering of sin, but the very real and heartbreaking loss of a child.

As in *Our Lady of the Fishing Boats*, Brown contrasts political conflict with Marian gentleness. King Herod's officials deem the locals 'terrorists' (an anachronistic usage hinting at Brown's conflation of biblical characters and contemporary setting), but Mary provides water and wine for an injured 'comrade' of Herod's soldiers, and she binds his wounds with oil and strips of linen in an allusion to the second sacrament of healing.[67] Mary's love for her supposed enemy is a mother's love, and her role is again a domestic one, as she stays indoors, spinning thread in order to weave a robe for a village child. Afterwards, she reflects on divine love, and murmurs some of her youthful *Magnificat*:

> The first stars went through the sky like a troop of pilgrims. The wind got up at nightfall and blew gently from the west, bringing to her the smells and sounds of the sea, from far off, from very far off, incense of salt, tiny shells trundled in the breaking surf.
> 'My soul doth magnify the Lord,' said the woman, alone in her door. Then the wave of night, star-crowded, broke over the village.[68]

Here, much of the Virgin's iconography swarms together. Mary is the *stella maris* but she is also earthbound: she is a mother who spins and weaves, she is a sorrowing bereaved parent, and she gives glory to God and participates in His plan for humanity's redemption with joyful cooperation. Brown uses multiple facets of her cult in this unpublished short story.

Bruzelius argues the cult of the Virgin 'leaves women – or at least mothers – in the same position as of old: they purchase speech at the price of suffering. Within this context happiness and contentment are either nugatory or nonexistent.'[69] She claims that the writing of Julia Kristeva, Adrienne Rich and others who try to re-vision motherhood from a feminist standpoint, 'remains conditioned by the idea that maternal speech exists only because it can be validated by maternal suffering: only the woman of sorrow, bound in a uniquely painful relation with her offspring, may give tongue.'[70] It is certainly true that this suffering Mary, the grieving *mater dolorosa*, speaks more freely than any other version of Mary in Brown's work. She is notably vocal, defending herself by saying, 'I only gave a drink of water to a thirsty man', when villagers accuse her of helping Herod's soldiers.[71] We may well argue that in only allowing Mary to speak freely after the purchase of pain, Brown reinforces both negative and conservative values. However, in using Mary's *Magnificat* as the main structural and thematic presence in this short story, Brown reminds us that Mary's declaration of assent was first uttered during the Annunciation, prior to the death of her child. She was not silent when faced with the trembling angel that Muir describes so evocatively; she sang loudly and joyously. In 'Magnificat' this joyful praise has not ceased

– Mary's voice is still heard and she is the heroine of the tale, capable of clear-sighted sympathy and kindness.

This story is lent yet another dimension by a reading of the *Magnificat* as a song about social justice and the vindication of the oppressed. Lines from the *Magnificat* that reflect God's love for the very poorest are sung by Mary after the villagers discover that Herod is dead. Their spiritual rather than material riches are emphasised by the narrator:

> Then the sun came out again and it seemed as if the rain dripping from the sleeves and fingers of the people were diamonds and emeralds and opals. They turned their faces to the light. Their faces shone like the faces of blest spirits.
>
> *He hath put down the mighty from their seats* sang Mary from her spinning wheel on the doorstep, *and he hath exalted the humble and the meek.*[72]

Later, along with the apostle Simon Peter, Mary dispenses Communion in what we are encouraged to believe is the villagers' first Mass, meaning that Brown's text fits in well with the earliest narratives about the Mother of God, which 'often presented Mary as continuing Jesus' work of preaching and healing, as companion to the apostles'.[73] Brown makes sure to mention that the very poorest beggars and lepers receive Communion from Mary, so that here, as elsewhere, Mary is not a distant or remote Goddess – she is accessible to the lowliest members of society. The powerless, hungry and humble are exalted in Mary's *Magnificat* and she acts out of love for the poor, so that she at once fulfils her various titles as 'mother of divine grace', 'refuge of sinners' and 'comforter of the afflicted'.[74]

Christopher Whyte argues that 'the gender ideology of [Brown's] world is starkly repressive' because he identifies his female characters 'overwhelmingly with the reproductive function'.[75] It might well be argued that by depicting Mary's motherhood in a highly positive light, Brown reinforces the restricted roles available for women in his fiction and poetry. 'Magnificat' may well be read as a story of confinement and restraint, where Mary lingers on after the death of a son whose birth was the only happiness she could ever have imagined. But this view fails to take into account that Brown responds, albeit subtly, to the age in which he writes, as well as to theological orthodoxy concerning Mary. In Brown's play and short story, Mary offers solace and healing in a century in which Brown, born three years after the First World War, then lived through the Second World War, the Cold War and the Falklands War, and would, in 1994, have been aware of civil war in Rwanda and Serbian attacks on Bosnia. In his unpublished, apocryphal works with Marian subjects, Brown returns to an essentialist vision of the female reproductive capacity but uses it in, arguably, a new way – one that responds to his age. Both of his 'apocryphal' Marian works reflect contemporary world politics, and both of these pieces politicise the Holy Family, pointing out their status as refugees living in occupied territory. Brown is not often read as either a contemporary commentator or as a writer who uses gender as a source of potentially revolutionary energy, but both *Our Lady of the Fishing Boats* and 'Magnificat' reflect these ideas. Brown's emphasis on Mary's reproductive capacity is not, then, a conservative, essentialist or traditional standpoint, but a protest.

III. Enculturation

Brown's appropriation of the Virgin's iconography illustrates the diverse and colourful symbols, prayers and rituals associated with hundreds of years of Marian devotion. Over the centuries the Church has adapted and used these different images of Christ's mother in order to spread the Gospel message across the globe. Missionaries and priests have woven Mary into the religious traditions and artistic makings of various cultures, so that she becomes – among others – the Mexican, Chinese and Brazilian Mother of God. Mary is used as part of enculturation – the assimilation of the riches of local culture into Church teaching, mission and art. Brown 'encultures' Mary very firmly to his native Orkney, but how else does he depict her?

Until now, Brown's novel *Time in a Red Coat* (1984) has been read, as Timothy C. Baker notes, 'as allegory or fairy tale: it appears to be a collection of universal truths about the nature of human life presented through diverse myths and stories.'[76] The novel has been discussed most extensively by Baker and Berthold Schoene, and while both critics agree that the novel's European and Asian settings mark a complex departure from Brown's usual Orcadian *milieu*, neither Baker nor Schoene is eager to trace the text's engagement with Mariology. In fact, despite Roderick Dunnett's observation that the novel's heroine 'is herself a kind of Marian figure', critics have ignored this aspect of *Time in a Red Coat* entirely.[77] Nevertheless, Brown's novel is filled with hints, signs and symbols taken from Mary's place in global cultures, the Rosary and the Book of Revelation.

In his analysis of *Time in a Red Coat*, Baker stresses the novel's 'poetic representation of the human hatred of war and search for a peaceful community'.[78] Brian and Rowena Murray also note the text's commitment to depicting trauma and violence, arguing that it is 'an anti-war story' which ruminates on various instances of twentieth-century conflict.[79] The backdrop of war across continents will by now remind us of the vague, eerie settings of 'Magnificat' and *Our Lady of the Fishing Boats*, with their civil guards, terrorists, comrades and informants. However, in this text, there is no Orcadian Bethlehem, and no woman named Mary. Brown presents his reader with a strange, often-silent Chinese princess. She is born under the sign of water, and follows the 'dragon of war' so that she can offer healing and consolation in its wake. This is a role already associated with the Virgin, as Warner reminds us:

> The Virgin, like Athene, presides over peace and over war. She exists
> on earth and through the places and things she has consecrated by her

touch, and gives those things the right to victory. [. . .] In the ninth century the defenders of Chartres against the Norsemen had flown the Virgin's tunic from the staff of their bishop, and in local legend the wonder-working relic single-handedly turned back and defeated the invaders.[80]

The 'red coat' of Brown's novel displays remarkable similarities to the Virgin's tunic in the tenth-century Siege of Chartres. This garment begins life as a dress that has the young princess 'swathed in white silk' (*TRC*, 16) and cloistered under the watchful eye of her guardian, Mistress Poppyseed. However, the violence and turmoil of war throughout history stain the white silk dress so that it becomes a deep, blood red. The princess' tunic takes on the role of wonder-working relic, but it also records the progress of centuries in its increased shabbiness and in its symbolic change in colour from innocence to experience.

Baker argues that to read the novel as a Christian allegory would be 'reductive', and he claims that its Christian symbolism comprises 'only brief elements in a complicated narrative'.[81] He acknowledges Schoene's assertion that, in *Time in a Red Coat*, 'it is young people of the next generation who, self-confidently brushing aside the bleak disillusion of old age, make sure that communal life will continue and repeat itself', but neither critic looks closely at the religious significance of children in this text.[82] It is children (as in Brown's 'apocryphal' work about Mary) who recognise something spiritual in Brown's princess, while adults drastically misread her:

'Here's an angel coming,' said the child.

A young woman was coming up between the fields, in a gown that had lately been white, but now the dusts and flower-juices of a hundred miles had stained it. Birds had passed over it. Thorns had torn it here and there.

'Angel!' said the woman. 'I'll give you angel. Bring the other bucket here. The only angel that'll be coming to this village soon will be the Angel of Death, and it looks to me *he*'ll get a good harvest, at least. You listen to too many stories. The only angels are over there painted on the walls of the church.' (*TRC*, 24–5)

The woman's reproach betrays her failure to see the possibility of divine presence manifested on earth. Her religious perspective is limited to the painted angels that she sees on church walls, but these are meant to be a reminder, rather than the one and only source of religious beauty. In this comparison between the spiritual atrophy of adulthood and the special religious insight of childhood, Brown recycles a favourite trope. The young innocent, Saul, of *Our Lady of the Fishing Boats* gazes on angels, while nearby, Hamnavoe's grizzled old fishermen see only snowflakes. In this section of *Time in a Red Coat*, the female child calmly identifies an angel, while her mother grimly predicts the oncoming threat of war and death.

However, the spiritual qualities of Brown's young innocents signal more than his rehashing of a familiar literary motif. In this novel (and elsewhere in his Marian opus) Brown very clearly alludes to the child visionaries of nineteenth-century Europe.

As the idea of the Virgin's youthful purity took hold in the nineteenth century, her apparition appeared most frequently to single women, children and adolescents, particularly in France, 'where a sentimental view of both children and religion was rampant'.[83] Brown borrows the idea of European child visionaries for his late novel, and, in a phrase echoing the fourteenth-century mystic, Julian of Norwich, he acknowledges that the role of children in *Time in a Red Coat* was to make 'a pure sweet promise that indeed all shall be well'.[84] The novel's princess recognises the connection between the purity of childhood and her appearance to young visionaries. She says, dreamily, 'There's always a child. In every winter place, a child. In every broken and burnt place. They come, they drink round me like spring butterflies. I don't know why that should be. It happens' (*TRC*, 108).

Descriptions of the young princess' face and clothing also contribute to Brown's careful reinterpretation of the accounts of child seers. Before the princess sets out on her quest to slay the dragon of war, she sits, captured, in Mistress Poppyseed's house. We are told: 'At first glance, it could have been an ivory doll sitting erect in the tall chair, a doll swathed in white silk and carefully carved from ivory by a master. Then the doll gave a yawn, and it was a girl' (*TRC*, 16). This description is remarkably similar to the vision reported by the sixteenth-century St Teresa of Avila, who claimed that on the Feast of the Assumption, the Virgin cloaked her 'in a great white robe of shimmering light'.[85] She continued:

> Even though I could not make out many details, I could see that the beauty of our Lady was extraordinary. I was able to perceive the general form of her face and the amazing splendour of her garment. It was not a blinding white but rather a soft luminosity. [. . .] Our Lady appeared to me as a very young girl.[86]

This renowned Counter Reformation saint's vision surely influenced the depiction of Brown's heroine, who appears in various dreams and visions throughout the novel. In fact, Brown's reader is so besieged by the language of dreams, hallucinations and apparitions in *Time in a Red Coat* that it quickly becomes his least realistic and most highly fluid literary work. It would be easy to suggest that Brown's heroine is an amalgam of various fairy tale archetypes, but though she is certainly dreamlike, she is also (arguably) based on very real historical devotion, as the allusion to St Teresa of Avila's vision indicates. The princess is described in this way:

> To many she seemed the image of some girl they had admired or even been in love with, long ago, a thousand miles away [. . .] or a marvel-

lous figure that entered their dreams sometimes, so beautiful and good that they awoke resentful of the grey light of morning. (*TRC*, 94)

In this mystical-sounding account, Brown's heroine becomes the Madonna of the Rosary, who offers salvation and protection during wartime across the centuries. The Rosary's mystic origins have been attributed to the vision of St Dominic during the Cathar wars; Dominic claimed to have been given the Rosary by Mary so that humanity could use it to implore her for aid. Indeed, the Virgin is intimately connected with protection in times of war and instability. Boss identifies that 'promotion of the rosary has come to be a mainstay of devotions associated with modern Marian apparitions', while Trevor Johnson writes that the Madonna of the rosary 'was figurehead of the militant (and militaristic) Counter-Reformation'.[87] Notably, during the travels of Brown's heroine, she finds herself in a Germanic-sounding countryside, where churches have been burned to the ground. A blacksmith's wife tells her: 'Fat Luther and the fat Pope, they're not getting on with each other, that's what it's all about as far as I can gather …' (*TRC*, 83). Brown's princess is, then, more than a vaguely fairy tale heroine. She appears to people in reveries and apparitions, offering protection and consolation in troubled places in the manner of Christ's Virgin Mother. She is especially influenced by images of Mary during the Counter Reformation, a period which initiated a powerful resurgence of Marian devotions and theological writings.

Critics have not only overlooked the historical grounding for Brown's Marian princess, but also the fact that she is surrounded by Mariological symbolism. At her birth, the Palace Masquer announces, 'The child has come to us in the sign of water. She will be a water princess' (*TRC*, 14). Schoene notes the clear Christian association here and argues that 'Brown makes water, often referred to as the source of all life on earth, assume the role of redeemer in his story of suffering and violence'. He adds:

> our 'water princess', all dressed in white, is represented by the fish, a traditional symbol of Christianity. She is everyman featuring as main protagonist in a universal narrative in which the whole story is to resolve itself once and for all.[88]

But if this novel is read under the lens of Marian allegory, it yields much more precise themes and echoes. Water is of course primarily an image of nourishment, purity and – under a sacramental world view – baptismal grace. And water imagery does indeed function as the princess' main symbolic attribute. But water is also an abiding feature of the Virgin's iconography; Warner calls Mary 'the eternal mistress of the waters'.[89] Instead of representing 'an anonymous symbolic figure of mythic extraction, embodying The Redeemer for the whole of mankind', Brown's heroine represents (as she does in his unpublished play and short story) the mother of this Redeemer.[90] She is a mediating maternal focus for the war-weary inhabitants of the continents through which she travels.

The role of mediatrix and mother is most clearly displayed in Chapter 5, 'The Inn'. This is a key stage in the heroine's development within the novel, where she becomes less the angelic child, and more the image of a consoling mother. Baker identifies Brown's heroine as being subject to several different interpretations at this point in the text: 'she is Mitzi, the inn-keeper's dead wife; she is the snow princess of a child's fairy tale; she is a ghost; she is an external observer of events.'[91] However, her character is also explicitly linked with Orthodox icons of Mary – the *Theotokos* – where she holds the infant Christ in her left arm. In this chapter of Brown's novel, narration is focalised through the grief-stricken innkeeper's thoughts. When he awakes from sleep:

> Through the window, six opaque green whorls in an oak frame, an unearthly light was flooding into the inn, as if it was sunk in the sea. He squinnied at the icon on the wall, the Blessed Virgin and the Child. So: an inn too, an inn in midwinter, and in a crib in that inn had begun the true history of man, after the false start in Eden. Yes, with that sleeping infant the world had woken to full knowledge of itself. There, on the Virgin's arm, silent, reposed The Word that was to flood the whole universe with meaning. (*TRC*, 47–8)

This chapter is the novel's hallucinatory high point: the innkeeper confuses his grandchild for his dead wife, his thoughts wander to other wars, and his memories swarm into the text so that the reader cannot be certain whether Brown's focalised narration is reliable. This narration is certainly less than lucid, and the watery image of the Virgin serves to heighten the dreamlike, liminal, uncertain atmosphere. The inn is even built at the foot of a crossroads, perhaps reminding us of Mary's weeping at the foot of the cross. Most significant to this scene, though, is the icon of the Virgin and child, which is no backdrop or cursory detail.

Traditionally, an icon is a sacred image which makes the divine real and present for its audience or reader. It is no surprise that the novel's princess appears shortly after the innkeeper studies the icon of the Virgin and Child. She is spiritually summoned by the innkeeper, who dreams of the nativity. In his dream he becomes the innkeeper who greets Mary and Joseph, and 'he saw with a start that the girl was with child [. . .] a first low sweet moan was on her lips. The purity of the girl's face touched him' (*TRC*, 48). Through the icon, Christ's birth is really made present for the man. Mary becomes the 'tremulous girl', to whom he says, consolingly: 'There, my dear, it'll soon be all over. Then think how happy you'll be with the little new-born one in your arms' (*TRC*, 19). Notably, these words are almost identical to those of old Willag's, in *Our Lady of the Fishing Boats*, written around twenty years previously. Brown's previous Marian writings were not wasted in this, his last and most sustained reflection on the God-bearer.

As Brown's old, dreaming innkeeper finishes contemplating the icon of the Virgin, the novel's princess (a Mary in disguise) appears, and in effect saves the lives of the man and his granddaughter. This little granddaughter who (of course) possesses spotless spiritual vision, gives 'a cry like a little bell' (*TRC*, 51) and offers the princess a bed, while the old man remains unsure of her. Several references are made to the princess' white gown, the effective battle talisman of the text, which may remind us of the Virgin's clothing, especially (according to tradition) the tunic she wore during the Annunciation. Mary's clothes have long been seen as powerful relics, because they were believed to be 'steeped in her holiness by direct communication with her pure and incorruptible body'.[92]

When she is asked what brings her to an inn in the middle of winter, the princess reiterates her mission. She says wearily that she must '"kill the Dragon"' (*TRC*, 52). The dust jacket of the novel's 1991 reprint explains succinctly that the task of the girl is 'to slay the burgeoning dragon of war before it destroys the world that she loves …', but to date critical appraisals of the novel have left the symbolic potential of this dragon rather unexplored. Little has been made of the text's thematic link with Brown's poetry collection *Fishermen with Ploughs* (1971), which depicts a ninth-century Norwegian tribe fleeing 'starvation, pestilence, turbulent neighbours (what the poet calls, in the shorthand of myth, the Dragon)' (*CP*, 89). Nor have critics explored the novel's connections with the Book of Revelation, where a woman – often read as Mary herself – is attacked by 'a great red dragon, having seven heads and ten horns' (Revelation 12:3).

John the Apostle is traditionally identified by the Church as author of Revelation. Amid apocalyptic scenes of chaos, darkness and turmoil, he reveals:

> And there appeared a great wonder in heaven; a woman clothed with the sun, and the moon under her feet, and upon her head a crown of twelve stars: And she being with child cried, travailing in birth, and pained to be delivered.
>
> And there appeared another wonder in heaven; and behold a great red dragon, having seven heads and ten horns, and seven crowns upon his heads.
>
> And his tail drew the third part of the stars of heaven, and did cast them to the earth: and the dragon stood before the woman which was ready to be delivered, for to devour her child as it was born.
>
> And she brought forth a man child, who was to rule all nations with a rod of iron: and her child was caught up unto God, and to his throne.
>
> And the woman fled into the wilderness . . . (Revelation 12:1–6)

Rather than a male child, it is the princess who is born at the start of *Time in a Red Coat*, but she too is born after 'a long labour, full of pain' (*TRC*, 11) that mirrors these scriptural pangs of childbirth. She also utters 'after a silence, one thin lost cry' (*TRC*, 13) and she too is a Marian figure, like the woman characterised by lunar and solar imagery who combats the dragon of Revelation. Revelation discloses that 'when the dragon saw that he was cast unto the earth, he persecuted the woman which brought forth the man child. And to the woman were given two wings of a great eagle, that she might fly into the wilderness' (Revelation 12:13–14). Brown's novel relays that at the birth of the princess, 'Very far off, an eagle (a throbbing needle point) rose above the mountains and wheeled north, and soon was nothingness in the veils of mist' (*TRC*, 2). Brown's first chapter closes dramatically, saying, 'Hooves splashed through the goldfish ponds. Scent of trodden roses was everywhere. Hooves broke the branches. Hooves reared against the first stars' (*TRC*, 15). The four references to hooves clearly point to the four horsemen of the Apocalypse in Revelation and signal the destruction to come. Indeed, the last sentence of this chapter tells us, 'It is now the time of the dragon' (*TRC*, 15).

The language, texture and imagery of Revelation continue to underpin the novel throughout. For example, where Revelation relates that 'the serpent cast out of his mouth water as a flood after the woman, that he might cause her to be carried away of the flood' (Revelation 12:15), in Brown's novel we see the princess almost submerged and drowned. In Chapter 4, 'River', a soldier's corpse collides with her small boat. When she is asked by a ferryman where she is going, the girl replies, 'to the war and the wounds' (*TRC*, 39), while in Revelation we are told, 'the dragon was wroth with the woman, and went to make war with the remnant of her seed' (Revelation 12:17). Brown uses the imagery and character of Revelation to underline his novel about war and to reinforce the Marian aspects of his heroine, but perhaps he suggests more broadly that a loss of faith in the consolation that the Virgin can offer may bring about wider sorrow. Indeed, he may even argue through this Midrashic novel that the loss of Marian veneration and the neglect of Marian piety are more serious and even demonic, as signalled by the dragon. Nevertheless, by the end of *Time in a Red Coat*, the princess' coat has become white again, as attentive readers of Revelation may expect. In the last book of the Bible, the marriage of the Lamb and his wife are heralded by her 'fine linen, clean and white: for the fine linen is the righteousness of saints' (Revelation 19:8) and the Lamb's 'vesture dipped in blood' (Revelation 19:13). The Lamb's armies in heaven 'followed him upon white horses, clothed in fine linen, white and clean' (Revelation 19:14).

This novel is ultimately the high point of Brown's Marian oeuvre, most of which is, ironically, 'apocryphal', like many of the early legends of the Virgin herself. There is further irony in the critical misreading of *Time in a Red Coat*, a novel which has never been seen as explicitly influenced by Marian motifs, devotions and iconography. Critical writings have expressed dissatisfaction with a Catholic reading of this text, and have even seen this type of analysis as reductive. Taken as a whole, Brown's unpublished poetry, play and short story all feed into the depiction of the princess in *Time in a Red Coat*. His apocryphal works on Mary – particularly his play – are early structuring devices in which Brown experiments creatively with the images and titles of the Virgin's many cultic representations. These unpublished works are windows into Brown's creative process – one rich with symbolism and a long historical legacy of Marian devotion. Trevor Johnson argues that 'Mary's regal status can [. . .] be read as a sign of her supereminent position among the saints of the Church – a position of such central importance that she [holds] the office of highest authority after that of Christ.'[93] Brown affords her this authority, even in her most humble and vernacular depictions.

Ultimately, Brown's writing on the Virgin Mary serves as a major rebuttal to many of the criticisms that have been levelled at him throughout his career. Brown is not the merely instinctive and intuitive poet that Bold often describes. His Marian writings are grounded in close observation of the ways that Mary's cult has changed and developed over the centuries, and consequently he presents her in a variety of forms: as stone image amid a pre-Reformation agricultural society; as glittering Queen of Heaven; as a young croft-wife nursing a bairn in her arms; as a grieving older mother; as a young girl appearing in religious apparitions, and as the God-bearer, *Theotokos*. Brown's critics are often displeased with his devotional poetry, demanding that he fit into the more conventional mould of the 'condition of Scotland' novel, or the urban realist narratives of twentieth-century Scottish fiction. Critics have also seen religious readings of his work as reductive. Brown may have taken criticism of his devotional poetry so badly that much of his work on Mary remains unpublished, despite the fact that it engages with his own immediate context significantly more than has been appreciated.

However, Mary is a major feature of Brown's overarching sacramental vision of all material reality. She is a mediator of God's grace, and made appropriate to the Orcadian landscape to which she is often encultured. Orkney's stars, waves and wild flowers cluster around Mary. Children of untarnished spiritual vision in these texts lead their audience by the hand, and attempt to show how faith was once celebrated, before the 'fall' that placed new emphasis on narratives of progress and efficiency. Brown's Marian texts are not always wholly successful – the political subtext to *Our Lady of the Fishing Boats* is certainly unlikely to make much of a mark on children, Brown's original intended audience. *Time in a Red Coat* was not an overwhelming critical success, its subtly embedded religious foundations and allegorical overtones being out of fashion in its 1980s context. Perhaps it is difficult, too, for Brown's readership to feel any degree of warmth or empathy for the Marian figures in his writing. Although the Madonnas in his poetry and the grieving mother of 'Magnificat' are sympathetic figures, they are far removed from readers' everyday lives. Winnie Melville of *Greenvoe* and even the convert-writer Colm of 'The Tarn and the Rosary' are more accessible, familiar, flawed and emotional protagonists.

However, where Brown's published output on Mary is often characterised by reticence, reserve and shyness to publish, his work on Orkney's patron saint is, by contrast, all boldness and experimentation. It is to St Magnus that the focus of this book will now turn.

Notes

1. Scott-Moncrieff, *Death's Bright Shadow*, p. 113.
2. Mention of Mary is mostly confined to the Gospel of St Luke, where she speaks four times.
3. Hall, 'Wo/men only? Marian devotion in medieval Perth', p. 124.
4. O'Brien, 'Mary In Modern European Literature', p. 521.
5. Rendall, *Steering the Stone Ships*, p. 46.
6. Anonymous, 'New Year's Song', in Marwick (ed.), *An Anthology of Orkney Verse*, p. 47.
7. Ibid., pp. 45, 46.
8. Vloberg, 'The Iconographic Types of the Virgin in Western Art', p. 550.
9. O'Brien, 'Mary In Modern European Literature', p. 529.
10. Alternative verses are included in NLS Acc. 4864.3.
11. Bold, *George Mackay Brown*, p. 40.
12. De Flon, 'Mary In Nineteenth-Century English and American Poetry', p. 505.
13. Bold, *George Mackay Brown*, p. 30.
14. Ibid., p. 28.
15. See Rendall, *Steering the Stone Ships*, p. 54. Some well-known tales about the island are reproduced by Joseph Ben in his sixteenth-century *Description of the Orkney Islands*. See Ben, 'Description of the Orkney Islands', pp. 266–71.
16. Warner, *Alone of All Her Sex*, p. 130.
17. St Bernard of Clairvaux, quoted in Campbell, *Mary and the Saints*, p. 40.
18. Warner, *Alone of All Her Sex*, p. 262.
19. Crawford, 'In Bloody Orkney', p. 25.
20. Brown, 'Our Lady of the Waves', *Selected Poems 1954–1983*, p. 36.
21. Dust jacket of Brown's *Selected Poems 1954–1983*.
22. Rubin, *Mother of God*, p. 131.
23. Ibid., p. 194.
24. Brown, 'A Prayer to Our Lady for a New Child', March 1965, NLS Acc.4864.3.
25. Ibid.
26. Brown, *Northern Lights*, p. 132.
27. Carmichael, *Carmina Gaelica*, p. 133.
28. Hopkins, 'May Magnificat', in *The Major Works*, p. 139.
29. McBrien, *Catholicism*, p. 1109.
30. Ibid.
31. Hopkins, 'May Magnificat', *The Major Works*, p. 140.
32. Brown, 'Rosary', 6 April 1965, NLS Acc.4864.3.
33. Ibid.
34. Muir, *An Autobiography*, p. 273.
35. Ibid., p. 274.
36. Edwin Muir, 'The Annunciation', in *Collected Poems*, p. 224.
37. Brown, 'Annunciation' [n.d.], NLS Acc.4864.3.
38. Warner, *Alone of All Her Sex*, p. 289.
39. Vloberg, 'The Iconographic Types of the Virgin in Western Art', p. 56.

40. Atwan and Wieder (eds), *Chapters into Verse*, pp. 13, 16–17.
41. Jeffrey (ed.), *A Dictionary of Biblical Tradition in English Literature*, p. 494.
42. Greeley, *The Catholic Imagination*, pp. 97–8.
43. Warner, *Alone of All Her Sex*, p. 182.
44. Brown, *A Spell for Green Corn*, pp. 90–1.
45. Brown, *Our Lady of the Fishing Boats* (1964), two manuscripts (MS 1 and MS 2), NLS Acc.4864.9. All further references will be to MS 2, unless indicated. Another, clearer, draft of the play (dated 1966) also exists in Brown's papers in the University of Edinburgh's Special Collections. See EUL MS 3115.5.b.
46. Brown's elegy 'The Seven Houses: In Memory of John F. Kennedy' appears in *The Year of the Whale* (1965) alongside 'Our Lady of the Waves', indicating that Marian devotion as well as contemporary politics were on his mind at this time. These ideas are married in *Our Lady of the Fishing Boats*, though perhaps not altogether successfully.
47. Brown, *Our Lady of the Fishing Boats* (1964), MS 2.
48. Ibid.
49. Ibid.
50. Ibid.
51. Francisco Suarez, 'The Dignity and Virginity of the Mother of God', quoted in Warner, *Alone of All Her Sex*, p. 43.
52. Bruzelius, 'Mother's Pain, Mother's Voice: Gabriela Mistral, Julia Kristeva, and the Mater Dolorosa', p. 218.
53. Brown, *Our Lady of the Fishing Boats* (1964), MS 2.
54. Ibid.
55. Ibid.
56. Muir, *An Autobiography*, p. 263.
57. Brown, *Our Lady of the Fishing Boats* (1964), MS 2.
58. Ibid.
59. Brown, 'Magnificat' (1994), OLA D124/18/2/6.
60. Rosemary Radford Reuther, quoted in Johnson, 'The Marian Tradition and the Reality of Women', p. 98.
61. 'Magnificat' [n.p.].
62. Johnson, 'The Marian Tradition and the Reality of Women', p. 104.
63. 'Magnificat' [n.p.].
64. Ibid.
65. Rubin, *Mother of God*, p. 109.
66. Bernard of Clairvaux, quoted in De Visscher, 'Marian Devotion in the Latin West in the Later Middle Ages', p. 183.
67. 'Magnificat' [n.p.].
68. Ibid.
69. Bruzelius, 'Mother's Pain, Mother's Voice: Gabriela Mistral, Julia Kristeva, and the Mater Dolorosa', p. 226.
70. Ibid., p. 217.
71. Mary is also the only villager, apart from the Rabbi, who can read a notice pronouncing Herod's death. Brown is keen to stress her intelligence.
72. 'Magnificat' [n.p.].
73. Rubin, *Mother of God*, p. 152.
74. These titles are taken from the Litany of Loreto, a Marian litany approved by the Church in 1587.

75. Whyte, *Modern Scottish Poetry*, pp. 170–1.
76. Baker, *George Mackay Brown and the Philosophy of Community*, p. 96.
77. Dunnett, 'George Mackay Brown at Seventy', p. 7.
78. Baker, *George Mackay Brown and the Philosophy of Community*, p. 96.
79. Murrays, *Interrogation of Silence*, p. 195.
80. Warner, *Alone of All Her Sex*, p. 304.
81. Baker, *George Mackay Brown and the Philosophy of Community*, p. 101.
82. Schoene, *The Making of Orcadia*, p. 251.
83. Warner, *Alone of All Her Sex*, p. 302. See also Maunder, *Our Lady of the Nations: Apparitions of Mary in Twentieth-Century Catholic Europe*, pp. 50–4, 64–73.
84. Brown, quoted in Baker, *George Mackay Brown and the Philosophy of Community*, p. 98.
85. Starr (trans.), *Teresa of Avila: The Book of My Life*, p. 267.
86. Ibid., p. 268.
87. Boss, 'Telling the Beads: The Practice and Symbolism of the Rosary', p. 391; Johnson, 'Mary in Early Modern Europe', p. 366.
88. Schoene, *The Making of Orcadia*, pp. 250, 249.
89. Warner, *Alone of All Her Sex*, p. 262.
90. Schoene, *The Making of Orcadia*, p. 254.
91. Baker, *George Mackay Brown and the Philosophy of Community*, p. 99.
92. Warner, *Alone of All Her Sex*, p. 292.
93. Johnson, 'Mary in Early Modern Europe', p. 159.

CHAPTER 4

Magnus

On 20 October 1994, George Mackay Brown wrote to Sr Margaret Tournour:

> A learned Norwegian wrote an article in 'The Orcadian' last Thursday, attacking St Magnus and the whole conception of Sainthood. Yesterday morning I felt I ought to reply. Those learned people judge everything by the light of common day. So I wrote a reply, to the effect that common people knew a saint when they had experience of one: and clever people are like Wordsworth's Peter Bell: 'a primrose by the river's brim / A yellow primrose was to him / And nothing more ...'. Many of them are essentially ignorant.[1]

This was not, by Brown's late standards, a measured response. Indeed, Brown's article of reply to Erik O. Paulsen's 'Well, is St Magnus really a saint?' is a strongly worded piece, which condemns Paulsen's work as 'at best a grey and uninteresting' comment. Brown writes that Paulsen has presented 'the prose rather than the poetry' in his examination of the life of St Magnus, and he chastises the *Orcadian*'s readers, noting, 'I was sorry to see, on the week after Mr Paulsen's article, that not one Orcadian had spoken up on behalf of their saint.'[2] This prickly response seems at first to be incongruous with Brown's public persona at this late stage in his life. He was usually careful to avoid any sort of theological debate, writing to Sr Margaret in 1992: 'if in any company a religious argument however friendly develops, I either shut up or go away: my mind doesn't work logically, only imaginatively. Slowly one comes to learn one's limitations.'[3] However, despite his deep need for privacy, Brown could not sit idly by while the sainthood of St Magnus was called into question. Brown's article of reply, 'The Magnus Miracles were Manifold', expresses his passionate, lifelong commitment to an Orcadian saint who was central to his faith and creative career.

In fact, Brown had been aware since his youth that St Magnus (born c. 1075) was viewed as rather an odd historical figure by many of his fellow islanders. He writes in his autobiography that Orcadians 'considered [St Magnus] to be a queer fish, one of those medieval figures, clustered about with mortifications and miracles that have no real place in our enlightened progressive society' (*FI*, 52). But for Brown, the importance of discovering St Magnus in *Orkneyinga Saga* cannot be overstated. Brown depicts the martyrdom of Magnus in a large number of works, and across a variety of literary forms and styles. As such, he has done more for this historical, religious figure than any other modern writer; indeed, the *Saga*'s 1981 Penguin edition is dedicated to Brown. His work on St Magnus is, therefore, of vital importance to understanding Brown as a Scottish Catholic artist.

The critical reaction to Brown's corpus of writings on St Magnus has (at times) been as muted as the public reaction to this saint. Bold writes: 'It may be that Brown had lived so long with his faith in Magnus the saint that the writing of [the novel *Magnus*] was done more in the nature of a religious duty than a stimulating act of creation.'[4] Similarly, Douglas Gifford's contention that Brown's work is characterised by 'a predictable denouement' and 'an artless obviousness of situation and image' is also based on 'the explicit miracle that ends *Magnus*'.[5] Gifford's view is typical of criticism that finds Brown's Orcadian locus, subject matter and religious history to be creatively stifling. But Brown's fascination with St Magnus can instead be seen as catalytic – a force of inspiration for creative work in a variety of literary modes, which shows him to be an experimental, diverse and prolific devotional writer.

Any examination of Brown as twentieth-century Scottish hagiographer has to investigate the ways in which *Magnus* (1973) – the novelistic high point of his hagiographic accounts – might be situated within a wider sphere of Catholic writing, as well as within the textual conventions of hagiography and Norse belief and culture. This chapter will consider the ways in which Brown adopts, develops and subverts the cult of St Magnus in literary terms. It will consider Brown's different formal treatments of this medieval Catholic saint, particularly in terms of the novel, which some have called 'practically a Protestant form of art'.[6]

I. History, Hagiography and the Cult of Saint Magnus: The Sagas

The earliest *vitae* (or biographies) of St Magnus are: a Latin Life – *Legenda de sancto Magno* – which is taken from the *Vita Sancti Magni*, a narrative composed by an Orcadian priest named 'Master Robert'; *Orkneyinga Saga* (*The Saga of the Earls of Orkney*); *Magnús saga skemmri* (*Magnús saga the shorter*); and *Magnús saga lengri* (*Magnús saga the longer*). It is generally agreed by saga scholars that the Latin Life is the original source for the sagas, of which *Orkneyinga Saga* is the earliest: Haki Antonsson dates it from the first half of the thirteenth century.[7] While, recently, there has been disagreement on some of the finer points of dating the Sagas, most scholars are in agreement with John Mooney's claim that:

> A comparison of the three versions of the 'Life of St Magnus,' may be held as showing the *Orkneyinga Saga* and the *Short Saga* to be biographical sketches of Magnus as EARL OF ORKNEY, and that of the *Longer*, Magnus as a NORTHERN SAINT.[8]

While this book will not become embroiled in dating historical events, folios and manuscripts, it is essential to bear in mind the different sources for St Magnus' hagiography as re-created by Brown. While critics have, in the past, looked mainly to *Orkneyinga Saga* as the source text for Brown's depiction of Magnus, many of the events in his version of Magnus' life are in fact taken from these other accounts – particularly from the longer, more 'saintly' reconstruction. Brown read saga literature extensively, and it is *Orkneyinga Saga* that he singles out as 'magnificent stories [. . .] told by a genius' (*FI*, 64). However, John Mooney's *St Magnus, Earl of Orkney* (1935) details the variations in the St Magnus legend as told by the *longer* saga, and, as this was a book that Brown discovered early on and treasured, we can be sure that he was aware of the often quite different young Earl that this saga depicts.[9]

Orkneyinga Saga details the history of the Viking Earls of Orkney, and especially the life, death and posthumous miracles of Magnus Erlendson, the Earl whose execution was ordered by his cousin Hakon Paulson on the island of Egilsay c. 1117 after a feud to gain sole control of Orkney. The *Saga* tells of Magnus' early refusal to fight at the Battle of Menai Strait (c. 1098), where he sat chanting psalms on the prow of a Viking ship. It reveals that on the day of his martyrdom, Magnus prayed, and then asked his reluctant executioner to strike him hard on the head with the axe (to avoid being beheaded 'like a thief'). The Saga states that '[w]ith that he crossed himself and stooped to receive the blow. So his soul passed away to Heaven' (*OS*, 95). Soon, the first of many miracles occurred:

> The place where this happened was rocky and overgrown with moss, but soon God revealed how worthy Earl Magnus was in His eyes, for the spot where he was killed turned into a green field. In this way God showed that it was in the cause of justice that Magnus had died, and that he had reached the verdant fields of Paradise, called the Land of the Living. (*OS*, 95)

Many of the details of the Magnus legend will come into play later in Brown's re-creation of this, and other, sagas accounts.

Magnús saga the shorter, composed in the second half of the thirteenth century, is most similar to *Orkneyinga Saga*, probably because it uses its predecessor as a template. However, the fourteenth-century *Magnús saga the longer* (that is generally agreed to be hagiographical and not simply historical in focus) departs from these accounts in a number of respects. *Magnús saga the longer* takes its cue from Magnus' original hagiographer, Master Robert, and says that while Magnus Erlendson has a model childhood where he shows great ability in the study of 'holy writings', he gets into bad company as a youth, and joins in Viking expeditions.[10] Unlike *Orkneyinga Saga*, which only exalts Magnus' virtues and praises him robustly, the *longer* saga reveals:

> he lived like a Viking with robbers and mercenaries from theft and loot, and he was as bad a killer as any one of them; but it seems

plausible that he did this more because of the perverted morals and the instigation of evil men than because of his own bad character ...[11]

While Brown does not utilise the dramatic repentance and conversion that comes as a consequence of Magnus' early reckless and brutal career, he does do something similarly creative. By filling in the gaps and silences of *Orkneyinga Saga*, he imaginatively re-creates Magnus not just as a holy Viking Earl, but also as a northern saint. His midrashic, hagiographical agenda is therefore akin to the longer saga.

But how does this violent warrior square with the man who later refused to fight in the Battle of the Menai Strait and chanted psalms aloud in the prow of the Norsemen's longboat? Several contemporary critics have speculated on this.

II. Twentieth-century Historical and Critical Perspectives

In her discussion of twentieth-century interpretations of late-medieval hagiography, Julia M. H. Smith points out that today's accounts of saints' lives draw attention to 'the ways in which stylistic revisions might effect changes in emphasis and create an image of sanctity modified to suit the preoccupations of a later age'.[12] It is worth bearing Smith's cautionary note in mind when considering the numerous critical interpretations of Magnus' life and death that have appeared over the course of the twentieth century. These modern accounts of Magnus' martyrdom are strikingly imbued with the language and ideology of modernity.

In his *History of Orkney* (1932), the Orcadian author and historian J. Storer Clouston takes a pragmatic, down-to-earth view of Orkney's patron saint. Clouston calls St Magnus

> a zealous and sincere but somewhat flamboyant christian [sic], highly temperamental, a poor judge of councillors – accepting bad advice at least as often as good, apt to prove square when the hole was round and round when the hole was square, probably lacking humour and certainly deficient in ordinary workaday commonsense, dearly loveable to his friends who understood and appreciated, and an alien to the rest ...[13]

Clouston's *History of Orkney* was read by Brown early on, and is at least as useful as the Sagas in tracing the formative influences that shape his own interpretation. Berthold Schoene criticises Clouston's history for being 'ingenuous' and 'misogynist', adding that '[t]he most outstanding deficiency of Clouston's book is its obsessive hero-worshipping stance towards the past'.[14] But these are all criticisms that have been made of Brown, too. Clouston's work would have been decisive in shaping the young Brown's understanding of his Orcadian heritage, and – if nothing else – is valuable in helping us to understand Brown's developing understanding of the St

Magnus legend. Elements of Clouston's fanciful, impractical saint can certainly be seen in Brown's later versions of the tale, particularly in *Magnus*, where – after Magnus Erlendson comments enigmatically on his spiritual destiny – one of his men thinks, exasperatedly, 'God help the people of Orkney who have an incompetent like this in charge of their affairs' (*M*, 129).

Clouston's contemporary John Mooney views St Magnus rather differently. In 1935, he writes:

> Heroic servant of the Lord! The North in that year of Grace, 1098, was in need of a protest like thine against the wars of plundering and massacres by covetous and ambitious princes. In this year of Grace, 1934, the hearts of men and women who worship the God of Love are praying and longing for the consummation of the same ideal as inspired the young nobleman from Orkney more than eight centuries ago.[15]

Mooney's enthusiastic endorsement of Magnus is a post-war assertion, endowed with the language of conquered imperialism. Using vocabulary that reveals his own historical context, Mooney continues, 'It may be supposed that Magnus, the conscientious objector, would not have been eager to put himself unnecessarily in the way of Magnus, the warrior.'[16] In fact, this reading of Magnus as a committed Viking pacifist has been the dominant strain of most subsequent historical accounts of his life. In 1978, Edwin Sprott Towill suggests:

> Had [Magnus] lived today he would probably have been a member of the Fellowship of Reconciliation, perhaps even of the C.N.D.! The physical fear of pain and death was obviously far greater to him than to many other martyrs therefore such heroism as he showed was so much the nobler. The history, even of those war-like Viking days, should have some place for those who saw no heroism in senseless killing.[17]

This ringing eulogy is very much a product of its time, replete with the language of contemporary anti-war movements and organisations in a post-Vietnam cultural moment. Towill virtually ignores the religious and miraculous aspects of the St Magnus legend, focusing instead on the figure of Magnus as an example of anti-war peaceful protest.

In 1960, Brown's fellow convert George Scott-Moncrieff emphasises Magnus' rebellion against the established order, calling him 'the Saint of Bad Form, for it was by flouting accepted convention that he established his title to martyrdom'.[18] And when discussing his 1976 chamber opera *The Martyrdom of St Magnus* (which is based on Brown's *Magnus*), Peter Maxwell Davies notes that St Magnus was 'the first pacifist – the first Viking Pacifist anyway'.[19] More recently, Gilbert Márkus claims that while Magnus 'was no pacifist', his 'example of conscientious objection in Wales many years previously was now being followed by his enemy's crew'.[20] Accordingly, as

Maria-Claudia Tomany points out, St Magnus 'is now venerated mainly for his pacifism'.[21] The descriptions of pacifism and conscientious objection in many of these narratives are wholly modern, post-World War, post-Holocaust and post-Vietnam constructions that re-create a medieval saint to suit the modern age. It is worth remembering Smith's warning in light of the anachronistic critical vocabulary of twentieth-century 'pacifism' and 'conscientious objection' to describe St Magnus, especially considering what we know of the saint as Viking raider in the *longer* Magnus Saga.

Nonetheless, these descriptions of Magnus' pacifism are important when considering Brown's fusion of medieval legend with a Second World War concentration camp in his novel *Magnus* (1973). Twentieth-century perspectives of this particular Norse saint as a pacifist, freedom fighter and peaceful protester have influenced Brown's work, and his writing has clearly affected subsequent interpretations. However, Brown's saint is of a somewhat different religious tincture to the one seen in works by Mooney and the religious pamphleteer D. P. Thomson (1876–1974). Timothy Baker notes that in their works, 'Magnus becomes a far more familiar type of saint, one who has led a godly life and can be used as an example for the reader to follow.'[22] This is unsurprising, given these authors' religious beliefs (neither were Catholics: D. P. Thomson was a Church of Scotland minister and Kirkwall businessman John Mooney was father of the Rev. Harold Mooney, minister at Deerness for over fifty years). As Thomas DuBois points out, after the Reformation, '[m]inisters sought to reeducate their flocks to regard saints as figures to emulate rather than as intercessors to rely upon'.[23] But in all of Brown's accounts of Magnus' martyrdom, he is a very Catholic saint, distinguished not just by his holy life, but especially by his readiness to provide supernatural aid to those who plead for his intercession. Brown's saint may be influenced by interpretations which shape him in the mould of twentieth-century pacifism, but in his unique versions of Magnus' life and death, Brown very firmly sets out the theological territory of his Scottish Catholic imagination.

The vexed interpretations of sainthood are, in fact, a feature of the scholarly reaction to Brown's writings on St Magnus. As already noted, Brown's novel has frequently left Scottish literary critics rather puzzled and perplexed, and often their analysis primarily reflects critics' personal views on issues of dogma and religious belief. The Murrays acknowledge the importance of Brown's Magnus writings within his overall canon, and note that '[t]hroughout his writing life, Brown wrote about the Magnus story in many different forms. Technically, he did something different in each. Thematically, he shifted emphasis in each telling.'[24] This slightly hazy appraisal follows their diagnosis of the 'existential frustration' characterising Brown's contemplative prose passages in *Magnus*. The Murrays read these passages as 'generalising on sacrifice, reflecting on poetry, art and music ...'[25] Alan Bold more accurately considers this contemplative writing to be 'an erudite essay on the symbolism of the Roman Catholic Mass'.[26] But, as noted earlier in the discussion of Bold's criticism of Brown's Marian works, he cannot disguise his ambivalence towards Brown's religious subjects. He argues: '[a]s a Catholic [Brown] tacitly assumes that the martyrdom was ordained by God and in the novel we have to take Brown's faith for granted.'[27] Bold later complains that Brown is in danger of 'sacrificing his own creative gift on the altar of Catholic dogma', and he concludes that Brown

> owes it to his non-Catholic readers to explore the man Magnus instead of dogmatically accepting his sanctity. [. . .] my own admiration for *Magnus* is qualified by a reluctance to accept wholeheartedly its dogmatic elements (for I cannot see anything particularly saintly in a man being murdered – and that is what happens in the novel for a non-Catholic reader) ...[28]

It would seem that Bold's hesitancy to suspend disbelief and engage with this Catholic story on its own theological terms means that he simply rejects it wholesale. Meaningful reflection on Brown's deep textual engagement with hagiographic saga sources is not a feature of this criticism, and Bold is not interested in the different possibilities for the life of Magnus according to the different literary forms in which Brown depicts him. Ultimately, Bold is unwilling to delve very far into the textual warp and weft of this novel because he has no time for sainthood and other elements of Catholic 'dogma'. Moreover, he feels that Brown owes something to his non-Catholic readers – and that he ought to explain or justify his fascination with a medieval saint for those who either have a different, or no, devotional perspective. But perhaps the assumption that non-Catholic readers will be alienated by Brown's historical novel is unfair. Bold rather assumes that these readers will share the exasperation and puzzlement felt by the Scottish literary critical establishment about Catholic fiction, but there is no guarantee that they did, or will. The Hogarth Press was so delighted with *Magnus* that it became the publisher's Booker Prize submission for 1973.

Interpretations of Brown's twentieth-century re-creation of a twelfth-century *vita* are made problematic by critical stances which are hostile to religion, and which reflect only the idea that the Church is a centre of power which must be challenged. It is from a more critical interrogative stance that this book will continue to examine Brown's creative rendering of the St Magnus legend, particularly in light of how the novel *Magnus* deals with saga material, and how it strays from this.

III. Magnus and the Poetics of Hagiography

On 18 October 1992, almost two decades after *Magnus* was first published, Brown writes to Sr Margaret Tournour about a collection of poems, *Stained Glass Windows*, which he is writing on the lives of saints. He notes: 'I think I won't consult any saints' lives: I just want to get a tone and an atmosphere (facts get in the way).'[29] Schoene recognises the tension between historical

fact and fictional embellishment in Brown's hagiographic work where he
says, '*Magnus* is a heavily interpolated text that frequently replaces fact with
fiction, or faith.'[30] However, believing the three sagas and the Latin *Life*
of Magnus to be factual accounts is somewhat naïve. Brown's reaching for
'tone and atmosphere' in fact equates his artistic process with the accepted
traditions of hagiography, as the Jesuit scholar Hippolyte Delehaye suggests:

> Inspiration apart, hagiographers do just as poets do: they affect com-
> plete independence of, sometimes a lordly contempt for, historical
> facts; for real persons they substitute strongly-marked types; they
> borrow from anywhere in order to give colour to their narratives and
> to sustain interest; above all, they are ever mindful of the marvellous,
> so apt for heightening the effect of an edifying subject.[31]

In the introduction to the posthumously published *Stained Glass Windows*
(1998), Brown states: 'The saints' tales come out of imagination, as all
art must do.'[32] He admits that he 'did not undertake any historical study
into the lives of Saint Thomas More and Saint Margaret Clitherow', but
'made them up as I went along, as the ballad-makers of the past did, on
imagination's harp'.[33] Delehaye would have approved of this qualification
of Brown's, as in *The Legends of the Saints* he notes that 'it would be unjust
to condemn an author in the name of history if he only intended to write
imaginative fiction. Some hagiographical documents are clearly of this
kind; they are parables or stories designed to bring out some religious
truth or moral principle.'[34] In fact, this subject is very much on Brown's
mind a year later, when he writes to Sr Margaret that he has been working
on a poem about the Irish princess and nun St Sunniva. He confesses:
'One doesn't believe in the factual truth of many fragments of Dark-Ages
sanctity. But they preserve and enshrine, perhaps, another, deeper kind of
truth.'[35] It is this 'deeper kind of truth' that Brown attempted to convey in
his hagiographical novel *Magnus* of 1973.

The major alteration that Brown makes in his novelistic *vita* of St Magnus
is a new preoccupation with the theology of the body, or, rather, the importance of the body because of its sacramental potential. Brown inscribes
this new bodily emphasis in *Magnus* by focusing very particularly on the
activities of Orkney's medieval peasants, on Magnus' decision to remain
in a non-consummated marriage, and on his death. This latter area of
focus is one in which Brown turns Gifford's accusation of 'predictable
denouement' on its head, for the narrative switches not only in tone and
style, but also uses prolepsis strikingly so that the twelfth-century martyrdom is suddenly transported into the twentieth century. This is Brown's
most experimental and political version of St Magnus' *vita*. Bold notes that
'[a]nachronism is, in fact, one of the main stylistic features of Magnus' but
does not elaborate further.[36] However, in a letter to Sr Margaret in 1990,
Brown writes, 'I'm glad you enjoy Magnus – bits, at least. Time is all mixed
up, intentionally: to show, I suppose, that a martyr is a martyr for all time.'[37]

The novel begins with a divine, panoramic perspective. Orkney is viewed from above, and we are told that 'the wild geese flew over', while 'the peasants put their slow patient scars on the fields' (*M*, 11). Immediately, the agricultural process of ploughing is described using the language of bodily wounds. The earth is wounded in preparation for the fertility and fruitfulness that will be restored by the sanctifying 'harvest' of Magnus Erlendson's death. It is worth remembering here *Orkneyinga Saga*'s claim that 'the spot where [Magnus] was killed turned into a green field'. The first fruits of martyrdom were seen in Orkney's rejuvenated soil. Brown is eager to embed this idea into his novel from its very first page.

Meanwhile, the larger metaphorical meaning of Mans and Hild's ploughing is reinforced by the concurrent marriage of Magnus' parents, which will produce Orkney's saint. The peasants hear 'fragile choir voices' and a 'web of sacred song' as the marriage takes place nearby (*M*, 16). After the wedding feast, a narrator intrudes to reveal that 'a great sacrificial host surged between the loins of bridegroom and bride, and among them a particular chosen seed, a summoned one, the sole ultimate destined survivor of all that joyous holocaust' (*M*, 25–6). Brown begins his *vita* with an agricultural process that prefigures the conception of a great saint, but at the same time he hints at a 'holocaust' – a premonition of Magnus' death, and the execution in the concentration camp of the penultimate chapter.

However, if the fertility and divine panorama of the opening chapter are a celebration of human sexuality, then Magnus' own experience of sex is entirely different. *Orkneyinga Saga* relates that after celebrating his wedding, he lived with his bride for a decade 'without stain of lechery'. In order to avoid sexual temptation 'he would plunge into cold water and pray for aid' (*OS*, 90). Brown renders Magnus' self-enforced chastity in deeply sensual terms:

> March fell, a cold wave of light, over the islands.
> It laved the world.
> It passed through the bodies of the young men and girls. It left them cold and trembling for love.
> The wave surged on. The sun climbed. In April the body of Magus took a first kindling, blurrings of warmth and light. A slow flush went over his body. [. . .]
> The hill was opened by the plough. Fire and earth had their way with one another. Was everywhere the loveliest spurting of seed and egg and spawn.
> Girls felt into the rockpool, flowed, climbed out into the sun with sweet silver streaming bodies. They shrieked.
> Magnus burned. (*M*, 68–9)

Brown's writing suggests God's plan for the fruitfulness of the world. His description of 'the loveliest spurting of seed and egg and spawn' (*M*, 69) indicates that God's plan for human sexuality is something wholly good and worthwhile. But is Magnus' chaste marriage not, in this case, contrary to God's will – even heretical? It is certainly one of the most puzzling aspects of the saint's life. George Scott-Moncrieff insists that Magnus and his wife's unconsummated marriage 'was an unconventional act, but one that exalted the highest aspect of human love'.[38] Sigrid Undset likewise finds that, '[t]o non-Catholic historians the Jarl's actions must have seemed foolish and in bad taste, to Catholics it is quite comprehensible'.[39] However, this is open to question, especially in light of Brown's representation of the saint's struggle with sexual desire. We might argue that Magnus' sexual stance actually spurns Church teaching on human love and productivity.

Perhaps Magnus' unusual marriage followed the scriptural advice of St Paul, who noted that '[i]t is good for a man not to touch a woman' (I Corinthians 7:1), but if that were not possible, 'let them marry: for it is better to marry than to burn' (I Corinthians 7:8–9). Brown's Magnus follows this advice, as he 'burns', and decides to marry a girl from a noble Scottish family. However, as a result of Magnus' rejection of the sexual union with his wife in Brown's novel, we find that 'She was like a bee imprisoned in a burning window' (*M*, 71–2) and '[s]ubtle witherings began to appear in her flesh before the summer was over' (*M*, 72). Clearly, for Magnus' bride their chaste marriage leads only to unfulfilled longing and unhappiness. Brown notes that 'Magnus saw it too. He wept for the bitter ordinances of time' (*M*, 72). However, it is possible that Brown accentuates this part of the Magnus legend because it fits nicely with a new hagiographical element of his own design. In the chapter 'The Temptations', we are told:

> It was said, concerning the holy martyr Magnus, that to gain his soul's kingdom he had to suffer five grievous temptations, and but that he was upheld then and ever and near the hour of his blessed martyrdom by a certain comforter that was sent to him, his soul might have been overborne by the evil one and brought down into the fires of hell. (*M*, 67)

In depicting Magnus' sexual (and other forms of) temptation, Brown's language mirrors the narrative method of Graham Greene, whose 'decadent relishing of the melodramatic language of Hell [. . .] almost reclaim[ed] the gothic rhetoric of anti-Catholicism'.[40] The language of eternal damnation is particularly virulent where Magnus' sexuality is concerned. The text does hint at a reason for Magnus' chastity – that his is a political marriage where there is no love. The novel warns that 'the bodies of a man and woman [who take part in] lust unsanctified and uncreative [. . .] are bound upon a wheel of torment that will carry them down into uttermost burning depths' (*M*, 70). Perhaps Brown's saint refuses to consummate his marriage because his union is simply one of political expediency, rather than love.

But it is also likely that Brown's emphasis on Magnus' chastity comes from his interest in other hagiographical narratives. Leslie A. Donovan notes that 'sexual temptation is normally presented as a one-sided activity in female saints' lives'. She writes that 'it is the pagan male adversary who is tempted by the woman saint's physical beauty and her denied sexuality'.[41] His denied sexuality means that Magnus Erlendson's nickname, 'Magnus the Maiden', makes a great deal of hagiographical and historical sense.[42] Elsewhere in Brown's poetry about the lives of female saints – particularly in the cases of the virgin martyrs Cecilia, Tredwell and Sunniva, who each choose celibacy – the idea of the virgin body is seen as 'the supreme image of wholeness [and is] equated with holiness'.[43] In 'Saint Sunniva', Brown depicts the lives of the saint and her companions as ones of quiet religious observation and tranquility. They live in an all-female religious community and their purity is so striking that it makes 'Rough-tongued Orkney sailors / Fall silent at nights.'[44] Even 'The skipper with the tarry hands / Folds them, a rough dove', such is the power of the women's religious devotion. Soon, though, Sunniva and her companions are killed by falling rocks, and:

> There, the long silver bones,
> There, Sunniva the saint
> Sweet-fleshed, in a rose of sleep
> Between rosary and square bronze bell.[45]

Brown's insistence that Sunniva remains 'sweet-fleshed' is a nod towards her saintly incorruptibility, but it also highlights her perpetual virginity. Sunniva's virginity signals holiness, but also expresses power, strength, courage and self-sufficiency. Donovan writes that in hagiography, '[t]he male saint generally achieves his spiritual heroism either by resisting temptation or by refusing to abandon his faith. In contrast, women saints' lives show their subjects heroically preserving their virginity against physical assault from male antagonists.'[46] Brown's St Magnus not only resists 'five grievous temptations' and refuses to abandon his faith (going so far as to refuse to fight because of it), but he also chooses to remain a virgin. As such, Magnus fulfils and transcends the gendered expectations of saintly heroism.

The close focus on Magnus' chastity is moreover connected to the novel's little-explored notions of the theology of the body. Magnus' physical pain is consistent with the idea of vicarious suffering – a very prominent theme in the French Catholic novel, and something that has not yet been identified by Brown's critics. In reply to a friend's mockery of his chastity, Magnus announces:

> Pain is woven through the stuff of life. Ingerth is suffering now, because of me. I suffer too, because of Ingerth and everyone I have had dealings with. Is God to blame for all this suffering? What an empty question! Look at the agony on this crucifix I have round my neck. This crucifix is the forge, and the threshing-floor, and the shed

of the net-makers, where God and man work out together a plan of
utter necessity and unimaginable beauty . . . (*M*, 73)

The broken and wounded body of Christ is paralleled and imitated willingly by Magnus, and signals a more widespread need for sacrifice and
healing throughout the Orcadian locus. As Magnus reflects on his own suffering when gazing at the crucifix, he becomes a hero set in the mould of
the 'mystical' or 'miraculous' novel, in which '[t]he incarnation is revealed
to characters when they discover that their sins or their suffering bring
them into an analogical relationship with the suffering God in Christ'.[47]
Magnus does not engage in early Viking expeditions as he does in the *longer*
saga, but the novel suggests that he causes wider suffering by refusing to
surrender to Hakon's desire for sole leadership of Orkney. Crops are tram-
pled and ordinary peasants, like Hild and Mans, are harried, oppressed
and killed by both Magnus' and Hakon's soldiers. Thus, the bodily struggle
that Magnus endures is symptomatic of a far wider and more expansive
theme of brokenness in the text; there are literal and figurative wounds
throughout.

A good deal of critical attention has been paid to Brown's egalitarian
impulse in *Magnus*. Butter recognises that saga writers 'were interested only
in aristocrats, not at all in low characters such as tinkers, and hardly ever
in ordinary soldiers and workers', but Brown is keen to place these lowly
characters at the very heart of his new rendering of the myth.[48] This reflects
his assertion to Sr Margaret that 'common people knew a saint when they
had experience of one'. The pain suffered by Brown's lowly characters is
highlighted throughout, from the 'immensity of their labour' during the
opening scenes of ploughing ('Hild stumbled [. . .] she felt as though her
shoulder had been wrenched from its socket. She groaned') to the painful
rowing on board a Viking ship, where Mans 'lurched back and fore on the
thwart with dead shoulders [. . .] He thought the hour of his death had
come' (*M*, 17, 52, 55). Griffiths explains that the central characters of the
French Catholic novel 'take on suffering to expiate the sins of the world, or
the sins of others', and the plot 'revolve[d] around the miraculous results
of that sacrifice'.[49] Although Magnus Erlendson has traditionally been read
as the novel's sole redeemer, Mans and Hild are in fact the first redemptive
figures in the mould of those identified by Griffiths. They take on suffering
to expiate the sinfulness of wider political struggle, and, in their aching
shoulders at sea and on land, they re-enact the imagery of crucifixion.

The tinkers Jock and Mary also suffer gruelling pain. They frame the
text, running across Mans's crops at the start of the novel where, in the
midst of the language of fertility and ripeness, Magnus is about to be conceived, and they are the witnesses to the saint's first posthumous miracle
at the end of the novel. But they do not escape Orkney's civil war. Mary
begins life as 'a dark lithe creature' with 'large flashing eyes: as if they drew
their light from the clear well of the sun' (*M*, 15). However, Mary's sight

becomes gradually dimmer as the political situation worsens, and by the final chapter she is blind (though her sight is restored by the new saint, Magnus). Mary's blindness has many narrative functions and echoes. The darkness of war is inscribed onto Mary's body so that she becomes a symbol of destructive political violence, but her blindness also allows Brown to transpose one of the miracles of *Orkneyinga Saga* into the life of an ordinary person. In the *Saga*, the sceptical Bishop William is struck blind after he shows he is unwilling to believe in the saintliness of Magnus, but his sight is restored when, 'seized with a great terror, [he] went to Earl Magnus' grave and prayed there in tears' (*OS*, 104). In *Magnus*, on the other hand, the miracle is granted to the tinkers Mary and Jock, the poorest and most marginal of all Orkney's peasants. During the miracle scene, Brown includes a prayer to St Tredwell, an Orcadian saint very much like St Lucy, who put her own eyes out when she rejected the lustful advances of a suitor. In this way, Brown's hagiographical knowledge is deftly interlaced with French Catholic themes of suffering and the saintly subject of the Icelandic sagas. This narrative tapestry is then augmented with a new focus on the common man and woman of medieval Orkney.

The novel's ultimate physical sacrifice comes, of course, when Magnus gives his life for the greater good and his body becomes a sacramental gift to the people of Orkney – it renews the very soil, which becomes verdant and peaceful. To date, no critic has connected Magnus' martyrdom with the death of the 'whisky priest' in Greene's *The Power and the Glory* (a novel strongly influenced by the French Catholic novel of vicarious suffering), which it very obviously parallels.[50] In Greene's novel, '[t]here is a triumph of faith at the expense of the political world', as there is in *Magnus*, but more importantly, through the death of Greene's 'whisky priest',

> execution is a final participation in the Cross, and the text implies the
> full stature of the religious aesthetic in the final pages of the novel. In
> this way Greene actualizes a distinctly Catholic tradition of an analogi-
> cal aesthetic, of putting on the form of Christ as the standard of one's
> true self before God. [. . .] The doctrine of Christ is imaginatively
> understood in *The Power and the Glory* as a theological aesthetic of
> transformation into an *alter Christus*. The lowly whiskey priest is raised
> up in participation with Christ who sacrifices himself for love's sake.[51]

Magnus becomes just such an *alter Christus*, his martyrdom foretold early on by his reflections on the broken body of Christ on the cross, and made complete by his sacrificial death on Egilsay. Even the technical features of the death scene in Greene's novel are adopted by Brown in his own text. In *The Power and the Glory*, the experience of the reader is made strange during the execution scene by the switch in narrative focalisation from the saintly main protagonist to an observer, Mr Tench. In *Magnus*, the narrative during the killing is focalised, not through St Magnus, but through the unwilling executioner in the Nazi concentration camp.

Brown also makes sure to foreshadow the novel's posthumous miracles with Magnus Erlendson's early eagerness to heal wounds. As a new hagiographic addition, he has Magnus Erlendson tend to a wounded soldier during battle: 'The fingers of Magnus Erlendson went skilfully between the broken flesh and the unfolding linen …' (*M*, 62). He also makes sure to depict the young Magnus, 'a rather small boy with a sensuous mouth and restless eyes', sorrowing over a wounded seal. We are told that he smiles at his red-headed cousin (and future enemy) Hakon, before he 'turned his face once more to the centre of pain' (*M*, 32). In Brown's novel, Magnus is a protector of the innocent. He is 'small' (as evidence from his skull, found in St Magnus Cathedral in 1919, supposedly suggests), while Hakon is an image of Judas Iscariot, red-headed and ambitious, the witchcraft he is associated with in the saga narratives signalled by the name of his falcon, 'Warlock'. Brown does not include any of the information from *Orkneyinga Saga* about a poem, composed in Magnus and Hakon's honour, which details their success in killing their enemies. Brown's Magnus does hint: 'At the beginning Hakon and I did things well together. We destroyed the Vikings – in Shetland we smoked them out like wasps' (*M*, 78). However, the only occasion where Magnus finds his hands red with blood in Brown's novel is when he tends to the wounded seal in childhood. Brown eagerly emphasises this Orcadian saint's curative powers even before his death.

Magnus is also a mystic in Brown's version of his *vita*. In 'The Killing', the chapter where experimental language and style, time shifts, and long sections of meditation and contemplation on the Eucharist and the Mass merge rather surreally, we see Brown adopt an archaic-sounding prose that is far more ornate than his typically sparse, *Orkneyinga Saga*-inflected language. This newly elaborate language is closer to the style of the *longer* saga:

> Fell then a sudden death-dread upon the ships, and voices that urged return, and hands were held out yearningly towards the hither healthful shore. The jarl Magnus maketh true response, 'Fare yet forward, not I but God is helmsman here.' (*M*, 123)

This section is then retold in the bare language of *Orkneyinga Saga*, with Magnus prophetically foreseeing his death and martyrdom in the form of a vision about a bridal feast in heaven. He muses, '"But there's this wedding feast. There's this coat that I ordered a while ago. I hope I'll have time to see these things when I'm in Egilsay"' (*M*, 129). His men are baffled. Whereas *Orkneyinga Saga* stresses Magnus' handsomeness, popularity and intelligence, Brown makes his saint a far more enigmatic and mystical figure. In the *Saga*, Magnus says, '"On with the journey [. . .] let it turn out as God wills"' (*OS*, 92), but Brown's young Earl is far more elliptical, strange and mysteriously connected with his spiritual path. In *Orkneyinga Saga*, a proactive Magnus makes three offers that will save his life, while in *Magnus* his friends make these offers for him as he contemplates the Mass.

This mystical Magnus, who contrasts so sharply with the hard-headed men around him, also highlights the way that Brown dramatises true spiritual insight. Magnus is very similar in the scene above to Brown's creative rendering of St Brandon, an Irish monastic saint of the sixth century. Brown's play *The Voyage of Saint Brandon* was anthologised along with *The Loom of Light*, his dramatic interpretation of the Magnus story, in *Three Plays* (1984).[52] This rendering of St Brandon's *vita* reveals far more about the practice of writing hagiography than it does about Brandon himself. It is a work which self-consciously demonstrates the Catholic imagination at work in the creative process, and which also sheds light on Brown's characterisation of Magnus. In the play, St Brandon leads a quest to find 'the island of the blessed' with a small group of monks. A rook 'speaks' to Brandon, telling him that 'Only an innocent old man like yourself would think us beautiful', but Brandon announces:

> BRANDON Brother bird, I take leave to differ with you. Nothing that has come from the hand of God is ugly – however different in form and hue and function. What is more perfect, an elephant or a flea? Neither. They both issued perfect from the hands of the Creator on the Fifth Day. Likewise a star and shell. We should shout *Gloria* to every natural thing on the face of the earth. To me you are a gracious company of birds, beautiful beyond telling. (*VoB*, 102)

Brandon's surroundings are transfigured for him through his graced vision. The key to his perspective lies not in madness, nor in blind optimism, but in a particularly creative imagination. An explicit connection is made here between imagination and faith. Brandon can receive God's message and guidance through birds because his imagination allows him to. As Brown admitted in an interview with Isobel Murray, when confronted with 'squalid little scenes' of intense ordinariness, Brandon 'throws the shining garment of the spirit over them'.[53] He continued: 'Blake had the same, well, the same kind of vision as old Brandon, you know. He saw what really mattered in everything, all the objects and things that he saw around him.'[54] Brandon's fellow monk, Malachi (a rationalist scholar), has no faith in divine mediation via the imagination, and thus, Brown suggests, he is not a true believer: he is deaf to God's word and his heart is closed. Malachi does not possess the sacramental view of all matter that Brandon (and Magnus) has in abundance.

Brown's play also contains a new focus on the narrative method of hagiography, which reveals much about his own rewriting of Magnus' *vita*. Each scene begins with a scribe reading his account of the monks' journey across the seas. This is taken virtually word for word from Jacobus of Voragine's thirteenth-century compendium of saints' lives, *The Golden Legend*, highlighting that Brown would have been familiar with the narrative method, tone and content of this work. Brandon offers advice to his scribe, saying that he 'should not write the story of the voyage [. . .] in strictly factual terms' (*VoB*, 148). And although the record of events is not, therefore, entirely accurate, it is hagiographical, because it draws spiritual wisdom from events that may well be embellished or even fictional. This narrative method was key to Jacobus of Voragine's compilation of *The Golden Legend*, as William Granger Ryan points out:

> Jacobus interlards his argument with narrative, most frequently stories of miracles. That most of these narratives were at least partly fictional – or better, the product of generations of oral retelling – in no way diminished their effectiveness. They served an important purpose: they humanized and dramatised the doctrinal point to be made. In them men and women were seen as living the doctrine.[55]

Brandon sums up this narrative technique well, where he suggests, 'Always, when you come to write the story, keep a little room for the creator and the creation and the harmony between them. That gift is called imagination' (*VoB*, 148–9). Brown followed this religious-artistic manifesto wholeheartedly in his hagiographic work. Seen under this lens, Schoene's observation that Brown 'frequently replaces fact with fiction, or faith' seems too simplistic.[56] Brown works within an ancient hagiographical tradition, but cuts, embroiders and embellishes as he weaves his twentieth-century interpretation. And Bold's contention that *Magnus* 'was done more in the nature of a religious duty than a stimulating act of creation' again reveals more about this critic than it does of Brown's novel, with its stylistic shifts, miraculous ending, medieval sources and dramatic leap forward eight centuries in time in the penultimate chapter.[57] As Peter Brown argues, 'long after the issue of the rise of the cult of saints has been removed from its confessional setting in post-Reformation polemics, scholars of every and no denomination still find themselves united in a common reticence and incomprehension when faced with this phenomenon'.[58] This is notably the case in twentieth-century appraisals of Brown's hagiographical novel.

The differences between *Magnus* and the *Orkneyinga Saga* are – as Brown would claim of St Magnus' miracles – manifold. In the novel, Magnus appears to have had a good and blessed childhood, which is not blighted by his actions as a Viking, as in the *longer* saga. Brown's Magnus does not escape the ship after the Battle of Menai Strait and hide up a tree, as he does in both *Orkneyinga Saga* and the *longer* saga (neither does Brown have him suffer the ignominy of throwing a stick at dogs barking at him from the foot of his hiding-place). In *Magnus*, no brothers or sisters are mentioned, despite the Sagas' insistence that Magnus' older brother played an active role in battle. Brown makes Magnus the first-born child: he wrote to Ernest Marwick that 'for dramatic purposes it will be necessary to forget about Erling'.[59] In *Magnus*, the future saint does not travel to Norway to meet King Eystein, who grants him his paternal inheritance, and also, intriguingly, Brown does not have Hakon visit a Spaeman in Sweden, as he does in both *Orkneyinga Saga* and the *longer* saga. Where the sagas connect Hakon to witchcraft, Brown seems far more sympathetic to his villain, perhaps signalling a wider sense of forgiveness and the love for the sinner that is at work in his corpus more generally.

But *Magnus* was not Brown's only rendering of the legend. His other works on Orkney's patron saint yield more treasures about this author's late twentieth-century Scottish Catholic imagination.

IV. Magnus and the Forms of Devotion

Brown's writing on St Magnus spanned six decades, and included poetry, short stories, a novel, plays, text for a 'son-et-lumière' production, and an opera libretto adapted from Brown's novel by Peter Maxwell Davies for a chamber opera of nine scenes. Brown's very earliest Magnus poems, published in the *New Shetlander* in 1947, are testament to his long-term curiosity about the potential for the legend to be conveyed in this form.[60] But how does Brown's interpretation of St Magnus' *vita* change as he adapts it to different literary forms? And what do these other Magnus writings tell us about Brown as a Catholic artist?

Magnus is certainly the most discussed and generally best regarded of Brown's renderings of the legend, but Schoene's criticism of the novel – 'Brown's major problem as a twentieth-century Catholic writer is grounded in his refusal to conform to the religious disillusionment and relativism of our postmodern age' – immediately highlights the subversive nature of the Catholic novel.[61] T. R. Wright notes that 'novels are the expression in literary form of "problematic" ages of doubt', while Marion Crowe argues that '[r]eligious faith seems more naturally adapted to poetry'.[62] The idea of the novel format as coming of age in the eighteenth century, a period informed by a context of increased secularism, and an empirical world rather than 'the world of chivalry and myth', has led critics and writers, like Orwell, to deem it 'practically a Protestant form of art; it is a product of the free mind, of the autonomous individual'.[63] Nevertheless, Catholic writers such as Graham Greene, Flannery O'Connor and Muriel Spark have used the novel format effectively and subversively. The realist (and non-devotional) norms of the novel are countered by these writers, all of whom challenge popularly accepted notions of miracles as fraudulent or imagined, and faith as an old-fashioned delusion. Brown too offers an alternative world view in response to Schoene's observation of postmodern religious disillusionment and relativism in contemporary fiction, because he resolutely insists on the miraculous, and never more than in his works on St Magnus.

Marina Mackay argues that if we see character development as the central preoccupation of the novel tradition, then 'we can see why Roman Catholic novels might have been marginalized: characters in these novels do not always conform to liberal ideas of character development.'[64] This is certainly relevant when considering the reception of Brown's novels, and particularly his plays. Brown's critics have rarely considered the provocative difference that Catholicism makes to these liberal ideas of character development. Donald Campbell, for instance, notes that 'narrative takes priority over character and [. . .] all too often [Brown's] characters make no dramatic journey and serve simply as ciphers by which the story is told'.[65] However, Brown's characterisation can be better understood within the tradition of Catholic fiction, in which 'we see the self manifest itself with less predictability'.[66] Unpredictable selfhood is a key feature of *Magnus*. What could be less predictable than transposing the saint's execution scene onto one eight centuries later? The text then switches back to its medieval setting and presents its reader with a miracle, without offering any alternative explanations or possible rationalisations. Brown's novel signals its Catholicity here, and reveals 'the bogus coherence of the closed and consolatory narrative' so embedded in the realist novel.[67]

Woodman's analysis of the tropes of twentieth-century Catholic fiction speaks pertinently to Brown's miraculous dénouements:

> As these novelists work and rework the perennial Catholic themes of suffering and death, sin and expiation, they do so with special consciousness of writing in a Protestant and then increasingly a secular and materialist country [. . .] If their work is sometimes highly reactionary or melodramatic or shows signs of what has been termed a special 'Catholic neurosis', they still combat with vigour the archetypal British heresy of Pelagianism: the view that we are 'saved', so to speak, not so much by God's grace as by our own moral decency. In seeking to shake that complacency these novelists characteristically highlight paradoxes of grace and providence that subvert and transcend ordinary human morality.[68]

The miracle which ends *An Orkney Tapestry* – the blueprint or first major rendering by Brown of the St Magnus legend – is one of these moments. We see Jock the tinker pray for his wife Mary's eyesight to be restored in a scene which deliberately eschews pious sentiment. This scene is represented as stage drama, despite the text's relaying of the legend in prose up to this point. The dramatic format means that the action is vivid and immediate, highlighting again that Brown saw Magnus as a 'martyr for all time'.[69]

In *An Orkney Tapestry*, and later in *Magnus*, Mary is ungrateful, comical and curmudgeonly when her sight is miraculously restored, while Jock is rather mercenary when his prayers at St Magnus' tomb are not answered immediately. He thinks, cunningly, that at least Mary's blindness means that they can still earn money from begging. The Murrays read the miracle as a reward for piousness: 'Magnus is seen to be working miracles [. . .] for those with Jock's faith.'[70] However, Elizabeth Huberman declares that Jock's plea for intercession is 'more in the spirit of a desperate gamble than of true belief', and while she recognises that the tinkers are seemingly rather irreverent recipients of a divine gift, she argues that their experience 'is more convincing testimony to the reality of miracle than a chorus

of hallelujahs. If this could happen to them, it could happen to anyone.'[71]
Here, Huberman signals Brown's challenge to Pelagianism. God's grace
works through Magnus, not because the tinkers are especially devout, or
because of any good deeds, but because Magnus is holy, and his name
has been invoked. Mary does not thank those who show her pity and give
her food (in fact, she refuses to share any of this when she comes across a
wounded soldier) and she is equally petulant when miraculously given her
sight back. Nevertheless, she is transformed. She seems young again and
the spirited beauty of her youth is restored; particularly in *Magnus*, where
the narrative voice marvels, 'She turned her glimmering face this way and
that' (*M*, 205). The Murrays' uncritical reading of this ending fails to note
that the miracle is especially powerful because of its ordinariness and its
lack of blinding glory.[72]

Therefore, Brown's rendering of the St Magnus legend counters liberal
humanist and realist visions of the novel format, as well as contemporary
Scottish literary fashions. His novel is neither urban, gritty nor realistic; it is
in direct contrast to the prevailing 'condition of Scotland' novels that are
produced during the period. Once more, it is striking to see just how much
more *Magnus* has in common with the French mystical novel that so influenced Greene, where miraculous intervention was often used 'to stress the
importance of the spiritual life that lay behind the appearances of reality
depicted by the realist novel'.[73] *Magnus* is so unlike its contemporaries that
Richard Griffiths has seen it 'more as a poem than a novel'.[74] This is not
surprising, given its defiantly Catholic vision of the world – one drenched
in the possibility for miracle, grace and redemption.

Brown's rendering of the Magnus legend in *An Orkney Tapestry* also strays
from realistic novelistic conventions when it alludes to exegetical readings
of the Bible's rich variety of literary and narrative forms. Brown's biblical
Tapestry deals with history, legend, myth and hagiography in a variety of
formats, including short story, stage drama, polemic and ballad. This text
has its own Genesis chapter – an Orcadian creation account – which sets
out the geography of the islands' land and seas. And Brown's Orkney Bible
contains both Old and New Testaments, with Old Testament types prefiguring the coming New Testament Messiah. In the section dealing with the
Battle of Clontarf – a tale taken from *Orkneyinga Saga* – Brown anticipates
Christ through the symbolic raven of knowledge in Earl Sigurd's magic
banner. The text then suggests a typological relationship between this
medieval battle, Magnus' martyrdom and Christ's sacrifice:

> The Battle of Clontarf and the Martyrdom of St Magnus are both set
> in the season of The Passion and Easter. The actors move about under
> the Cross. The fearful song of the Valkyries after the battle, about the
> garment of war woven from entrails, is not unlike the medieval hymns
> that picture Christ in his Passion, clothed in wounds and blood.
>
> Clontarf was fought on Good Friday. It was Easter Monday when

Magnus came to the stony field in Egilsay. To Hakon was made over entire now the heraldic coat-of-state. Magnus gave his clothes to Lifolf and knelt on the stone and went naked (it seemed) into the ecstasies of death. Yet all through history the shuttles are flying, perpetually, secretly, silently. (*OT*, 83–4)

In the limited space that *An Orkney Tapestry* affords Brown (for he covers many subjects other than St Magnus), he sets out Magnus' *via dolorosa* and martyrdom, and presents him as a type of Christ – an Orcadian *alter Christus*. Magnus' emulation of Christ by passing his clothes on to his murderers, his prayers, and his forgiveness of his unwilling executioner all mirror the plot and sacrificial theme of the biblical crucifixion.

In his introduction to *Three Plays* (1984), which includes his Magnus play *The Loom of Light*, Brown writes: '[o]n to the stark framework of the play I rigged the novel *Magnus*'.[75] It seems clear from his letters to Marwick around this time that Brown was working on both his St Magnus novel and play simultaneously, with the play 'shaping itself quickly' and providing a blueprint for the novel.[76] Brown's depiction of the passing of time is the major difference between his play and his novel. In *Magnus* Brown makes one startling leap forward in time, from twelfth-century Orkney to twentieth-century Nazi Germany, but in his play Brown consecrates time through monks who begin each scene by chanting the setting and timeframe. This echoes the structure of Eliot's *Murder in the Cathedral* (1935), where the martyrdom of another twelfth-century saint, Thomas Becket, is introduced by a chorus – the Women of Canterbury. But, as Brown's monks 'sing every day the seven-fold office' (*LoL*, 3), he ensures that *The Loom of Light*'s structure is primarily liturgical.

In Scene One, 'Seedtime' (which is named 'The Plough' in *Magnus*), the chorus tells us:

The year 1075 since Bethlehem and Herod.
    There is a king in Norway, who is king also of Orkney, Shetland, Caithness, the Hebrides, Man, all the broken coastlines of the west.
    In Orkney the king keeps two earls, black earl and red earl.
    In winter, once the harvest in is, the earls move ivory chessmen beside a fire in the Hall.
    The croft women turn perpetual wheels of wool and stone and malt.
    The monks in a green holm sing every day the sevenfold office. They wear the long bright coats of chastity, poverty, obedience.
    It is spring – the red earl will sanctify desire with ceremony. And in spring fishermen and peasants go out to break the new furrows, salt and clay. (*LoL*, 3)

Here, the chorus sets out the play's major, recurrent imagery, which Brown used first in *An Orkney Tapestry*. The theme of divine providence working through the looms and 'shuttles' of time is explored using the imagery of weaving: this is made clear in the 'perpetual wheels of wool' and the monks' 'long bright coats'. Weaving imagery reaches a climax in the later Scene Three – 'Song of Battle' – where Magnus recites scriptural fragments from his Psalter. In his recitation of psalm 45:13, Isaiah 63:1 and Genesis 37:23, Brown ensures that Magnus proclaims his affinity with biblical metaphors of spiritual clothing:

> MAGNUS ERLENDSON 'The King's daughter is all glorious within. Her clothing is of wrought gold. She shall be brought to the king in raiment of needlework ...'
> [. . .] 'Who is this that cometh from Edom, with dyed garments from Bosra, this beautiful one in his robe, walking in the greatness of his strength?'
> [. . .] 'The coat that Isreal gave to his beloved son, Joseph, a beautiful garment of many colours, it was taken from him. Steeped in the blood of beasts it became one colour ...' (*LoL*, 18–19)

Here, Magnus indicates his knowledge of the biblical idea of clothing as an expression of one's spiritual standing before God. In *Magnus*, the inner struggle that the saint has with sexual desire is realised through the spinning imagery and the 'coat-of-state' motif; this also dramatises the struggle between loyalties to inherited earldom and spiritual calling. In the stage drama of *The Loom of Light*, we have no objective narrator to relay Magnus' dreams, visions and contemplative thoughts about his status as Earl. Instead, we are presented with an actor reciting psalms and other scriptural passages which incrementally repeat the imagery of spinning and weaving. This creates a ritualistic and liturgical effect that is entirely missing from Brown's novel. In *The Loom of Light*, Magnus becomes a priest uttering psalms, who awaits choric response.

While Diane Murphy warns that medieval saint plays 'are not direct offshoots of the liturgy, nor are they entirely secular productions', Wright argues compellingly that '[i]t is difficult sometimes to draw the line between liturgy and drama'.[77] As a convert who would have paid special attention to (at first) unfamiliar Catholic liturgy, and as a Catholic writer who is concerned with countering secular and positivist notions of a world apparently abandoned by God, Brown draws on the tropes and motifs of early religious dramatic narratives. Often, medieval plays 'present a realistic view of the concerns of ordinary people' – a trope which Brown synthesises deftly in his depiction of the irascible peasant, Mans, who complains as much in *The Loom of Light* as in *Magnus* about the unfairness of the feudal system.[78] But the saints take on another role in medieval plays:

> The saints, despite their humanity, are also expected to be larger than life. They do not simply experience the problems and contradictions inherent in the social order, they solve them. [. . .] This attainment of an ideal is not conceived as a unique solution brought about by one

individual's piety, but as a reprieve of Christ's redemption of mankind as a whole. Implicitly or explicitly, the enactment of saintly legends relies on the concept of *imitatio Christi*, the imitation of Christ. The end result of portraying a saint's biography on stage is therefore very similar to the intent of biblical drama.[79]

This could not be a more appropriate description of Magnus in *The Loom of Light*. Brown's hero does not bargain for his life, as he does in *Orkneyinga Saga*. Hakon makes these offers for him but is shouted down by his men, so, while he becomes the play's Pontius Pilate, Magnus willingly accepts his death like Christ. The Mary who watches over Magnus is not his mother, but the tinker Mary. Brown's dramatic rendering of the saint is thus strikingly akin to the agenda of the miracle plays of the Middle Ages. Magnus is not just another character experiencing societal problems. In his role of *imitatio Christi*, he solves these.

However, Brown recognised that his play could have been fussy, confused and made melodramatic by excessive period features. He writes on 15 April 1972:

> The St Magnus play is going along fine. [. . .] The scene I had most qualms about – the martyrdom – will turn out well, I think. (I fear we will have to rely heavily on choric work after all – it's the only way of taking women into the play and they are always the stronger sex in Orkney as far as drama is concerned. Some of the speeches, to be quite frank, will be difficult for amateurs to utter – we will have to face that – but intentions are acceptable in heaven if not entirely on earth.[80]

Brown identifies the most problematic aspect of the play here, if unintentionally. His chorus, while technically necessary to inform the audience of the play's change of scenes, cannot relay all the information that Brown wishes to communicate. Instead, Brown includes extremely literary stage directions that will make very little impact on an audience. In another nod to Eliot's Women of Canterbury (or perhaps the biblical Women of Jersualem), Brown tells us that his 'women of Egilsay' are '*smitten with new light, with springtime, with a never-more-expected hardly-yet-to-be-believed re-surgence of flesh and spirit*' (*LoL*, 33). He also adds directions that ask a great deal of the play's actors: '*During this reading a man enters the church. He kneels a little apart from the women. The light falls brokenly on his face: desperation, uncertainty, outrage, fear, doubt, shift and mingle under a cold mask*' (*LoL*, 34). And Brown makes sure to include the dramatic use of light and the visually impressive ceremonial aspects of the Easter Triduum: '*The young monk returns with a black cloth which he drapes over the crucifix. He puts out the candles one by one. The monks sing on with deepening sorrow into the darkness of Good Friday*' (*LoL*, 32). As a result, *The Loom of Light* is potentially a very moving piece of theatre. However, the characters who, at various points, enact the drama of the Mass through their positions as celebrants, priest, willing sacrifice, or who enact more direct biblical parallels, are unable, through no fault of their own, to realise Brown's whole vision for his St Magnus mystery play. Brown may have realised this, too. The typescript for *The Loom of Light* includes Brown's marginalia, which suggests that the 'literary stuff' is not to be performed on stage, as it is only for book readers.[81]

As a consequence, *The Loom of Light* is arguably most valuable for what it reveals about Brown's knowledge of medieval miracle plays, and how he implants their features into his dramatic blueprint for *Magnus*. Wright observes:

> [T]he mystery cycles achieve their most effective theological teach-
> ing through their 'staging' of the history of the world, presenting a
> 'moving picture', an animated stained-glass window, of the medieval
> theology of time, God's artefact, which is not mere linear progress but
> full of vertical meaning, figural significance: 'The events chosen for
> dramatisation are those in which God intervenes in human history, to
> express his will.'[82]

In Brown's play, time is depicted as a consecrated entity, but in *Magnus* the dimensions of time and space are interrogated and disrupted; time is no longer linear but ripe for God's intervention. Traditional teleology is dislocated so that the traditions of the saint plays of the Middle Ages invade the relatively new novel format. Murphy notes that 'playwrights of the Middle Ages were not constrained by the unities of time, place, and action. [. . .] They are a hybrid form that regards the death of the protagonist as triumphant rather than tragic.'[83] Fittingly, at the end of the chapter 'The Temptations' that Brown inserts into *Magnus* (so that it becomes a novel of eight chapters rather than a play of seven acts), the novel format is overrun and disrupted by the sudden intrusion of stage drama. Magnus ultimately 'takes his sword out into the sunlight' – a sign that he is no pacifist after all, and that he recognises some blood will have to be spilt for him to make his sacrifice.

However, in terms of the representation of this sacrifice, the novel is utterly different to Brown's play, and this is because of its dramatic time shift. Where in *The Loom of Light*, the saint's execution is over quickly (Brown writes in a letter of 29 March 1972, 'I see this too as being highly ritualistic – an utter eschewment of crude melodrama'), in *Magnus* the exe-cution is transposed into one in Nazi Germany.[84] The future saint foresees this during his time in the Egilsay Church, where he hears Mass:

> The pain of the dead (the man knew) is soothed by a healing word
> or thought. But perhaps the pain of all history might be touched with
> healing by a right action in the present. [. . .] He saw himself in the
> mask of a beast dragged to a primitive stone. A more desolate image
> followed, from some far reach of time: he saw a man walking the
> length of a bare white ringing corridor to a small cube-shaped interior

full of hard light; in that hideous clarity the man would die. The recurrence of pattern-within-flux touched him, momentarily, with wonder. (*M*, 141)

Later we hear the explanation for Magnus' waking vision: he has foreseen the execution of an unnamed figure by Lifolf, the cook in a Nazi concentration camp:

> The room I stood in was a whitewashed cube. There was a single electric bulb in the ceiling. Into one wall about eight feet from the floor three steel butchers' hooks had been screwed. A short noose hung from the right-hand hook. (*M*, 178)

From the setting of April to the unnamed prisoner, who 'spoke as though it were some kind of game at a party' (*M*, 178), recalling the *Orkneyinga Saga*'s, 'As cheerful as if he'd been invited to a feast' (*OS*, 94), the scene is testament to the cyclical nature of history that Brown paints, where Magnus' surrender of ego and will to other people's sinfulness echoes throughout time. Christ's broken body is the template to be re-enacted willingly in the broken body of Magnus, the unnamed prisoner, and other holy men and women who offer healing to the brokenness in their societies and communities. Brown expresses this idea two years before his death in his reply to the article by Paulsen, writing: 'This murder was not so much an event in history as a symbolic act, a ritual, a timeless moment, a sacred dance, a pure imitation of Christ.'[85]

Once more, Brown is not quite as singular as might initially be thought in his strange welding together of medieval and twentieth-century martyrdom. As a result of his incarnational perspective, as Ross Labrie states, Brown is able 'to recognize the jointure of time and eternity and the "immanence" of Christ in human life'.[86] Labrie continues:

> This knitting of the timeless and the temporal leads the Catholic writer, as Berrigan wrote [. . .] 'to exist at any given point of time' as if one were existing 'at the end of time.' Similarly, for [Thomas] Merton the nurturing spirit of history was the 'free and loving will of God' through which the present moment was ripe with the possibilities of the eternal.[87]

Brown's novel dramatises the cosmic sweep of history in a particularly Catholic way; Magnus' martyrdom is an echo of Christ's sacrificial death that reverberates throughout time. It is not an isolated incident or historical event, but something that continually nourishes and gives grace to those with a measure of imagination and small deposit of faith. Brown's Catholic imagination is a site where medieval drama, European novels and Norse sagas coalesce, and out of these sources Brown creates a text that runs against contemporary literary fashion. Brown was clearly pleased with *Magnus*. He wrote in his autobiography that he considered sections of the novel 'to be among the best writing I have done. Few readers will agree with me. But it's always like that, I think. "What thou lovest well" is often looked at coldly by others' (*FI*, 171).

In his reply to Erik Paulsen's doubtful account of Magnus' sainthood, Brown claims: 'The scientist has taken the place of the artist and the contemplative nowadays' and, most tellingly: 'The Magnus poem – for that is what it is – went like a flame through all the northern parts of Europe.'[88] Brown's identification of the legend as 'a poem' is important. It is worth remembering that Brown also reprimands Paulsen for presenting 'the prose, rather than the poetry' of Magnus' martyrdom – a remark which chimes curiously with Griffiths' observation of Brown's novel *Magnus* 'more as a poem than a novel'.[89] Hilda Spear has also claimed Brown as 'a poet in everything he touches', and, as highlighted previously in the discussion of the novel's realist roots, literary criticism has often found that 'religious faith seems more naturally adapted to poetry'.[90] Brown wrote a spate of St Magnus poems towards the end of his life, including limited edition collections on the sole subject of the martyrdom. Poetry provided a hymn-like structure for Brown. This form encapsulated his songs of faith and expression of devotion to St Magnus in a way that the novel, with its realist and secular roots, could perhaps never maintain. Perhaps this is no surprise, given poetry's 'violation of the literal', particularly in the Romantic and Symbolist movements, which demonstrated 'rebellion against rationalism and positivism respectively'.[91]

Brown's early poetry on St Magnus immediately indicates his preoccupation with seeing the finger of God in nature. 'Saint Magnus in Egilsay', from Brown's second collection, *Loaves and Fishes* (1959), retells the legend. The poem opens with the line 'Since Time folded his breath about the world' (*CP*, 31), a signal of the wider providential plot that allows Magnus' death to be a healing reflection of Christ's redemption of humankind. However, after Magnus is implored, 'Bow your blank head' in stanza two, the poem's final stanza offers us a rich burst of devotional lyricism that revels in the saint's connectedness with the natural world:

But O what love came then! Root, stalk, and flower
Twined in a riot through the acre of death
And larks cut lyrical nests deep in its turf.
Parched loin, and stringless tongue, and peal-blind eye,
Sailed up that sound, fingered that dust, and saw
The red ploughs cleave their snow and curve for ever
    Across the April hill. (*CP*, 32)

Magnus' execution is something that puts the machinery of God's grace into action, and we read Catholicity not just in formal devices like plot and structure, as with Brown's novel and play, but in his poetry's lexicon, which is focused through a sacramental lens. There is more than a hint of Hopkins in these exclamatory, rhythmic lines, which allude to 'The Sea and the Skylark', where Hopkins hears 'the lark ascend' and notes, grimly, 'man's last dust'.[92] The cataloguing of Orkney's 'riot' of animate nature is reminiscent, too, of 'Duns Scotus's Oxford', which Hopkins describes as 'Cuckoo-echoing, bell-swarmèd, lark-charmèd, rook-racked, / river-rounded'.[93] Furthermore, Romanticism influences Brown's poetry so that 'root, stalk, and flower' (akin to Hopkins' 'folk, flocks, and flowers') take centre stage, rather than the consecration of time, a saint's personal struggle with his spirituality, or inextricable movement towards sacrifice. The natural world reflects and celebrates Magnus' redeeming sacrifice, and, in his depiction of the sacral Orcadian land, Brown echoes Wordsworth's view of nature 'as a sacrament, a symbolic revelation of God'.[94]

In Brown's other Magnus poems, it is the regenerative, healing effects of Magnus' death that matter most – the saint's inexorable steps towards execution do not really feature here. In 'April the Sixteenth', from *Winterfold* (1976), six stanzas catalogue the gifts and devotional offerings that Orkney's ordinary people bring the saint. Suffering is recognised in much simpler language than the previous poem:

> And the poor of the island
> Came with their hungers,
> Then went hovelwards with crossed hands over the hill. (*CP*, 155)

In 'Song for St Magnus: 16 April' from *Northern Lights* (1999), we see Brown's most personal lyric on the saint yet. The poem's seven stanzas (Brown thought seven a 'good religious number') implore Magnus to remember those who are suffering and most in need of help:[95]

> Keeper of the red stone, remember well
>   Sufferers today, those
>   Who are to cross the dark firth,
>   People in hospitals,
>   In hospices, eventide lingerers,
> Children who look at daffodils
>   (Both with the dew on) each
>   To break today in spring tempest. (*CP*, 402)

As the poem progresses, it becomes a prayer for intercession. Brown's prayerful vision expands from a focus on local 'fishermen / From Noup Head to Rora' to beseeching St Magnus for aid across the continents:

> Be present at the fires
>   Of women in Bosnia and Somalia
>   Kneading dough smaller than fists. (*CP*, 403)

Finally, in 'St Magnus Day 1992', a poem written for his friend Sr Margaret, Brown writes one of the simplest and least decorative of his St Magnus poems. In virtually all of his poetic output, Brown absolutely refrains from using the first person singular pronoun, preferring instead to study other states of mind, or 'inscapes', and disliking 'confessional poetry'.[96] But in the first stanza of this private poem (which was after all a gift not meant for publication), we read Brown reflecting on his own ordinary surroundings:

> Outside my window daffodils
> Dance in the north wind.
> In another garden
> A blackbird
> Clothes, before leaves, a tree in song.

> It is Saint Magnus Day. (*CP*, 446)

The poem widens its vision in free verse and simple language to include a collective 'we', and the idea of humanity as a tribe redeemed continually by sacrifice is presented:

> But for that company of heroes
> But for those
> Whose blood purified the roots and sources
> The daffodils
> Would be a measurable disturbance of earth and air today,
> That blackbird
> A graph on a cold grid of sound.

> But the poor still dance (thank God).
> Because of the saints
> We, a throng out of winter,
> Dance now in coats brighter than Solomon. (*CP*, 446)

The poem's insistence on the eternal redemption of humankind through 'saints' and 'heroes', and the assertion that the suffering poor 'still dance' might be unpalatable for some. There is, perhaps, no real engagement with suffering and poverty in these lines, which are ultimately brimming with optimism. However, Brown's combination of Magnus' redemptive message and his introspective musing about the personal effects of sacrifice are unique to his poetry. Brown's voice does not intrude in *Magnus*, despite the novel's various switches in tone (from saga-esque to hagiographic to journalese) and its remarkable leap across the centuries. The 'literary stuff' that encroaches in *The Loom of Light* is still third person narrative, and far removed from the ordinary workaday world of gardens and blackbirds. But, more than any other medium, poetry allows Brown to connect personal devotion to St Magnus to his own immediate and personal context. Moreover, his poetry on Magnus suggests that if we are able to make the leap of imagination into the leap of faith, so that the heroes of sagas become our own saints, then their power is transformative. Brown claims that without Magnus' sacrifice eight centuries ago, daffodils would only be 'a measurable disturbance of earth and air', and the blackbird would merely be 'A graph on a cold grid of sound'. Orkney's patron saint has vouchsafed peace and the beauty of the natural world. In Brown's article defending Magnus' sainthood in 1992, he writes, 'We live in a dull prosaic time, when most people get their nourishment from the tabloid press, and TV soap operas, not from the great life-giving legends.'[97] All of the artworks that Brown created about Magnus depict the saint as a regenerative hero, but perhaps it is in his poetry that we see Brown's personal devotion most clearly.

In a television script written in 1980, Brown could be accused of taking a typically conservative stance. His language certainly takes on an almost apocalyptic timbre:

> Perhaps [Magnus] would be saddened by the materialism that is rampant in western society; the blind worship of Progress that sees no other goal or trophy worth striving for: only what can be possessed, accumulated, immediately relished by the five senses, in ever more bewildering variety. While, in other parts of the earth, people are slowly starving. While the earth and its resources are being systematically robbed, in a cold fury of greed. While beautiful species are being hunted to extinction, so that a passing fashion can be indulged, and fleeting hungers satisfied. While weapons of unthinkable world destruction are poised for the moment of panic or insane rage that will set them loose.[98]

This short extract hints at Brown's lifelong devotion to St Magnus, and reinforces his belief that the saint not only stood courageously against violence, but defended the natural world against the destructive forces of greed, ambition and ruthless exploitation. Yet, as impassioned as this argument for the sainthood of Magnus Erlendson is, it does not reflect the energy and sheer creative verve with which Brown reinscribed his legend into Scottish literature. Critical writings have been slow to recognise Brown's pioneering artistic project concerning the Magnus story. Instead of an innovator, he has been labelled a polemicist, a moralist, romantic and reactionary – all frequently arrived at (but ultimately unimaginative) assessments of this modern Scottish Catholic novelist.

In his Magnus writings, Brown resituates a largely forgotten Norse saint within a Scottish and Scandinavian hagiographical context, but simultaneously he reintroduces St Magnus into Scotland's twentieth-century literary consciousness. As with his creative work on the Mother of God, Brown does not only adopt and subvert biblical sources. His Catholic imagination feeds on the apocryphal, hagiographic and saga writings of medieval Scotland. As he paints a landscape of saintly heroism in the twelfth century, he adds textures of the French Catholic novel, medieval miracle plays, biblical drama and Catholic liturgy. And he restores Orkney's ordinary people to the noble canvas of the skalds and saga-men, so that they receive the first fruits of redeeming miracle.

Brown also subverts and experiments with form in his work on Magnus.

His playfully midrashic rewriting and expansion of the life of Magnus means that he opens up new possibilities for storytelling, meaning and interpretation. His vertical, God-centred theology of time disrupts the novel format, and forces his reader to grapple with a challenging and provocative medieval story that contains all the political difficulties of the current age. Perhaps most significantly, Brown's Magnus writings show his keen typological interpretation of Magnus as another Christ, an echo of the sacrifice on Golgotha that gave Orkney 'the greatest day in all our island history'.[99] Brown's deft, experimental treatment of the martyrdom of Magnus is no less fascinating than his writings on the life of Christ, which will be the subject of the chapter to come.

Notes

1. Letter of Brown to Sr Margaret Tournour, 20 October 1994, MFA.
2. Brown, 'The Magnus Miracles were Manifold', p. 14.
3. Letter of Brown to Sr Margaret Tournour, 5 January 1992, MFA.
4. Bold, *George Mackay Brown*, p. 110.
5. Gifford, 'Scottish Fiction Since 1945', p. 15.
6. Orwell, *Inside the Whale and Other Essays*, p. 39.
7. Antonsson, *St Magnús of Orkney: A Scandinavian Martyr-Cult in Context*, p. 6.
8. Mooney, *St Magnus, Earl of Orkney*, p. 15.
9. Brown calls Mooney one of Orkney's 'intelligent countrymen' (*OT*, 23–4) and notes that Mooney is the author of *Saint Magnus, Earl of Orkney*.
10. Mooney, *St Magnus, Earl of Orkney*, p. 300.
11. Tomany, p. 143, quoting from Finnbogi Udmundsson's 1965 edition of *Magnúss saga lengri*.
12. Smith, 'Review Article: Early medieval hagiography in the late twentieth century', p. 71.
13. Clouston, *A History of Orkney*, p. 68.
14. Schoene, *The Making of Orcadia*, pp. 54, 55, 57.
15. Mooney, *St Magnus, Earl of Orkney*, p. 97.
16. Ibid., p. 99.
17. Towill, *The Saints of Scotland*, p. 100.
18. Scott-Moncrieff, *The Mirror and the Cross: Scotland and the Catholic Faith*, p. 30.
19. Davies, 'Pax Orcadiensis', p. 21.
20. Márkus, *The Radical Tradition: Saints in the Struggle for Justice and Peace*, pp. 43–4.
21. Tomany, 'Sacred Non-Violence, Cowardice Profaned: St Magnus of Orkney in Nordic Hagiography and History', p. 128.
22. Baker, *George Mackay Brown and The Philosophy of Community*, p. 62.
23. DuBois, *Sanctity in the North*, p. 24.
24. Murrays, *Interrogation of Silence*, p. 146.
25. Ibid., p. 144.
26. Bold, *George Mackay Brown*, p. 106.
27. Ibid., p. 101.
28. Ibid., pp. 106, 109–10.
29. Letter of Brown to Sr Margaret Tournour, 17 October 1992, MFA. The poems in *Stained Glass Windows* (1998) are surely inspired, at least in part, by their

great predecessor *The Golden Legend*: a compendium of *vitae*, dated around 1260 and compiled by an author known as Jacobus de Voragine.

30. Schoene, *The Making of Orcadia*, p. 218.
31. Delehaye, *The Legends of the Saints*, p. xxxii.
32. Brown, *Stained Glass Windows*, unnumbered introductory pages.
33. Ibid.
34. Delehaye, *The Legends of the Saints*, p. 50.
35. Letter of Brown to Sr Margaret Tournour, 9 September 1993, MFA.
36. Bold, *George Mackay Brown*, p. 102.
37. Letter of Brown to Sr Margaret Tournour, 20 October 1990, MFA.
38. Scott-Moncrieff, *The Mirror and the Cross: Scotland and the Catholic Faith*, p. 34.
39. Undset, *Saga of Saints*, pp. 176–7.
40. MacKay, 'Catholicism, Character, and the Invention of the Liberal Novel Tradition', p. 225.
41. Donovan, *Women Saints' Lives in Old English Prose*, p. 11.
42. Scott-Moncrieff, *The Mirror and the Cross: Scotland and the Catholic Faith*, p. 34.
43. Warner, *Alone of All Her Sex*, p. 72.
44. Brown, 'Saint Sunniva', in *Stained Glass Windows* [n.p.].
45. Ibid.
46. Donovan, *Women Saints' Lives in Old English Prose*, pp. 13–14.
47. Bosco, 'From *The Power and the Glory* to *The Honorary Consul*: The Development of Graham Greene's Catholic Imagination', p. 58.
48. Butter, 'George Mackay Brown and Edwin Muir', p. 21.
49. Griffiths, *The Pen and the Cross*, p. 103.
50. Brown writes in his autobiography that, during his early reading of other Catholic authors, 'Graham Greene's *The Power and the Glory* impressed me deeply; for here was a hunted and driven priest, and in many ways a worthless one, who nevertheless kept faith to the end, as better martyrs had done in other places' (*FI*, 54–5).
51. Bosco, 'From *The Power and The Glory* to *The Honorary Consul*: The Development of Graham Greene's Catholic Imagination', pp. 63, 68.
52. Brown writes that *The Voyage of Saint Brandon* 'is based on the Temple Classics edition edited by F. S. Ellis (London, 1900). It was originally printed in William Caxton's *The Golden Legend* of 1843.' *Three Plays*, p. 81.
53. Murray, 'A Sequence of Images: George Mackay Brown', p. 32.
54. Ibid., p. 33.
55. Ryan, 'Introduction' to *The Golden Legend*, p. xvi.
56. Schoene, *The Making of Orcadia*, p. 218.
57. Bold, *George Mackay Brown*, p. 110.
58. Brown, *The Cult of Saints: Its Rise and Function in Latin Christianity*, pp. 12–13.
59. For more on Erling, see Mooney, *St Magnus, Earl of Orkney*, p. 41. Letter of Brown to Ernest W. Marwick, 29 March 1972, OLA D31/30/4.
60. Early typescripts of poems about St Magnus exist in Brown's papers at D31/30/2 OLA. 'Prayer to Magnus' was published in *The New Shetlander* 6 (1947).
61. Schoene, *The Making of Orcadia*, p. 230.
62. Wright, *Theology and Literature*, p. 111; Crowe, *Aiming at Heaven, Getting the Earth*, p. 11.
63. Crowe, *Aiming at Heaven, Getting the Earth*, p. 11; Orwell, *Inside the Whale and Other Essays*, p. 39.

64. Mackay, 'Catholicism, Character, and the Invention of the Liberal Novel Tradition', p. 229.
65. Campbell, '"Greenness in Every Line: The Drama of George Mackay Brown"', pp. 2–3.
66. Mackay, 'Catholicism, Character, and the Invention of the Liberal Novel Tradition', p. 229.
67. Ibid., p. 230.
68. Woodman, *Faithful Fictions*, p. xiii.
69. Letter of Brown to Sr Margaret Tournour, 20 October 1990, MFA.
70. Murrays, *Interrogation of Silence*, p. 145.
71. Huberman, 'George Mackay Brown's *Magnus*', p. 133.
72. In *George Mackay Brown and The Philosophy of Community*, Baker also notes that the miracle is 'small and quiet', p. 65.
73. Griffiths, *The Pen and the Cross*, p. 103.
74. Ibid., p. 229.
75. Brown, *Three Plays*, p. ix.
76. Letter of Brown to Ernest W. Marwick, 8 April 1972, OLA D31/30/4.
77. Murphy, *Medieval Mystery Plays as Popular Culture*, p. 26; Wright, *Theology and Literature*, p. 166.
78. Murphy, *Medieval Mystery Plays as Popular Culture*, p. 26.
79. Ibid., p. 27.
80. Letter of Brown to E. W. Marwick, 15 April 1972, OLA D31/30/4.
81. Brown, typescript of *The Loom of Light*, EUL MS 3111.3, f. 20.
82. Wright, *Theology and Literature*, p. 174.
83. Murphy, *Medieval Mystery Plays as Popular Culture*, pp. 27–8.
84. Letter of Brown to Ernest Walker Marwick, 29 March 1972, OLA D31/30/4.
85. Brown, 'The Magnus Miracles were Manifold', p. 14.
86. Labrie, 'The Catholic Literary Imagination', p. 12.
87. Ibid., pp. 12–13.
88. Brown, 'The Magnus Miracles were Manifold', p. 14.
89. Ibid.; Griffiths, *The Pen and the Cross*, p. 10.
90. Spear, *George Mackay Brown: A Survey of His Work and a Full Bibliography*, p. 204; Crowe, *Aiming at Heaven*, p. 11.
91. Wright, *Theology and Literature*, p. 146.
92. Hopkins, 'The Sea and the Skylark', *The Major Works*, p. 131.
93. Hopkins, 'Duns Scotus's Oxford', *The Major Works*, p. 142.
94. Wright, *Theology and Literature*, p. 146.
95. Brown, *A Spell for Green Corn*, p. 25.
96. David, 'Correspondences: An Interview with George Mackay Brown', p. 19.
97. Brown, 'The Magnus Miracles were Manifold', p. 14.
98. Brown, television script (1980), EUL MS 2843.7.1.
99. Brown, 'The Magnus Miracles were Manifold', p. 14.

CHAPTER 5

The Nativity of Christ

While *Magnus* can be read as the ultimate allegory of the Crucifixion in Brown's corpus, Brown's most direct and extensive treatment of the life of Christ centres on His birth. David Jasper and Stephen Prickett note that the birth of Christ has always exerted a powerful influence on the imaginations of artists, as it was the point where 'myth and history met, and the human and divine became one'. They add that 'it has always been a peculiarly poetic moment, celebrated by countless poems, paintings and pieces of music'.[1] Brown felt this too, and reflected in his *Orcadian* column that

> Literature has been a good handmaiden to Christmas, from the time of the medieval ballads and carols. No lyric so chaste and perfect as: 'He came alle so stille / There his moder lay / As dew in Aprille / That falleth on the spray'... (*RaD*, 198)

Brown's depictions of the nativity are among his most popular works. His annual Christmas stories for the *Scotsman* were eagerly anticipated by his reading public, and his poetic output on the nativity story spanned almost his entire poetic career.[2] Brown often approached the subject of the nativity directly, but he also used the familiar tropes, motifs and characters of the nativity story in a highly fluid, flexible and allusive way. Indeed, depicting the birth of Christ afforded Brown the opportunity to adopt several literary guises. In his nativity writings, he can be read as priest, bard, antiquary and social commentator. Brown adopts and critiques different religious perspectives on the poetic moment of Christ's birth, and he experiments with form, using parable, homily, short story and dramatic monologue to describe the infant Christ and his holy family.

Despite the popularity of his nativity works, these are the most notable site of divergence in belief between Brown and his Scottish literary critics. Alan Bold acknowledges the difficulty that Brown faced as the creator of modern nativity tales where he contends that 'the biblical account [of the life of Christ] is almost contemptibly familiar'.[3] And while they offer no comprehensive evaluation of Brown's festive works, the Murrays are rather apologetic about Brown's allusions to Christ in the Gospels, where they say: '[t]here may [. . .] be one too many Stations of the Cross poems for some readers'.[4] Elsewhere, familiar critical misreading of paganism appears regularly in appraisals of Brown's nativity writings.

This chapter will question critical interpretations of Brown's 'sacrilegious', 'heterodox' and 'contemptibly familiar' nativity tales.[5] Instead,

Brown's depictions of the Babe of Bethlehem can be read as inventive devotional works that combine popular appeal with a rich intertextual and theological engagement with the Christmas story.

I. Christmas Homilies

Brown's weekly 'Letters from Hamnavoe' (1971–6) and 'Under Brinkie's Bray' (1976–96) columns in *The Orcadian* were accessible, entertaining short essays that frequently dealt with history, culture and the arts in a succinct way. At first, these may seem like simple whimsy, but Brown's short festive articles are carefully wrought and liturgically structured pieces of work. In December 1971, he writes:

> ... deep under all the proverbs is the powerful instinctive feeling that winter should be winter and summer should be summer, and the loveliness and the flavour of each are squandered by a neutral neither-here-nor-there season. 'There is a time for snow and a time for sun'... 'There is a time for darkness and a time for light'... 'There is a time for the hearth and a time for the wind in the hill'... On such opposites the life of man is woven harmoniously and well. [....]
>
> We ask therefore this winter for one deep, immaculate snowfall, to keep the seeds warm; and for a swift, sudden thaw; and beyond the mud and wetness, in the new light, the first delicate tremors of spring. (*LfH*, 42)

In common with many of Brown's Christmas vignettes, this article takes on a homiletic tone and a liturgical structure, meaning that its author adopts the role of priest during Mass. The influence of the Book of Ecclesiastes means that the first paragraph can be taken as Brown's effective biblical reading of wisdom literature. This culminates in a prayer for intercession on behalf of the whole community, with nature harmoniously in tune with the imagery of the 'immaculate' Virgin. And if a sermon is missing from this essay, then it often appears elsewhere in Brown's journalism – particularly in his essays on Christmas and the nativity. In November 1989, he writes gloomily about 'the huge brash commercial wave' which drains meaning from the Christmas story. Brown decries the 'wash of money and profit' which distracts society from 'a poor child born into a world of power and money', but he ultimately concludes that 'the true meaning endures, no matter how it is covered up and bundled away. Enough sermonising for today' (*RaD*, 225). This lament could easily find its way into a Christmas homily, or sermon. Brown recognises this, where he writes, uncomfortably, 'I feel chastened, as though I had spent the morning writing a sermon; and I have no talent or training for such things . . . Excuse me this once' (*RaD*, 225).

Brown's distrust of the commercial aspect of the season at the expense of Christian worship is frequently apparent in these 'sermons', which (gently) chastise those whose 'getting and spending' threatens to overshadow the point at which God becomes man in the Christmas story. His writing may sound unnervingly like finger-wagging, but Brown is also keen to stress that the period of advent and the celebration of Christmas should be primarily about expectation and joy. In 'The Snows of Christmas' (December 1972), religious language is used again to describe seasonal weather; Brown describes snowy Stromness as 'a transfigured place'. However, despite the beauty of his surroundings, his fellow islanders complain when instead they could be 'rejoicing creatures in a new pure place ...' (*LfH*, 96). Brown finds that the familiarity of the Christmas story, along with the inconvenience of wintry weather, has blunted people's response to advent. But for Brown, wintry Orkney is absolutely alive with the coming 'good news' of Christ's birth.

For a writer so notably reticent to discuss his religious opinions in interviews, this medium provides a subtle and relatively overlooked insight into Brown's personal feelings about advent and Christmastide. Christmas journalism also provides a draft for later seasonal stories. The lines between fiction and journalism are blurred in December 1986, where Brown writes a very short fictional piece about a Cromwellian colonel, who, along with his lairds and ministers, enforces the abolition of Christmas in Orkney. A curiously Brown-esque character makes his way into the tale:

> There was an old man who lived by himself in the hills. I think he must have been a sailor at one time. Anyway, he could read his few books by lamplight. He turned the pages, and discovered a very old Celtic midwinter festival called 'Hogmanay'.
>
> The old sailor went from croft to croft telling the women that their ale hadn't been brewed in vain. He told the fiddlers to get their music ready. He told the children they could laugh and get presents after all (though, to be sure, it wouldn't be as beautiful and blessed a time as Christmas).
>
> So the islands rejoiced, a week late, for a century or two to come. (*RaD*, 156)

This is a curiously metafictional rendering of Brown's role as writer and journalist. The story's villains are puritans who attempt to obliterate the joy of Christmas, but they are hoodwinked by Brown's fictional substitute or doppelgänger – the old man who reads by lamplight and reminds his fellow islanders of the celebrations to be had. Here, Brown instructs his readers to appreciate the Gospel message despite their 'pallid money-crazed society' (*LfH*, 140). History, journalism and fictional parable coalesce, yet they are simultaneously held within a definite homiletic framework: Brown preaches that the burden of capitalism and the desire for personal satisfaction should not distract us from worshipping the divine.

Brown's choice of Hogmanay (the 'Celtic midwinter festival') as a surrogate celebration ought not to be read as incompatible with his Christian message. He writes in 'Return of the Light' (December 1990) that 'nobody can know for certain when Christ was born. The great feast of Christmas is set in the darkest time of the year, just after the winter solstice. It is a symbolical holiday ...' (*RaD*, 250). Nonetheless, his discussion of the winter season and interpretations of Christ's birth have not always been read as Christian.

II. Pagan Practice or Christmas Celebration?

In his discussion of Brown's story of the folk supernatural, 'The Last Trow', Simon Hall writes that 'everywhere' in Brown's work there exists a 'strange synthesis of the Christian and the pagan, so that he sees nothing incongruous in having a subterranean, pagan earth creature give a warning against a venal sin the like of which we might expect from a Christian God'.[6] Hall's surprise at Brown's lack of anxiety over these (supposedly) contending elements of his work mirrors a much broader critical distrust of Brown's synthesis of magical folk belief and Catholic ritual.

The sermonising 'trow' (troll) of 'The Last Trow' takes another shape in *An Orkney Tapestry*, where Brown's treatment of the celebration of Christ's birth may garner most accusations of unorthodoxy. In Brown's discussion of Orcadian lore, 'The Midwinter Music', he describes the winter's deepening darkness and the beauty of the Aurora Borealis, before stating: 'It is the season of The Nativity. It is also the time of trows' (*OT*, 126). Folkloric creatures and Christianity are yoked together in this, the testimony of Brown the antiquary, or folk historian:

> To the islanders the earth they tilled was an element of dark dangerous contending energies. [. . .] The trows belonged to the underworld, to the kingdom of night. Hideous shapes, they represented all the curses of unredeemed nature. The best way to contain the kingdom of winter and death was to lead a decent life, for the trows were among other things embodiments of the seven deadly sins; and it was best to observe duly the rituals of Christianity as well as other rituals that were old when the megalithic people built the stones at Brodgar. (*OT*, 126)

Brown's islanders identify the trows with 'unredeemed nature': they become miniature devils, embodiments of sin, and tempters who are intangibly wound up in the game of souls. There is no anxiety in Brown's description of the meeting of the folkloric and the scriptural, however. The trows may not necessarily be biblical, but in this imaginatively re-created pre-Reformation setting there are many devotions and practices which are unbiblical, and many tales which are apocryphal. And in fact this accurately reflects the folkloric and magical rituals of late medieval popular religion all over Europe, where theatrical and sacred performances, processions, blessings, dancing and singing all went beyond official liturgical practices, before these were 'swept away by the chastening ideas of the Reformation'.[7]

Brown constantly draws images of the devilish trow and the birth of heavenly Christ Child together, so that we hear of the 'trow-infested earth and the angel-fretted sky' (*OT*, 128). Brown displays not the slightest hint of concern that this description is 'strange' or unorthodox.

'The Midwinter Music' also emphasises the fruits of the earth, which some critics would undoubtedly regard as a major sign of Brown's covert paganism. The text details a crofter's patient turning of quernstones in 'fruitful sunwise circles' and we hear of the trows' eagerness to 'secretly turn the quern widdershins, against the sun' (*OT*, 127). As Rendall notes, '[s]ome thousand years after the arrival of Christianity in Scotland, the Presbytery of Dingwall was hearing that: in the parish of Gairloch, bulls were sacrificed, fertility offerings of milk were poured on the hills, sacred wells venerated and chapels "circulated sunwise ..."'.[8] Brown the historian inserts these very ancient practices into his Yuletide lore, but it is unhelpful to read moments like this as a breakthrough of paganism that represents a challenge to Christianity, rendering Brown somehow quasi-Catholic. Rather, these details signal their author's knowledge of beliefs that became gradually assimilated into Scottish Christian culture. Where in his Christmastime journalism Brown is the priest offering a sermon during the liturgy of the word, in this writing he offers us the liturgy of the Eucharist. Brown writes that on Christmas Day, '[t]here was nothing to be afraid of [. . .] The trows had returned to their burrows, defeated. Christ was born among the fields' and his body is broken up with 'the blood of summer' to be distributed among the communicants (*OT*, 129). Christ's birth and death are intimately linked in this celebration, with his body and blood being received in the Eucharist during the festival of his nativity.

Greeley's history of the Catholic imagination is helpful when considering Brown's mingling of pre-Christian practice and Eucharistic imagery. He argues that Catholicism has never feared '"contaminating" the purity of the spirit with sensible and often sensual imagery', and, he explains:

> On the face of it, this compromise with nature religion is strange. [. . .] Catholicism, in its better moments, feels instinctively that nature does not defile spirit but reveals it. Hence Catholicism [. . .] has not hesitated to make its own practices, customs, and devotions of the nature religions whenever it has encountered them ...[9]

These pre-Christian practices and devotions are clearly at work in 'The Midwinter Music'. While Greeley's analysis suggests that Catholicism has not always assimilated these customs entirely peacefully, in his work Brown is keen to portray a gradual, non-violent absorption of nature religion into Christian practice. In *An Orkney Tapestry* the night outside the family's croft is 'thick with trows' but Brown makes sure to remind us that '[i]t was possible that Our Lady and Saint Joseph with their as-yet-hidden treasure would come to their croft that night, seeking shelter' (*OT*, 128). In his journalism, Brown details the rituals of megalithic peoples at Maes Howe and the Ring of Brodgar, and writes, unworriedly, 'The early Irish monks applied these beliefs to the lives of men. They pointed out, gently, that indeed the promised Light of the World had come at Yule: the merest bud of light, a child in a poor stable in the east' (*LfH*, 49). Brown is eager to stress the peaceful medieval and early modern coexistence of the Christian, the magical and the folkloric. Although, as Eamon Duffy notes, 'A perfectly good Christian justification could be offered for these popular observances', their elements of 'parody and misrule' did not survive the Reformation.[10] Perhaps critical anxiety about Brown, the 'pagan pape', stems from our own modern unease with the idea of compromise with paganism – a legacy, arguably, of the Reformation dislike of para-liturgical ceremonies and magical practices. This unease plays powerfully into Scottish critical writings of the twentieth century.

Brown's short story 'A Winter Tale' from his 1976 collection *The Sun's Net* traces the Reformation dislike of Catholicism's appropriation of paganism to the present day. Brown writes the nativity back into a modern setting where belief in miracles has faltered and where the birth of a child in an abandoned croft brings life and hope back to a dying community. During Dr Clifton's night-time walk home from a dinner party, a stranger approaches him and pleads for help, while 'over the hill, a torn patch of sky appeared with a few stars shining in it'. The doctor delivers a boy to a young woman 'not much more than seventeen or eighteen years old' (*SN*, 24–5) and we are left with the idea that this modern 'Magus' has been granted the grace to witness a contemporary nativity because of his open-heartedness. Dr Clifton embraces island life and accepts that there are mysteries, particularly those of a religious nature, beyond his comprehension. Conversely, the island's minister denies (and thus is not witness to) miracles, saying 'we modern ministers, whether we like it or not, are living in an age of scepticism and pragmatism' (*SN*, 21).

The minister of 'A Winter Tale' also displays similarities to Brown, however. He tells the reader of his attempts to write a short Christmas sermon, and we learn that this becomes 'a description of Maeshowe and the midwinter sun' (*SN*, 44) – very similar to Brown's own festive local journalism. The Rev. Grantham also hints at a desire to become a priest, so that he might 'dispense supernatural comfort' in 'a little dark confession box full of whispers' (*SN*, 37). The island's parishioners would have none of this, though. Grantham describes their hostility to Christmas iconography:

> The crib – that was the trouble, it seemed, at first. They did not want a crib in the church. It smelt of idolatry. Didn't they have these cribs in Catholic churches at Christmas? They would have me know that this was a Presbyterian church, and always had been, and always would be. They would be very pleased if I reconsidered the crib. (*SN*, 41)

The islanders also note their discontent when the minister proposes a service of Christmas carols, with one parishioner, Andrew Sillar, declaring:

'Carols indeed! Carols is papish too. Our kirk is founded on the
sermon, the preaching of the word.' [. . .] 'Could you not see your
way,' said Obadiah, 'to preach a short sermon – it need be no more
than five minutes – half way through the service?'.... Andrew Sillar was
muttering away in the background about papedom and idols. 'When I
was young,' he muttered to Albert MacVicar and George Brinkie, 'we
didn't even keep Christmas in this island. That's a fact. "Christ's Mass"
– what could be more papish than that!' (*SN*, 41–2)

Like the conversation between the men in the smithy of 'The Tarn and
the Rosary', this section of the novel highlights a Presbyterian distrust of
Catholic liturgical and devotional practices. Despite its potential for couthy
descriptions of small-town religious life, this is no kailyard tale. The text
begins with a suicide, the island schoolteacher is full of contempt and fear,
and the minister is, by his own admission, 'an inadequate husband' and
'a weak pastor' (*SN*, 42). But without these darker elements of prejudice
and failure, the birth of the baby in the abandoned croft could become
saccharine. And in presenting his reader with a realistic version of flawed
humanity, Brown fulfils the task of the Catholic artist according to Flannery
O'Connor, who writes, '[t]he novelist is required to open his eyes on the
world around him and look. If what he sees is not highly edifying, he is still
required to look. Then he is required to reproduce, with words, what he
sees.'[11] Island life is not glossed over with a thick coat of sentiment in this
text. Brown does not 'tidy up reality'.[12]

Although Hall argues that 'Roman Catholicism has not suffered from
any marked prejudice or sectarianism in Orkney', Brown accurately por-
trays the opposition towards aspects of Catholic liturgical practice in some
strains of Presbyterian belief in stories like 'A Winter Tale'.[13] Rendall points
out in her study of Orkney church history that '[a]ny innovation to church
music could – and still can – be guaranteed to cause dissension in the pews.
Singing anything in kirk, other than unaccompanied psalms, was unthink-
able to most Presbyterians for generations.'[14] She notes that it was 1870
before the Church of Scotland published its first hymnal, but that even
this 'was fiercely resisted in some quarters' where the singing of hymns was
regarded as unacceptable as late as the 1950s.[15] However, these views are
not simply expressed because of a blank prejudice against Catholicism. In
fact, they are rooted in the Reformation dislike of Catholicism's gradual
assimilation and cooperation with paganism. In his essay, 'The Pagan
Origin of Christmas: A Reminder', the Free Presbyterian minister, Rev.
William MacLean (1907–85), writes:

Not only Christmas as a whole but also the festivities associated with
it are of pagan origin. Instead of the child Sol Invictus, there is the
popular Christmas crib with a doll as the Child Jesus. What a flagrant
flouting of the Second Commandment! How awful the blasphemy
in representing the eternal God in human nature as a doll! How

idolatrous and worthless the religion that has a doll for its god! [. . .]
How sad in this degenerate age of widespread apostasy to see profess-
ing Christians bowing at the pagan and popish shrine of Christmas!
How guilty are parents, who are under solemn obligations to bring
up their children in the nurture and admonition of the Lord, when
they lead them into these heathenish customs! 'For thus saith the
Lord, Learn not the way of the heathen . . . for the customs of the
people are vain' (Jer. 10: 1–3). Seek to honour Christ according to His
Word as our godly forefathers did. Have nothing to do with Christmas
parties, Christmas trees, Christmas gifts, the selling or sending of
Christmas cards or Christmas stamps. Avoid as you would the plague
the Christmas Eve Midnight Service and the Christmas Crib. They all
point to Rome. The observance of Christmas is largely responsible for
the subtle infiltration and advancement of Popery with its blasphemous worship and veneration of the Virgin Mary.[16]

This may be an extreme example of the Free Presbyterian Church of
Scotland's attitude towards the celebration of Christmas, but it nonetheless illuminates the views expressed in 'A Winter Tale', where some sections of the Orcadian community find Catholicism sinister, or threatening.
MacLean's is a sincere standpoint and the suggestion of a pagan basis for
the celebration of Christmas in winter is not unconvincing, but Brown's
writing on the subject proposes that it is not the literal and historical source
that matters in a Catholic view of the nativity, but the truth that springs
from it – that God took on flesh to become Christ. Brown is as uncon-
cerned with the integration of pagan practice into Catholicism as another
Catholic writer, André Dubus, whose narrator in 'A Father's Story' talks of
his daughter's spiritual outlook, saying: 'In truth she tends to pantheism, a
good sign, I think; but not wanting to be a father who tells his children what
they ought to believe, I do not say to her that Catholicism includes pantheism, like onions in a stew.'[17] This would be apt advice to the critic who
reads moments of pagan belief in Brown's work as a challenge to Catholic
orthodoxy.

Brown's short story collections often deal with nativity themes. *Winter
Tales* (1995) draws together winter and Christmas stories written over
several decades; many of which were first seen as the annual Christmas tale
in the *Scotsman*. These texts frequent borrow from the structure, pattern
and imagery of the nativity story, using parable, allusion and echo. In his
introduction to the collection, Brown deliberately aligns himself with the
'Celtic missionaries' who gave 'the mystery of light out of darkness [. . .]
breadth and depth', where he writes, 'I like to think I am part of that tradition' (*WT*, viii).

Sometimes Brown's nod to the nativity story is faint but distinct enough
to be recognisable, as in 'Dancey', which opens with a boy, 'William Ness
of the croft of Eard [. . .] walking into the tail of a blizzard, well muffled,

to see if any of his father's sheep were in trouble' (*WT*, 135). Typically, folk legend is conflated with a Christmas setting, as the boy finds a woman, stumbling and cold, in drifts of snow:

> After his faltering questions had got no answer, his first impulse was to turn and run home as fast as he could. Women from the sea still moved through the old men's winter stories, and that and a hundred other images were vivid and terrifying and beautiful in the boy's mind.
> The young woman turned and pointed back towards the cliff and the open sea, whose cold blue brightness was beginning to be blurred and stained by another blizzard. (*WT*, 135)

The regular reader of Brown might expect a selkie legend here (as young William does) but the bleak wintry imagery, alliterative 'b' sounds that mimic violent shivering, and William's echo of the shepherds who watched their flocks in Luke's Gospel, all alert us instead to the idea of the story as a festive parable. Both young William and Brown's reader may expect to be faced with the mythological supernatural, but here they are presented with a tale of the divine supernatural, where grace is bestowed. As Sallie McFague TeSelle notes, in parables 'people are not asked to be "religious" or taken out of this world; rather, the transcendent comes *to* ordinary reality and disrupts it.'[18] In the same way, the disruptive transcendent will reveal spiritual truths in the midst of Brown's bitterly cold winter setting.

Instead of the Christ Child in 'Dancey', we read about a baby girl saved from a shipwreck. The strange woman whom William Ness finds in the blizzard dies as the boy guides her to his family's croft, but not before she has pointed repeatedly to the sheep-fold in which she has sheltered her baby. In time the child is adopted and christened:

> The ship was so broken up that only her port of registration, Danzig, was found carved in a timber. Danzig the child was called too, when the minister came to christen her. And there was another complication, for nobody could tell whether the bairn from the sea was Catholic, Lutheran, Orthodox or Jewish. Drops of water were sprinkled on its head, and Mary Danzig cried a little, then slept. (*WT*, 143)

This story deliberately fictionalises the wreck of the Russian ship *Archangel* off the island of Westray in the 1730s, of which there was only one survivor – a baby, who was adopted and named 'Archie Angel' by a local family. Dancey, or Mary Danzig, is a creative response to this, but she is also a flicker of grace in the darkness of her winter 'birth' in the sheep-fold, or effective stable.

We learn that Dancey grows to be strong and kind. She tends to her suitor's old mother gently, but she is capable of strength that far surpasses that of the other island women. Among some of Brown's most lyrical prose 'laboured the great squat strong figure of Dancey. Only she did not stoop and gather like the other women; she swung a scythe with the men'

(*WT*, 150). Dancey is thus an image of Ruth the Moabite. After her husband's death, Ruth stays loyally with her mother-in-law, and '[t]hey came to Bethlehem at the beginning of the barley harvest' (Ruth 1:22), where Ruth gleans in the fields 'without resting even for a moment' (Ruth 2:7). Dancey's life is measured in the text by crops of corn and the movement of the sea; its accelerating 'slow wave of time', 'ponderous wave of time' and 'upsurge of time' pushing the story towards its climax, where Dancey saves the life that once saved hers (*WT*, 139–44). Her strength, derived from harvests of loaves and fishes, is not limited to physical labour in the fields, however, and the mysterious child from a Catholic country over the seas grows into a woman of courage, while the boy who saved her becomes 'a strange lonely man', warped and thrawn by a life-denying Calvinism:

> On a Sunday he would put on his dark suit and take his Bible and go to the kirk five miles away. But always alone, never one of the little groups of worshippers here and there on the road. Remote and stern, he listened to the sermon. During the prayers, he drooped his head a little. He did not open his mouth during the hymn and psalms. He would place one penny gravely in the collection plate, going in. (*WT*, 142)

Both William Ness and Dancey are outsiders. To her husband's old mother, Dancey is '"that foreign slut!"' (*WT*, 144) and to the island women she is 'a foreigner from God knows where' (*WT*, 142) – much like Ruth, when she arrives in Bethlehem from the country of Moab. However, it is William Ness who becomes the story's symbol of intense isolation, due to his sectarian religious practice. His faith is absolutely private, and though his worship is, in a sense, communal, he does not communicate with or even acknowledge other parishioners. Conversely, we are left with the impression that Dancey, the text's effective Christ Child, engages in communal worship – harvesting – which becomes the closest thing to the sacrament of the Eucharist that the island's Protestant environment has to offer.

The text moves from the deep chill of the winter solstice to the heat of summer:

> That year the elements of sun and rain and wind were so exquisitely measured and scattered upon the furrows that the little black-ploughed fields sown with barley and oats had shallow pools of green soon and then the sloping rectangles were all green, all crammed with murmuring and whisperings in the wayward wind of early summer, and jewelled after a shower; and at morning and evening the lark stood high above the ripening stalks, and the blue hemisphere rang with the rapture of its singing. [. . .]
>
> The weather kept faith with the crofters. The corn changed overnight, from green to bronze, not uniformly, but croft by croft would receive the blessing. Then, after the pledge and seal of the sun, it was time to put the scythes in. (*WT*, 149)

This paratactical passage is replete with references to worship and praise. The harvesters' encounter with the land is sacramental, and the prayerful murmuring and whisperings among the growing corn – an image of the soon-to-be-crucified Christ – lead to the lark's hymn of praise and joy in nature's cathedral, the 'blue hemisphere'. 'Faith' leads to 'blessing', which in turn leads to 'the pledge and seal of the sun', a pun on Christ, the mediator of the New Covenant. William Ness does not participate in the islanders' harvesting of corn, nor in communal worship, because he keeps his own meagre crop to himself. However, he is also prevented from harvesting his crop, after falling and breaking his leg. Dancey participates fully in this communion. Brown plays cleverly with the twin interpretations of 'communion' in the sense of sacramental encounter with the Eucharist (Holy Communion), and with communal life, and his female protagonist tends to William, despite his resistance and even violence towards her. In this sense, Dancey is disposed to receive the sacrament because of her goodness, while William's 'sin', his life-denying acerbity, denies him fruitful reception of the sacraments. 'Dancey' is underscored by layers of biblical allusion and midrashic exposition on the life of Ruth, but it is ultimately a straightforward parable of Christian faith. Belief should not be something secretive and hostile to the outside world, the text tells us. The birth of the fragile baby in the grubby stable shows us that Christ comes as an outsider, but one to whom praise should be offered freely, generously and openly. The imagery of 'sun and rain and wind' and corn, the 'bread of life', should be no obstacle to reading the story as Christian.

Similarly, Brown's 'A Time to Keep' from his collection of the same name (1969) uses the figure of the outsider and an image of the nativity to dramatise the importance of open, non-sectarian worship. The title of this short story is taken from the Book of Ecclesiastes. As mentioned previously, the poetic structure of this Book's proverbs seems to have appealed to Brown. In this text, the atheist crofter-fisherman Bill objects strongly to the influence of the kirk, and refuses to join the 'dozen women trooping across the fields' (*TK*, 41) on Good Friday. However, despite his withering dislike of Reformed Christianity, Bill is surrounded by symbols and images of Christ on earth. On Good Friday, the day that the Lamb of God is slain, two of Bill's lambs are born dead, while the waves of the sea and the hills of the land are hands that 'lay together, like praying, in the summer dawn' (*TK*, 50) in his mind's eye. Although he scorns the island women, who sit 'before the missionary with open mouths, listening to that fairy tale', Bill is naturally religious, despite his attempts to ignore the evidence of God in his environment. He maintains, rather arrogantly, that 'I and a few others in the island knew better' than the church's parishioners, and admires 'Mr Simpson, B.Sc., from Glasgow' who 'had not been our schoolmaster four winters for nothing' (*TK*, 42). However, the experienced reader of Brown should know by now to distrust the shadowy, rationalist figure of the schoolmaster, who represents all that is life-denying in Brown's literary universe.

Despite the fact that Bill resolutely insists that his 'two particular saints are Robert Burns and Tom Paine', religious language sneaks into his thoughts: he thinks 'no-one on God's earth could plough such a wilderness' (*TK*, 41) when looking at a rough patch of land. As in 'Dancey', however, it is the land that speaks most strongly of Christ's presence on earth, and this creeps into Bill's descriptions of his crop:

> My oats had heaved at the sun like a great slow green wave all summer. Now the sun had blessed it. The whole field lay brazen and burnished under a blue sweep of sky. And the wind blessed it continually, sending long murmurs of fulfilment, whispers, secrets, through the thickly congregated stalks. (*TK*, 54)

Like William Ness, this obstinate and hostile character is prevented from sacramental encounter, as his 'blessed' crops are destroyed by apocalyptic-sounding 'flattening, rotting, burning, [and] destroying' storms (*TK*, 54). Bill's rejection of God has, for the time being, meant that he denies himself fruitful reception of the sacraments. However, after Bill's wife, Ingi, dies in childbirth, he receives a small token of grace in the form of his baby son, and in what Schoene calls 'a pagan christening ritual'[19] he tells the child, '"Be against all darkness. Fight on the side of life. Be against ministers, lairds, shopkeepers. Be brave always"' (*TK*, 60). But this ritual need not necessarily be read as pagan. Instead, Bill is gradually succumbing to the Hound of Heaven, who draws close, and pursues Bill unceasingly.

Bill's very gradual conversion is indicated by the story's final scene, where he, his child and his new wife Anna become 'a perfect replica of the Holy Family'[20] at Christmas:

> We looked into the byre as we went past. It was warm with the breath of the five kneeling animals. [. . .]
>
> 'It was a beautiful service,' said Anna, 'just lovely. All about Mary and Joseph and the baby and the shepherds and the three kings. I wish you had been there. Who would ever think such things could happen in a byre?' (*TK*, 62)

While Schoene writes that Bill 'surprises us by approving of his wife's litany of intercessions' and notes that this text represents 'the closest Brown comes to writing a Christian manifesto', it is important to stress that 'A Time to Keep' also shows the gradual movement and assimilation of belief from paganism (or atheism) into Christianity.[21] Bill is a mirror image of Greene's Bendrix in *The End of the Affair*, who shuns Christianity and fights desperately against signs of God's presence in the universe after his lover, Sarah, dies. However, while Bendrix's final words in the text betray his belief in but rejection of God, Bill seems gradually to be accepting and welcoming Christ.

Another crucial idea at work in this text is that of the importance of the outsider. Its final 'nativity scene' remembers the tinkers, wandering folk and drunkard in the ditch; those who might be outside of society's approval, but who are (the text argues) very much loved by God. 'A Winter Tale', 'Dancey' and 'A Time to Keep' all have in common the outsider who learns, through open-heartedness, that Christ is accessible to all. Bill of 'A Time to Keep' is an outsider (he is considered an unlucky crofter, he argues with and is shunned by neighbouring fishermen, and he refuses to attend church) but one who is immersed in religious imagery, and who, very gradually, opens his heart to the idea of a loving Christ, who loves the outsider so much that He claims prostitutes, lepers and tax-collectors will enter Heaven before the pious and sanctimonious.

These texts also address the synthesis of paganism into Christian belief, and are unworried by this. They counter Reformation dislike of nature religions, and use the tropes and motifs of the nativity story in a fluid and highly allusive way. The Scottish literary critical tradition is as uneasy with pagan-sounding practice in Brown's literary tapestry as Free Presbyterianism is troubled by the pagan origins of the Christmas celebration. In his writing, Brown is troubled by neither of these things.

III. Nativity Players and Journeys of Faith

The short stories discussed above have elements of Christ's nativity woven into their very fabric. Brown's shorter fiction does not always use the nativity as fluidly, but his rendering of characters from the infancy narratives of Luke and Mark are more than simple retellings. These texts are formed by apocryphal narratives, previous poetic depictions, fine art and early dramatic accounts, which often depart strikingly from biblical tradition.

'Coarse merry rough-tongued men': The Shepherds

Brown's 'The Christmas Dove' is included in the short story collection *The Masked Fisherman and Other Stories* (1989) after first appearing in *The Tablet* in 1981. The Murrays call this one of Brown's 'pleasant variants on the Nativity', but, when considered more carefully, the text is more than a simple festive story.[22] It is steeped in biblical (and other) traditions which illustrate the facts of God made flesh. The story details the journey of a dove – a traditional symbol of the Holy Spirit in Christian art – from incarceration in a gilded cage, to the freedom of open plains and deserts, to eventual sanctuary in the stable during Christ's birth. While there is no mention of the Holy Spirit in the Gospel infancy narratives, Luke (3:22) tells us that at Christ's baptism 'the Holy Ghost descended in a bodily shape like a dove upon him'. However, Brown's dove is present at the moment of the incarnation, and, in accordance with spiritual gifts bestowed by the Holy Spirit, it 'scattered grey blessings on the sheep-fold' (*MF*, 137).

This text not only depicts a Catholic universe where a drama of salvation is played out. It is also full of comical, subversive details. These are mainly to be found in the description of Brown's three rowdy shepherds, 'each with a skin of wine', who complain bitterly about the price of alcohol (*MF*, 136). These shepherds are very much like the fishermen of Brown's unpublished *Our Lady of the Fisher Boats*, who drink Barbados rum and play cards. But Brown's boisterous trio are not new, voguish inventions. They echo the shepherds of the medieval Corpus Christi plays, who 'function as unconscious prophets' and

> ... sit in the fields, grumbling and quarrelling, gorging themselves and drinking – typical peasants enjoying a meal remarkable only for its size and variety. But their running commentary on the food before them is full of unwitting *double entendres* which alert the play's audience that this is no ordinary night, but the very night on which Christ is born for the feasting of mankind.[23]

Like their medieval predecessors, Brown's shepherds feast and complain, their anachronistic allusions to the soon-to-be-born babe fulfilling the convention of *double entendres*. As the youngest shepherd boy removes prickles from a ewe's leg, the dove flies off, frightened, and one of the shepherds mutters: '"A good sign, a dove [. . .] It's usually that hawk after a new lamb"' (*MF*, 137). The good news of Christ's birth is signalled by this man, but his unwitting reference to the evil intentions of Herod (the 'hawk') towards the Christ Child (the Lamb of God) may also remind us of the Passover. Just as the blood of the lamb smeared over the Israelites' doors typologically prefigures the new Lamb who will be crucified with nails, the shepherds' skins of wine are precursors to Christ's Blood. Meanwhile, the water and oaten crust that the young shepherd boy feeds the dove also hint at the Eucharist. The shadow of death looms over this merry pastoral scene.

Jeremy Wood notes that in art depicting the nativity, the Adoration of the shepherds reveals 'the moment when Christ's divinity was first recognised by mankind'. Wood explains that from the thirteenth century,

> Franciscan teaching, with its emphasis on a life of simplicity and humility, did much to remind people that the poor were the first to adore the Christ Child who was born in poverty himself. In many depictions of the subject, such as one by the Spanish painter Ribera [*Adoration of the Shepherds*, 1650], the shepherds bring gifts to someone who is even poorer than they are, carrying baskets of eggs, bread, and perhaps even a lamb, trussed sacrificially, with them.[24]

It is unsurprising that Brown's own depictions of the nativity, and specifically the adoration of the shepherds, are grounded in Franciscan thought, where modesty and humble simplicity are the guiding stylistic mode and, by extension, teaching. As already noted, Brown's depictions of the Virgin closely ally her with Franciscan conceptions of the life and teachings of Christ, and, in fact, it was St Francis who inaugurated the practice of the Christmas crib at Greccio in 1223, turning the Holy Family into a poor and dispossessed family. Brown's emotional portrait of the nativity scene in 'The Christmas Dove' is heavily inflected by these thirteenth- and early fourteenth-century artistic representations. His short story emphasises the lowly origins of the Christ Child and the poverty of the Holy Family as the dove watches the shepherd boy, 'with a small lamb in his arms', make his way towards 'the poorest house in the town' (*MF*, 138). As in Jusepe de Ribera's painting, Brown's shepherd boy brings a lamb with him as his gift to a family even poorer than his own.

The German novelist Heinrich Böll argues that things as simple as 'sharing food, drinking bouts, and card games . . . are sacred and possess authentic sacramental dimensions'.[25] Indeed, modern readers of the medieval Corpus Christi cycles may sense that the feasting, drinking shepherds nod in some way to the Eucharist. It is this sacramental dimension, and what Leah Sinanoglou calls the 'relics of the medieval habit of mind', that we find in Brown's nativity stories.[26] 'The Lost Traveller' (1991) contains the same Eucharistic prefiguring as 'The Christmas Dove', but through its narrator's weary, doubtful perspective, this story is transformed into a journey of faith – an interior search that is more extensive than any following of stars, and more elusive.[27]

Brown begins 'The Lost Traveller' by conflating the parable of the Prodigal Son with Luke and Matthew's nativity accounts. His narrator is a 'penniless tramp' (5), who dares not return to his father and brother and their prosperous wool business for fear of rejection. This man is welcomed by a group of shepherds – 'coarse merry rough-tongued men' (8) – who are engaged in 'drinking and throwing dice' in the village inn. Without recognising his prophecy of the Eucharistic feast to come, the lost traveller exclaims, 'that beer and bread was the most delicious supper I had ever tasted!' (5). His shepherd companions also comment anachronistically upon the life of Christ before it has even begun. These men become the soldiers casting lots for Christ's clothes in this description of their gambling and eating, but they also become communicants, receiving His body and blood, so that Christ is both the sacrificial victim of the Mass and the redeemer of humankind. Here, a new textual echo can be discerned in 'The Lost Traveller', because these activities are virtually identical to those of T. S. Eliot's shepherds in his 'Journey of the Magi' (1927). Eliot's Magus witnesses the same 'dicing for pieces of silver / And feet kicking the empty wine skins' in the moments before Christ's coming – symbolism recognised by Arthur R. Broes as 'an emblematic life of Christ in miniature'.[28] Eliot was a seminal influence on Brown's thinking about the poetic and fictional rewriting of biblical and other hagiographical narratives, as the traces of *Murder in the Cathedral* within Brown's *The Loom of Light* attest. And the traces of 'Journey of the Magi' in 'The Lost Traveller' are profound, from the paradoxical prefiguration of the Eucharistic feast in the moments leading to Christ's birth, to the weariness and discomfort of their respective narrators. Like Eliot's suffering Magus, who longs for death, Brown's narrator feels 'lost and bewildered' (3) after many years searching for God. He thinks initially that 'there is nothing at the end [. . .], only death' (6).

Alongside the weary narrator, we also see sinister notes signalled (as in 'The Christmas Dove') by animals hunting.[29] Instead of a hawk, there is a predatory wolf who lurks by the sheep-fold at night, his green eyes seen 'at the edge of the flames' (9). And, using similarly rich, gleaming imagery, the narrator notes that 'under the horizon, sat King Herod in his palace, and in the light of his golden lamps the emerald and opal and lapis lazuli glittered' (7–8). Despite his own poverty and these creeping threats of danger, the text's crestfallen narrator does not slip into complete apathy. The lost traveller's thoughts wander as he remembers 'long theological debates' and 'quests into the mind and heart of God' at the monastery in which he once lodged (1). He recalls the lives of the humble monks, and, suddenly, instead of a heavenly host appearing in the sky, we are presented with a mindscape of angels proclaiming God's glory:

> To them the earth and all the firmament proclaimed the glory of God. The humblest things were drenched through and through with the divine essence. In their silence, all created things proclaimed the eternal joy and praise. They believed it, in their holy innocence.
>
> I had once believed it too.
>
> Every created thing is a messenger of God, a choiring angel.
>
> *Glory to God*, sang the evening star . . . *Glory*, cried the thorn bush . . . *Glory*, sang the stone on the road . . . *Glory*, sang the fire in the hearth . . . *Glory*, sang the worm under the earth . . . *Glory*, sang the water-drops deep down in the well . . . *Glory*, cried the wolf in the mountain . . . *Glory glory glory* sang the mountains and the seas and the forests. (10–11)

The narrator's epiphany is a neat summation of Brown's own sacramental perspective. All creation sings of God, and discloses that the journey of faith need not end in blinding light and hosts of angels filling the night sky; conversion, or reconversion, can come from a quiet trust, or contemplation of the ordinary. This epiphany is the turning point of the text, which sets the rest of the nativity in motion. A shepherd boy excitedly informs the narrator about the arrival of 'foreigners' with 'laden camels' (12), before slinging a lamb across his shoulders and making his way to the nearby village. The narrator is poised to receive the spiritual fruits of the miracle of Christ's birth, and he notes, gently, 'So it was that I, the God-seeker who had lost his way, went down at midnight to the inn' (13).

We are left in no doubt that the sight of God made flesh will complete the narrator's reconversion. Like the newly converted magus of Eliot's 'Journey of the Magi', this narrator lives in a pre-Christian world. He knows nothing of the coming life, death and resurrection of Jesus, and so 'he thus acknowledges the miraculous presence without any hope of personal advantage'.[30] But the birth of the baby in the humble stable invites him to love. This text does not frown on disbelief; rather it welcomes the doubtful, and dramatises the often uncertain and wavering nature of religious faith. Marion Crowe writes that '[w]ithout allowing doubt a legitimate place in the human universe', Christian art 'risks becoming brittle and inhuman'.[31] 'The Lost Traveller' does not condemn questioning, nor does it suggest that doubt will ever go away entirely. However, in this short story, rather than the gifts given by the shepherds, Brown emphasises the gifts of grace and hope that are offered to all by the Christ Child.

'Tae be wan o them Kings': The Magi

Brown's nativity tales are not all poverty and meekness.[32] If the shepherds' adoration of the babe in the crib is an image of modest simplicity, then Brown's Magi are characterised by radiance and splendour. Although the Gospel of Matthew provides little information about the Magi's motivation or psychological state, there is plenty in the way of tradition, apocryphal accounts and artistic depictions to flesh out their roots, appearance and personalities. Wood notes:

> As the Annunciation to the Shepherds meant the manifestation of Christ to the Jews, so the Epiphany celebrates His manifestation to the Gentiles, and hence throughout the world. This universality is reflected in the supposed origin of the three Magi in the three known continents, Europe, Africa, and Asia, and it is the reason why one Magus is often shown as black.[33]

Brown's own depictions of the Magi are informed by these imagined origins. And just as the names Caspar, Melchior and Balthazar (established in the tenth century) 'almost certainly contributed to their imaginative power for late medieval lay Christians', the exotic splendour of the Magi also exerted a powerful creative influence on Brown.[34] In his nativity poetry, the three kings are notable for their rather two-dimensional psychological proportions. Rather than fully developed characters, the Magi are set-pieces, defined by their journey to worship Christ. They are allied with the colours yellow, red and black – which indicate their cultural and racial heredities as Asian, European and African – and they are usually unnamed. For example, in 'The Keeper of the Midnight Gate', Brown simply identifies his Magi as 'Daffodil-face, Ebony-face, Nut-face' (*CP*, 151).

The majesty and foreignness of these characters immediately foregrounds two difficulties in Brown's depictions of them. First, the Magi come from a very different background to Brown's usual Orcadian *milieu*, and, second, their 'exoticism' can be seen as rather problematic – even troubling, in its consequent signalling of a Western gaze imbued with assumptions of its own, more rational culture. These difficulties are certainly a feature of Brown's short story 'Magi – *The first magus, The second magus, The third magus*' from *Andrina and Other Stories* (1983). Brown's first

Magus, a boy named Hwa Su, is prince of a mountain kingdom and the son of an Emperor. The setting is vaguely Eastern and recalls some of the early descriptions of the setting of *Time in a Red Coat*, published two years later. While this novel's initially strange, surreal and somewhat grotesque quality (reminiscent of Mervyn Peake's *Gormenghast*) is missing from Hwa Su's kingdom, there is a shared narrative perspective. Brown's view of his Eastern palace, furnished with 'jade dragons that had stood for a hundred years or more in the alcoves' (*A*, 88), is occidental, and his descriptions of the kingdom's chaos and disorder point to the already mentioned, more 'rational' narrative perspective. Perhaps this is a deliberate strategy on Brown's part. Like Eliot, he may highlight the imperialist gaze of the reader who 'vaunts the superiority of Western culture' in their pity of the illiterate, ignorant Magus.[35] But there is no real hint in the text that we are meant to read against Brown's occidental language. Hwa Su's kingdom is character-ised by luxury, opulence and 'the richest silk hangings and golden cups' (*A*, 88), but it is still childishly irrational and disordered.

By contrast, Brown's 'Three Old Men', from the collection *Winter Tales*, is set in Orkney once more. Brown's vernacular nativity is far more creatively interesting and convincing than '*Magi – The first magus, The second magus, The third magus*', despite its rather unsubtle notes, for example 'Tommy Angel' – the boy that leads the old men to the stable. As with Brown's stories of the shepherds, anachronism is a key feature here. Christ is born in a twentieth-century setting, and the Magi are the comically confused Sam (an old shepherd), Ben (a retired skipper) and Willie (a miller). They make their way in darkness and falling snow across the countryside to a destination they have temporarily forgotten. They are explorers of a pre-Christian world, and so, while we should not count on them to understand the iconography of Christ's birth, we might feel that their dithering and clumsiness may prevent them from reading any signs accurately. Each bears a gift: Sam brings three golden sovereigns, Willie carries his fiddle in order to play a new tune he has composed (the title of which, 'Milling the Barley', has appropriately Eucharistic overtones), and Ben brings carved ivory from a voyage to Bombay. While Sam's golden sovereigns correspond easily to the gift traditionally associated with the first Magus, Willie's gift of music is not so far removed from the interpretation of the gift of frankincense in John Hopkins Jnr's carol *We Three Kings* (1857), where it is connected with 'prayer and praising, voices raising', and it may not be stretching credulity too far to suggest that Ben's ivory carving is a fitting substitute for the myrrh that Hopkins Jnr connects to Christ's 'stone cold tomb'. The attributes of these gifts have a long literary heritage, and go back at least as far as the medieval Chester miracle plays. In Chester IX, for example, the Magi discuss the symbolic meaning of their gifts:

FIRST KING The gold betokens royal power, the incense *the God-head*, and the myrrh death. [. . .]

SECOND KING The gold betokens love, the incense *prayers*, and the myrrh *human mortality*.
THIRD KING The gold represents *the Godhead*, the incense devotion, and the myrrh pure flesh. All are characteristic of Christ.[36]

It is highly likely that Brown would have had knowledge of the miracle plays. His work on the nativity in general indicates his interaction with these early examples of the Catholic imagination, and, after initial dismay with Old and Middle English at the University of Edinburgh, Brown 'delighted' in these subjects (*FI*, 114).

Brown's Magi are also akin to the kings of the Chester miracle plays in terms of their comic ineptitude and lack of solemnity. They are far less pious, noble and grandiloquent than many of their Victorian and twentieth-century poetic predecessors. Yeats' Magi wear 'stiff, painted clothes', their gravity accentuated by their 'ancient faces like rain-beaten stones'. Similarly, the luxurious opulence of Longfellow's Magi is seen in their robes 'of crimson silk with rows / Of bells and pomegranates and furbelows'.[37] Brown's comical old shepherd, skipper and miller are a world apart from these pious foreign dignitaries, and instead reach back to their medieval predecessors, who combined a 'richly boisterous world of simple folk and Christian feeling'.[38] Gladys May Casely-Hayford's Magi offer the Christ Child a little sermon, and 'told Him of the joy that wisdom brings / To mortals in their earthly wanderings', but Brown's old men are themselves in need of wisdom.[39] As Coghill observes, the medieval combination of the equally spiritual and silly Magi 'intensified the power to pray, as if the sublime could best be apprehended by those who are open to the ridiculous'.[40] Brown uses the same dramatic method in his characterisation of the Orcadian kings, and though they wheeze and grumble, the old men are witness to a miracle. We are told that 'the snow cloud was riven, and in a deep purple chasm of sky a star shone out' (*WT*, 105). As with all of Brown's creative work on the nativity, we are left with the nativity scene, or the immediate prelude to this, before the angle of vision is dimmed and the text ends. The impact of the conclusion to the Magi's journey is paradoxically stronger when it is described only very fleetingly.

The Brechtian impulse of 'Three Old Men', which makes the plot and chronology of Christian salvation strange, is more than a kind of witty anachronism. In this short story, Christ's birth is not an incident confined to the past, accessible only through the pages of an ancient text. In *Magnus* a saint's death is transposed onto the execution of a man in the twentieth century. When discussing the birth as well as the death of Christ, Brown's writing refuses to follow a linear narrative and conforms, instead, to a cyclical universal pattern of death, resurrection and redemption. His postmodern strategy of disrupted teleology is reminiscent of Spark's, and draws attention to its own artificiality to highlight the ultimate creativity of God. But instead of providing us with disquieting moments of prolepsis, as

Spark does in *The Prime of Miss Jean Brodie*, Brown situates Christ's birth, life and death in the recognisable present, showing that Christ is not a distant historical figure but a real presence in contemporary everyday life.

The act of creation, and in particular of writing, is one that is deeply inscribed in Brown's 'Magi', a prose poem included in *Voyages* (1983). This poem details the journey to Bethlehem – the first Christian pilgrimage – and presents itself as a literary artefact, or relic, in the form of a diary written by one of the Magi. The Magi are (once again) vernacularised and given a Norse identity: Caspar becomes 'Karlson' and Balthazar is 'Balth'. These Magi are greedy 'gold-seekers' with a price on their heads. Rather than following a celestial star, they pursue a far more earthly course:

> June 27: The map was plain in the mind of Balth. He drew it with his toe in the sand, and put an X where was the treasure. We have been to two islands. There is no word of the place. (*CP*, 202)

Christ's cross is placed prophetically in the mind of Balth, but this Magus is so off-course geographically and spiritually that he confuses the holy cross with an 'x' marking the spot of material riches. Matthew 2:12 relates that 'being warned of God in a dream that they should not return to Herod, they departed into their own country another way'. In this poem, the dream becomes a nightmare, and the diarist-narrator records:

> November 21: One night lately was full of shapes of terror. Sleeping then, after sunset, I dreamed I was a child in Orkney, and I owned the whole world, corn and buttercup and rockpool, and the men and women and animals put looks of love on me and on each other. Then to awake to the scarred face of Karlson, and mosquitoes, and smoke from a volcano, and a hidden mockery of parrots. (*CP*, 202)

Like Eliot's subdued and complaining Magus, Brown's diarist laments his toil, hardship and penury. His alienation from Orkney seems to signal his alienation from the world at large, and the impossibility of heaven without Christ. But 'Magi' ends with the ragged men witnessing a 'black boy mark[ing] the dust with a star' (*CP*, 203), a sign of the true journey to Bethlehem and a message of Christian commitment where Christ comes to the lost and the poor. This boy parallels the child in Lorca's 'Ode to Walt Whitman' – one of the 'fragments of truth and beauty, like treasures long lost' (*FI*, 55) that caused Brown's conversion – and becomes the poem's heralding angel who comments intertextually on the Magi's and Brown's conversion to the faith.[41]

Harris has argued that in Eliot's 'Journey of the Magi' the very act of writing is 'a kind of violence' because of its literariness.[42] He argues persuasively that by 'reducing the potency of the numen to a text', the Magus' scribe deadens the miracle of the incarnation by making the iconography of the nativity blandly familiar, and he remarks on Eliot's fear that '[c]reating inscribed images kills the Word'.[43] Brown's diarist-Magus could be accused of the same thing, and, indeed, Brown expressed anxiety about this very problem:

> There is occasionally the uneasy thought, that there is something suspect about playing the same Beethoven or Mahler recording over and over – something anti-life, in spite of all the beauty. Oughtn't music, and poetry, to be a spontaneous thing, like the old county fiddler reaching for his fiddle, and the story-teller gathering listeners about him at the fire? Then each reel and each tale differed in every performance, the tremble of life was in it . . . (*FI*, 182)

The potential violence that the inscribed image can have upon the incarnate Word is also an anxiety of Edwin Muir's, who famously decried 'King Calvin with his iron pen / And God three angry letters in a book'.[44] Muir worries here that committing the Incarnation only to paper (rather than approaching the world as another source of revelation) has caused a legacy of cultural decline, authoritarian control and lost artistic potential. The fears expressed by each of these poets might be traced to their experience of the reformed tradition, where images – as alternatives to the inspired word of God – are not to be trusted. The commandment not to 'make unto thee any graven image' (Exodus 20:4) may lie behind these fears, undermining the stance, taken often by Muir and Brown, that art is the handmaid of religion.

However, in Brown's case, we might argue that these anxieties are at least partially resolved. Where Muir condemns reducing the incarnate Christ only to text, Brown asks, '*In principio erat verbum.* Can it be that those beauties of literature and all the arts are a striving to return to that immaculate beginning? – the word lost in The Word' (*FI*, 57). Here he speculates that artists participate in the work of the Creator in making images, texts and music. Brown's rationale is one that taps into the very earliest Christian justifications for images of the life of Christ in art. The variety of forms and voices at work in Brown's nativity writings make them innovative, fresh interpretations, which aspire more to the impulsive spontaneity so characteristic of ballad and folktale. The shepherds and Magi who journey to visit Christ may well be Brown's balladic incremental repetition, but he injects doubt, revelry, fear and his own very distinctive Orcadian backdrop into these renderings.

In her discussion of Catholic literature, Una Cadegan notes a 'characteristically Catholic stance' towards ideas of innovation and repetition. She argues:

> Catholic views of repetition are shaped not primarily by notions of mechanization, but by liturgy. Seen in the light of liturgical repetition, innovation is not its opposite but its companion – newness consists in the fresh encounter with old forms, old gestures, old texts.[45]

This fresh encounter with a very old story is what we see in Brown's portraits of the nativity players. In an essay manuscript written in the last year of his life, Brown praises 'the universal hunger for narrative and truth'.[46] In his twentieth-century context, text is the medium through which Brown satisfies this hunger, as well as providing for it in his role as artist. This essay is notable for its emphasis on the power of spoken word to communicate the truths of the Incarnation. Brown praises 'the simplicity and lucency of folk-tales and parables' and allies his own work with the work of his creator, where he writes, '[i]t must have been argued, somewhere, that Christ was one of the greatest story-tellers: The Prodigal Son, The Good Samaritan, Dives and Lazarus.'[47]

IV. Christ and the Eucharistic Meaning of Nativity Tales

Brown's prose poem 'King of Kings' highlights the stark contrast between the regal kingship of the Magi and Christ's kingship – which is one not of primogeniture and wealth, but of God's taking on flesh in the lowliest circumstances possible. The Magi bring glittering treasures to the holy infant. But when questioned about their origin, 'Coal Face' murmurs 'the broken kingdoms of this world', and 'Bronze Face' explains that the purpose of these gifts is that they should '*shine now in the ceremonies of the poor*' (*CP*, 77). Here, the Magus becomes an unwitting prophet who foresees the Mass. Brown's poem fits in faithfully with a large number of examples of European religious art from the early fifteenth century on, in which 'the adoration of the Child by the Three Kings [. . .] appears as the prototype of the earthly liturgy'.[48]

While Sabine Schmid has noted that Brown's poetry on religious themes broadly 'enacts the Eucharistic process', here the focus will be principally on how the Christ Child in Brown's nativity works is offered up as a sacrifice, and is surrounded by Eucharistic symbolism.[49] So far, the works discussed here have focused on nativity 'players', those characters who surround the infant Christ at his birth and at the Epiphany. It is clearly an artistic challenge to represent the Christ Child as anything more than a babe in arms in nativity texts, and so Brown's literary strategy is twofold. He makes the humble material surroundings of the child reflect something of His later teachings, and he populates his texts with Eucharistic symbols and allusions.

Occasionally Brown depicts an older child – not absolutely identifiable as the infant Jesus, but allusive enough to guide the reader's response. In 'The Child in the Snow', a plaintive Christ Child appears to the narrator in a dream, and he tells us '"At midnight I dreamed / Of a thin lost child in the snow"' (*CP*, 285). The poem's lexicon is disorientating, hazy and otherworldly:

> 'I have heard it again, the low knocking'...
>> The fall of a frozen bird.
>> It is the sift of ash in the hearth.
>> It is the sound a star makes on the
>>> longest night of the year, a silver harp-stroke.

No one is out on a night like this.
You heard a mouse between the walls,
Or a lamb in the high fold, trembling.
Turn over. Let your brain
Brim with a winter hoard of dreams. (*CP*, 285)

Despite the images of vulnerability and the narrator's dreamy tone, there
are concrete markers of the Christ Child's call to love here. The 'low
knocking' evokes images of the adult Christ, seen in Holman Hunt's *The
Light of the World* (1853), where Christ, holding a lamp, knocks on a door in
deep darkness. This painting obviously recalls Revelation 3:20, where the
Son of Man implores, 'Behold, I stand at the door, and knock: if any man
hear my voice, and open the door, I will come in to him, and will sup with
him, and he with me' – a statement loaded with Eucharistic meaning. The
poem's star combines the stories of the shepherds and the Magi in Luke
and Matthew's accounts by singing like the heavenly host, and also acting
as an astrological sign. Its sound, the 'silver harp-stroke', conforms to Colin
Nicholson's observation that in Brown's work, 'harp' is 'a way of not saying
"psalm" [. . .] a plucking of the strings of the harp, or any song of a sacred
character'.[50] The poem's delicate musicality, low knocking, trembling lamb
and 'thin lost child' all highlight the fragility of the infant Christ. However,
these things also hint at His powerful and persistent call to grace. What may
at first glance seem to be a desolate poem of loneliness and isolation is, in
fact, a literary depiction of evangelisation. The story of the nativity can work
on the unconscious mind so that Christ comes as a boy in a dream, and
invites the dreamer to share in faith.

Ron Ferguson has noted the danger of making the babe of Bethlehem
too saccharine in nativity works. He traces the sentimental Christ child's
origins to the nineteenth century:

> Most of the 'facts' of Christmas turn out to be Dickensian hokum.
> There is no evidence that 'the little Lord Jesus no crying did make',
> and the exhortation that 'Christian children all should be, mild, obe-
> dient, good as He' owes everything to Victorian social control and
> nothing at all to the biblical story. [. . .] The Christ which many want
> put back into Christmas is a domesticated, toothless, religious pet.
> The anarchic prophet who was such a disturber of the peace that
> he was hung from a tree outside the city walls of respectability has
> been banished from decent society and replaced by a sanitised icon of
> mind-numbing blandness. The sentimentalised crib in the midst of the
> global shopping mall speaks of the corporate co-option of the radical
> message of Christianity.[51]

Ferguson goes much further than Brown's local journalism ever did in his
criticism of the consumerist grip on Christmas. His argument suggests that
the sentimental birth of the babe distracts us from the radical message of

His redemptive, sacrificial death. But Brown's 'thin lost child', surrounded by ethereal snowflakes, stars, dreaming and harp-strokes, is a tender, young infant, and no disturber of the peace. And the holy infant seen in 'The Twelve Days of Christmas: Tinker Talk' is no radical, anarchic prophet, but is, in the eyes of a tinker, 'a bairn / Poorer than me. / A white dream, surely' (*CP*, 279). Meanwhile, in 'Three Sons', Christ is 'The Word, the Star-child' (*CP*, 508), and in 'Christmas Poem', He is 'a glory / Whiter than snowflake or silver or star' (*CP*, 283).

However, Brown's representation of the infant Christ must be investigated with a keen critical eye. Is his Christ Child a sentimentalised babe in arms, whose depiction evades the reality of Christ's radical Gospel message? Ferguson is keen to stress that 'Mary's boy was seen as a threat to princes and prelates. He grew up to break the religious rules about insiders and outsiders.'[52] Brown's depictions of Christ are usually either typological (as in *Magnus*) or he transfers events to an Orkney setting – one in which a canopy of stars, an inn and a stable are entirely fitting. Rather than writing directly about the revolutionary adult Christ of the Gospels, he engages in an analogical project informed by centuries of tradition. His infant Christ is no less powerful for this. Brown borrows the trope of Christ Child as sacrifice, which comes directly from the medieval tradition of nativity and Corpus Christi plays. And it is important to note that the sentimental babe in arms is not simply a Victorian invention. This is in fact a feature of medieval devotional works, which Brown surely emulates. Leah Sinanoglou notes:

> Works like the pseudo-Bonaventura's widely-read *Meditationes Vitae Christi* emphasize the Child's humanity. They seek to kindle a joyous form of devotion by bringing Him to life as a winsome infant and inviting the reader to a sentimental response. But the miracle of the host become child is based on a harsher parallel tradition. Medieval writings, from early Latin tracts to late English popularizations, persist in conflating the Incarnation and the Passion, in fusing the Babe of Bethlehem and the sacramental Victim of the Mass.[53]

Perhaps unsurprisingly, given the influence of medieval literary motifs and themes on other elements of Brown's creative work on the nativity, his Christ Child also becomes the sacramental Victim of the Mass, surrounded by the imagery of his death, as well as his presence in the sacraments.

The depiction of the Christ Child as host has a long trajectory in European as well as vernacular art, plays and sermons. Ursula Nilgen notes that this can be found in the *antiphona ad offertorium* on the feast of the Epiphany, which 'places the offering made by the congregation during the Mass under the guiding image of the gift-bearing Magi', as well as in Latin Magi plays, where the Magi offer gifts at the altar, symbolising the manger.[54] Nilgen also traces the connection between the birth of the Christ Child and the Eucharist in the canon of the Mass in the Orthodox Church, where during 'the Transubstantiation of the offering, a utensil in the form of the star of Bethlehem, the askeriskos, stands above the bread lying on the diskos'. She explains that the prosthesis – the room used for the liturgy of Preparation – is called 'Bethlehem'.[55]

In Brown's nativity poetry we find something remarkably similar. In poems dealing with the journey of the Magi, the image of the guiding star is conflated with the instruments of Christ's death, before pointing to his presence in the sacraments. 'Desert Sleepers' has the three Kings sleeping under the protective presence of the moon, which reflects the Virgin's iconography where it is described as a '[w]ashed shell'. But soon,

> One woke. Twilight
> Silently
> Battered a bronze nail (a star)
> In the west. (*CP*, 254)

Just as the host is heralded by a star during consecration and transubstantiation in the Eastern rite, Christ, the 'living bread', is heralded by a star in Brown's poem, but this star is simultaneously a crucifying nail. The Second Magus of 'Stars: A Christmas Patchwork' confides that '[i]n our chamber / A star like a nail was the only light' (*CP*, 211), while in 'The Kirk in Orphir', stars pierce the seamen approaching a wintry Kirkyard 'like nails' (*CP*, 507). The iconography of Christ's death also becomes the explicit and abiding ornamentation in another poem about his birth, 'Christmas':

> 'Toll requiem', said sun to earth,
> As the grass got thin.
> The star-wheel went, all nails and thorns,
> Over mill and kirk and inn.
>
> The old sun died. The widowed earth
> Tolled a black bell.
> 'Our king will not return,' said root to bone,
> To the skeleton tree on the hill.
>
> At midnight, an ox and an ass,
> Between lantern and star
> Cried, *Gloria . . . lux in tenebris . . .*
> In a wintered byre. (*CP*, 509)

The first line of 'Christmas' foregrounds the ambiguity that characterises the whole poem. The simultaneous joy and grief of Christ's birth is signalled by the 'requiem' which could either indicate peace or a hymn of mourning; the poem seems at first to want to provoke the latter emotional response. Throughout, we see a heaping-up of heavily symbolic and contrasting images: the 'inn' of Christ's birth is situated alongside the mill which will provide the bread to be consecrated in the kirk after his death. The canopy of stars looming overhead do not glitter hopefully, but pierce the sky, as 'nails and thorns' will pierce Christ. The landscape laments the 'old sun'; a pun connoting Adam, God's first human being. Not he, but the new Adam, will return to 'the skeleton tree on the hill', an image skilfully condensing the meaning of Calvary ('the place of the skull') and the cross, an abandoned and desolate tree. The last stanza of 'Christmas' is of course a celebration; a shout of glory and a recognition of '*lux in tenebris*' – 'light in darkness'. The meaning of salvation history has been enacted through the birth of a baby in a wintered byre, but the weeping of his mother is not far off.

These poems provide a very keen sense of Christ's birth and death and the connecting imagery between the two. However, Brown is careful to imbue his nativity poems with the supreme Catholic encounter with God through his presence in the sacraments, and particularly in the sacramental encounter of the Eucharist, where Christ is '"the Word made Flesh", the mystical body'.[56] In Brown's poetry, this mystical body is still a babe in arms. His institution of the sacrament of Eucharist at the Last Supper has yet to be initiated, and His death and resurrection have yet to occur. But Brown's point is, once again, that God-centred time is very different to the passing of years under our own limited perception. McBrien notes that 'the human actions of Christ which are memorialized and represented in the sacraments, especially in the Eucharist, are not confined to the actual time in which they were first expressed'.[57] This was never illustrated so deftly as in the Latin tracts, English medieval drama and pictorial arts of the Middle Ages (such as mosaic cycles, free-standing sculpture groups, gospels, church art and 'independent pictorial representations of the Nativity or Adoration of the Child'.)[58] Brown borrows their Eucharistic symbolism and makes it the abiding theme of his representation of the Christ Child.

Wood notes that in sixteenth-century art,

> Christ begins his sacrificial life at the Nativity, and in some examples the parallel with the Mass can be made very plain. [. . .] Often the Eucharistic meaning of the Nativity is made explicit by showing the Christ Child lying on sheafs of corn (from which the bread of the host is made). In some fifteenth-century Nativities artists even showed the Christ Child lying on the corporal, that is, the cloth upon which the consecrated bread and wine are placed during the celebration of Mass, identifying it as such by showing crosses stitched at the corners.[59]

Similarly, in the *Adoration of the Magi* of the eleventh-century Bernward Gospels, 'the "manger" on which the Child lies [. . .] is copied to the smallest detail [. . .] from a portable altar', while in the retable by Jacques de Baerze from the Chartreuse de Champmol, 'the manger has been completely assimilated to the altar that it symbolizes'.[60] The Hebrew meaning of Bethlehem – 'house of bread' – is reflected in the depiction of Christ as the new bread. This became an influential and abiding idea due to a

Christmas homily by St Gregory, where he claimed that 'the place where the Lord is born was called beforehand the House of Bread, since it would come to pass that He would appear there in the flesh [. . .] The newborn Child lies in the manger to refresh all the faithful, namely the holy animals, with the grain of His flesh.'[61] As Sinanoglou points out, 'St Gregory's symbolic reading of the nativity story became a medieval commonplace [. . .] reflected in the frequency with which art and literature paired wheat and the Christ Child.'[62]

This pairing is explicit in Brown's 'Bethlehem', an elaborate, patterned and highly structured hymn of praise in which each stanza is comprised of six lines, each spoken in rotation by the Angel, Innkeeper, Our Lady, Captain of Herod's Guard, Shepherd and Magus. In each stanza the mother of God laments her seven sorrows, although Brown subverts the subject of each of these to reflect the Eucharistic meaning of Christ's birth. Instead of the second sorrow – traditionally that of the flight into Egypt – we hear Mary exclaiming, 'The second sorrow, a crooked plough' (*CP*, 148). The image of thwarted agriculture (and by extension the grief that accompanies Christ's death, which Mary cannot know yet but prophetically foretells) is continued by her third sorrow: 'black seed', and her fourth: 'soldiers in a cornfield' (*CP*, 148). However, the most explicit pairing of wheat and the Christ Child is in the penultimate stanza, where Mary says, 'The road of sorrows stops at The House of Bread', or – Bethlehem. She expands on the twin poles of grief and joy in the nativity story in the last stanza, saying: 'The last sorrow and the first joy are one' (*CP*, 149). Interestingly, in Hugo van der Goes' *The Nativity* (c. 1473–6) the sheaf of corn in the painting's foreground sits next to a vase of scarlet lilies (standing for Christ's blood at his Passion), and a pure glass of water next to the vase holds seven columbines, which alludes to the Seven Sorrows of the Virgin.[63] Brown's poem attempts to conjoin Christ's birth with wheat-symbolism and the sorrows of his mother in exactly the same way.

In Brown's nativity oeuvre, we are also encouraged to read the figures surrounding the infant Christ as His congregation and communicants, and the scene itself as a prefiguration of the Mass. In 'The Golden Door: Three Kings', each of the Magi reads the stars and astrological charts for signs of the coming saviour. The Second Magus' emotional account emphasises the vulnerability of the Christ Child. He asks:

> What wandered about the star streets
> Last night, late?
> It knocked for shelter at doors of gold, like a lost boy.
> My heart was bruised with the image.
> I am waiting now at sunset, again, with my charts.
> I had perhaps drunk too much midnight wine. (*CP*, 150)

This 'midnight wine' is of course a taste of the intoxication and love that the blood of Christ will bring, and may reflect the third petition of the *Anima Christi*, a prayer which implores, 'Blood of Christ, inebriate me'. The poem's early mention of a luxurious 'golden door' in the palace of the First Magi is a prefiguration of the 'Door of Corn' in the last stanza. Christ, the 'lost boy', is the keeper of this door, and will dispense grace to all who enter his kingdom.

In 'Stars: A Christmas Patchwork', the Second King emphasises the physical nature of receiving the sacrament, and the hunger for grace is emphasised:

> We went on slowly, seeking
> The inn.
> (Sweet the wine bowl, bread, bason of water
> After such brandings of sun and sand.)
> At the inn
> One candleflame in a bottle, athwart
> A tumult of flushed mouths. (*CP*, 211)

This experience clearly references the veneration of the host. The mere sight of the Christ Child leaves the worshippers with 'flushed mouths', so visceral is the experience of adoring the elevated host, which makes God present. In 'Desert Rose', a Magus records that 'a star lifted its head / And seemed to murmur to me alone' (*CP*, 280). The star becomes a choir at Mass, and, like the joyfully singing star of 'Epiphany Poem', this stellar object reflects the wider liturgical pattern of Brown's nativity poetry. It sings, in effect, the 'Sanctus' before Communion, at which time the Magus will receive the Blood of Christ:

> *Now to the House-of-Bread*
> *I guide three hungry gold-burdened men.*
>
> Midnight, the star throng, shed
> Dew in my cup like wine. (*CP*, 280)

Brown's nativity poetry also displays the symbolism so redolent of fifteenth- and early sixteenth-century paintings of the Adoration, where:

> the stable or the ruin of Bethlehem are shown furnished with a small table, usually uncovered. [. . .] It almost always stands directly beside the Madonna and serves as a depository for the gifts of the Three Kings, or for dishes and fruit, or sometimes a fish, a wine jug, and a piece of bread. [. . .] such by no means rare motifs as the fish, bread and wine confirm again unmistakably that, now as before, this piece of furniture was intended to depict and symbolize the altar.[64]

The table, laden with premonitions of the Eucharistic gifts, is seen in Brown's 'House of Winter', where, in a 'bitter house', isolated and lowly, a narrator tells us:

> Inside one chamber, see
> A bare thorn.
> Wait. A bud breaks. It is a white rose.

We think, in the heart of the house,
A table is set
With a wine jar and broken bread. (*CP*, 284–5)

Similarly, in 'The Solstice Stone', the Eucharistic feast is set at the heart of what is a pre-Christian site, reminding us again that no matter if the infant Christ is newly born, or even if he has still to be born, God transcends time as we know it, and His supreme encounter with His people is inscribed into even the most ancient, Neolithic sites and spaces. 'The Solstice Stone' provides a short account, narrated it seems by the stone itself. It is a living, speaking Maes Howe, which announces that it was confined to 'silence and darkness' before the coming of Christ, and it remembers: 'I was barren-ness' (*CP*, 518). With the coming of the heavenly star on the longest night of the year, the solstice stone has its true Christian potential unlocked. A new, unidentified narrative voice speaks:

A star unlocked the stone.
The stone was a white rose.
It was a dove.
It was a harp with a hundred carols.
It was a cornstalk.
It was the candle at sunset.
It was a fountain, cluster of arches.

On that stone lie the loaves and the cup. (*CP*, 518)

What has in the past been the entrance to a tomb, or possibly a pagan altar stone, is liberated or 'saved' by the freely given servitude of the Christ Child. As in the previous poem, 'House of Winter', Christ is 'a white rose', newly budded in a poor chamber, but His gifts after death and resurrection are already to be seen, as His saving grace has been set in motion. Gifford has criticised Brown for 'weakness' in terms of his 'poetry's recurrent perception of Christ perhaps over-dominating the often pagan element of his Orkney-based work', but the conflation of Christ and pre-Christian Orkney works harmoniously and well in this poem.[65] They are not radically separate entities, but connected in the cosmic sweep of salvation history. The Eucharist is the climax of all previous foreshadowing of the New Covenant, enacted through pagan ritual and sacrifice prior to Christ's birth. Indeed, in 'Dance of the Months: A Christmas Card', Eucharistic imagery is used in place of the Christ Child or any of the nativity players at all, so that the climax to the counting down of the calendar months ends with a neat and succinct tercet, which narrows the meaning of the nativity down to its bare essentials:

In the inn of December, a fire,
A loaf, a bottle of wine.
Travellers, rich and poor, are on the roads. (*CP*, 280)

Brown's 'Christmas Poem' from *The Wreck of the Archangel* (1989) is one
that was especially important to him, so much so that he framed it and
hung it on his wall:[66]

> We are folded all
> In a green fable
> And we fare
> From early
> Plough-and-daffodil sun
> Through a revel
> Of wind-tossed oats and barley
> Past sickle and flail
> To harvest home,
> The circles of bread and ale
> At the long table.
> It is told, the story –
> We and earth and sun and corn are one.
>
> Now kings and shepherds have come.
> A wintered hovel
> Hides a glory
> Whiter than snowflake or silver or star. (*CP*, 283)

This poem is central to Brown's writing on the nativity, and gives us a key
into the religious element of his creative output more broadly. 'Christmas
Poem' is initially a panorama in miniature of a remote Orcadian agricultural past, which stands for the labour, love and death of all people. The
Muir-esque fable of the life of every individual person is 'green' – hopeful,
cyclical, and bound to the conceit of life as lighted by daffodil-sun and
shadowed by wind-tossed oats and barley. After the fruit of labour, toil and
children, 'harvest home', a celebratory rural heaven, is reached. However,
the last quatrain puts all of this in context, for Brown. The poem is a tribute
to the one birth, life, death and resurrection that gives this cycle meaning,
and it is framed, or 'folded', in a familiar story about a vulnerable child
born in a poor stable.

The idea of folding is central to Brown's creative task in depicting the
birth of Christ, and all the symbolism and apocrypha connected with it.
As Philip Pacey explains, folding 'summarises its author's intention, his
belief that the role of art is to fold, in its fecundity, the seeds of countless traditions, and thence to enable their unfolding into a portion of
continuing Creation'.[67] Into Brown's short stories, poems and his early
play which deal with God made flesh are folded Scotland's often tumultuous religious history, liturgical and devotional patterns of expression and
thought, tenderness, humour, fear and lack of faith. A direct influence
from the pre-Reformation miracle plays and pictorial representations of
the nativity is discernible, as is the weight of influence from Brown's early

poetic hero, Eliot. Sometimes Brown's nativity poems reference the act of folding directly: its predominant nativity themes are signalled by the title of *Winterfold* (1976). Folding occurs in 'The Twelve Days of Christmas: Tinker Talk', where a shepherd 'folded a shivering lamb' (*CP*, 279), and in 'Bethlehem', where the shepherd says, 'the last of the ewes is folded now' (*CP*, 148). In 'The Warbeth Brothers at Christmas', monks are woken by a Christmas bell, from '[t]he comfort of the five folded senses' (*CP*, 506), and in 'Stars: A Christmas Patchwork', a priest in Bethlehem on the night of Christ's birth says, '[f]olded it is now, the dove, / Furled, star-folded' (*CP*, 211). Folding is a creative and caring act. Christ's birth is the creative work of God, providing protection, strength and, Brown would argue, freedom from the bonds of sin. In a similar way, the act of writing becomes protection from naysayers and life-deniers; it brings freedom from exile and a welcome into the love of a text which folds within it the life of Christ. More than all of his other work, Brown's nativity writings compel his reader to consider a sacramental universe, and to reflect on the immanence of God. As Brown and Loades suggest:

> All imagery forces us beyond containment, and though this may sometimes only make us move laterally or sideways to think of another earthly matter, the process has thus begun of thinking analogically, and analogy is of course the essence of religion: the words induce us to move beyond their literal meaning towards thinking of a new order of reality.[68]

Brown's sacramental writing on the nativity is the culmination of the creative devotional patterns found in his work about Mary, the mother of God, and Magnus, the Orcadian *imitatio Christi*. It may be helpful to think of Brown's work as a whole in terms of a 'ladder of love' in this regard, with 'the wintered hovel' hiding 'a glory / Whiter than snowflake or silver or star' as the ultimate folding, or embrace, on this journey.

Notes

1. Jasper and Prickett (eds), *The Bible and Literature: A Reader*, pp. 205–6.
2. Brown's first poem on the nativity, 'The Lodging', appears in his second collection of poetry, *Loaves and Fishes* (1959), while a sequence of poems on this topic appears in his final, posthumously published collection, *Travellers* (2001). He published several poems about the nativity in collections over the course of his life.
3. Bold, *George Mackay Brown*, p. 44.
4. Murrays, *Interrogation of Silence*, p. 123.
5. Murrays, *Interrogation of Silence*, p. 94; Schoene, *The Making of Orcadia*, p. 214; Bold, *George Mackay Brown*, p. 44.
6. Hall, *The History of Orkney Literature*, p. 128.
7. Wood, *Themes in Art: The Nativity*, pp. 15–19.
8. Rendall, *Steering the Stone Ships*, pp. 17–18.

9. Greeley, *The Catholic Imagination*, p. 10.

10. Duffy, *The Stripping of the Altars*, p. 13.

11. O'Connor, 'Catholic Novelists and Their Readers', p. 177.

12. Ibid.

13. Hall, *The History of Orkney Literature*, p. 145.

14. Rendall, *Steering the Stone Ships*, pp. 181–2.

15. Ibid., p. 182.

16. MacLean, 'The Pagan Origin of Christmas: A Reminder', pp. 368–9.

17. Dubus, 'A Father's Story', in *The Substance of Things Hoped For: Short Fiction by Modern Catholic Authors*, p. 156.

18. TeSelle, *Speaking in Parables: A Study in Metaphor and Theology*, p. 3.

19. Schoene, *The Making of Orcadia*, p. 155.

20. Ibid.

21. Ibid.

22. Murrays, *Interrogation of Silence*, p. 218.

23. Sinanoglou, 'The Christ Child as Sacrifice: A Medieval Tradition and the Corpus Christi Plays', p. 505.

24. Wood, *Themes in Art: The Nativity*, pp. 38–9.

25. Böll, quoted in Crowe, *Aiming at Heaven, Getting the Earth*, p. 13.

26. Sinanoglou, 'The Christ Child as Sacrifice: A Medieval Tradition and the Corpus Christi Plays', p. 505.

27. Brown, 'The Lost Traveller' (1991), OLA D124/18/1/4. All further folio references will appear in the text within parentheses.

28. Eliot, 'Journey of the Magi', in *Later Poems 1925–1935*, p. 30; Arthur R. Broes quoted in Harris, 'Language, History, and Text in Eliot's "Journey of the Magi"', p. 839.

29. In 'The Christmas Dove' the gentleness and fragility of the dove is tempered at all times by the hawk, who becomes the text's Herod – a hunter who massacres the innocent. While the dove is greeted as '"bird of peace"' (*MF*, 137) by one of the Magi, the hawk sits, 'furled, nourishing himself with dreams of blood and death' (*MF*, 138). However, by the end of the text the dove sees a shepherd boy hesitating at the doorway of a stable, and he 'flew on to the boy's shoulder, and paused there a moment, and flew up to a cold rafter, and furled there, under the stars' (*MF*, 138). Brown's use of the dove, now 'furled', signals the Holy Spirit's protective and consoling presence, and takes in theological, artistic and theatrical conventions. The dove is at once guiding star, consolation, and sign that the Holy Spirit will be made known corporally through Christ.

30. Harris, 'Language, History and Text in Eliot's "Journey of the Magi"', p. 843.

31. Crowe, *Aiming at Heaven, Getting the Earth*, p. 16.

32. 'Tae be wan o them kings' is taken from Brown's poem 'Stars' (*CP*, 25).

33. Wood, *Themes in Art: The Nativity*, p. 47.

34. Duffy, *The Stripping of the Altars*, p. 216.

35. Harris, 'Language, History and Text in Eliot's "Journey of the Magi"', p. 841.

36. Chester IX, quoted in Wilson, 'The "Stanzaic Life of Christ" and the Chester Plays', p. 423.

37. W. B. Yeats, 'The Magi', and Henry Wadsworth Longfellow, 'The Three Kings', *Chapters into Verse*, pp. 38, 40–2.

38. Coghill, 'The Case for University Drama', p. 163.

39. Gladys May Casely-Hayford, 'Nativity', in Atwan, Dardess, and Rosenthal (eds), *Divine Inspiration: The Life of Jesus in World Poetry*, p. 43.
40. Coghill, 'The Case for University Drama', p. 163.
41. Similarly, in the poem 'A Dream of Christmas' an old man laments that the pursuit of riches, or 'ore', has 'wintered [him], hearthstone and heart'. As the old man dies, 'At the garden gate / A black boy stood with a golden apple' (*CP*, 519).
42. Harris, 'Language, History and Text in Eliot's "Journey of the Magi"', p. 845.
43. Ibid., p. 842.
44. Muir, 'The Incarnate One', *Collected Poems*, p. 228.
45. Cadegan, 'The Cultural Work of Catholic Literature: An Exploratory Analysis', p. 30.
46. Brown, 'Tablet Essay' (1996), ms [n.p.], OLA D124/2/3/11.
47. Ibid.
48. Nilgen and Franciscono, 'The Epiphany and the Eucharist: On the Interpretation of Eucharistic Motifs in Medieval Epiphany Scenes', p. 313.
49. Schmid, *'Keeping the Sources Pure'*, p. 174.
50. Nicholson, 'Unlocking Time's Labyrinth: George Mackay Brown', p. 106.
51. Ferguson, 'How true is the Christmas story?', p. 2.
52. Ibid.
53. Sinanoglou, 'The Christ Child as Sacrifice: A Medieval Tradition and the Corpus Christi Plays', p. 491.
54. Nilgen and Franciscono, 'The Epiphany and the Eucharist: On the Interpretation of Eucharistic Motifs in Medieval Epiphany Scenes', p. 312.
55. Ibid.
56. Tomko, *Sacramental Realism*, pp. 4–5.
57. McBrien, *Catholicism*, p. 791.
58. Nilgen and Franciscono, 'The Epiphany and the Eucharist: On the Interpretation of Eucharistic Motifs in Medieval Epiphany Scenes', p. 314.
59. Wood, p. 9.
60. Nilgen and Franciscono, 'The Epiphany and the Eucharist: On the Interpretation of Eucharistic Motifs in Medieval Epiphany Scenes', p. 314.
61. St Gregory, quoted in Sinanoglou, 'The Christ Child as Sacrifice: A Medieval Tradition and the Corpus Christi Plays', p. 494.
62. Ibid., p. 494.
63. Wood, *Themes in Art: The Nativity*, p. 27.
64. Nilgen and Franciscono, 'The Epiphany and the Eucharist: On the Interpretation of Eucharistic Motifs in Medieval Epiphany Scenes', p. 315.
65. Gifford, 'Renaissance and Revival', p. 2.
66. Murrays, *Interrogation of Silence*, p. 217.
67. Pacey, 'The Fire of Images: The Poetry of George Mackay Brown', p. 69.
68. Brown and Loades (eds), *Christ: The Sacramental Word: Incarnation, Sacrament and Poetry*, pp. 4–12.

The Last Things

In the manuscript draft of an essay written for *The Tablet* in the last year of his life, Brown muses over 'the universal hunger for narrative and truth', and reflects on the life of the medieval peasant, who would have known 'that Christ was one of the greatest story-tellers'.[1] This essay, which was drafted less than a month before Brown's death, shows the continuities of his faith over time. It has much in common with his earliest (fictional) conversion account, 'The Tarn and the Rosary', where the young convert writer, Colm, states:

> I'm telling you this as a writer of stories: there's no story I know of so perfectly shaped and phrased as The Prodigal Son or The Good Samaritan. There is nothing in literature so terrible and moving as the Passion of Christ – the imagination of man doesn't reach so far – it *must* have been so. (*H*, 189)

Having marvelled at the power of biblical narrative in his essay, Brown's focus shifts to Orkney's elemental landscape – one not so different to the surroundings gazed upon by his Orkney ancestor, centuries ago. If stories could tell this forebear something about the Christian life, then the rhythms of agriculture and the seasons of the year could tell him something about God Himself:

> He who had watched the fields under snow in winter, and set plough to them in spring, and seeded them and watched anxiously for the ripening under rain and sun and wind, and reaped and threshed and winnowed, and seen the loaves brought out of the oven by his wife – he knew well what Mass was on Sunday morning in the village church. He needed nobody to interpret to him what was the meaning of 'I am the bread of Life.' He had no need of the theologians to expound transubstantiation to him. He knew that he was made out of dust, like Adam, and to dust he would return. In between were the seventy marvellous and anxious years, in which he hungered, in the body and in the mind and in the soul.[2]

These two sources of divine revelation – the story and the earth – nicely illustrate Catholicism's dual acceptance and veneration of sacred scripture and sacred tradition. Both are equally important to understanding the Catholic sacramental universe, where all reality is utterly immersed and suffused with Divine presence. Brown felt strongly that his Orcadian ancestor would have understood this as he listened to parables from a holy book, and watched the analogical drama of salvation play out across the sea and land.

Thomas W. Smith argues that 'for Catholics, as for all Christians, Christ is the ultimate mediator, and in a sense nothing else compares with Him. Yet precisely because Catholics hold that God-in-Christ redeemed all aspects of creation, everything else can be seen as an analogous mediator as well, including the writer's art.'[3] Brown's work reflects this theology at all times, and in different ways. The mediating force of literature, the motherly love of God, the intercession of a heroic saint, and the birth of God made flesh all show that for Brown, Catholicism is not simply a rejection of his childhood Presbyterianism. His faithful fictions on each of these subjects communicate what Brown regarded as something much more profound – the fullness of life with Christ. As with the medieval peasant, who watched time and again the endless cycles of agricultural renewal, Brown rewrote his conversion narratives in a number of different ways, and he wrote, again and again, short stories, poems and plays about Mary, Magnus and Christ. Brown's incremental repetition of archetypal characters – the greedy innkeeper, the spiritually alive child, the boisterous shepherd – displays a marked Catholic impulse in itself. Repetition becomes prayer-like, and reflects what Brown would regard as the constancy of Divine love. Floods, drownings at sea, ruined crops and death will always blight the lives of his characters, but God is a constant, offered every Sunday during the Mass – a continual and sanctifying source of grace.

In Brown's fiction, poetry and plays, biblical characters find new Orcadian homes, so that it is not unusual to see Ruth the Moabite gleaning in Orkney's green fields, and it is quite fitting that apostolic fishermen wrench a living from the intersection of the cold North Sea and the Atlantic, while ploughmen re-enact the Stations of the Cross as they wound the earth. The Magi journey across drifts of northern, wintry snow to find a bairn being tenderly cradled by a young girl in an Orkney byre, and shepherds drink, fight, joke and jostle, unwitting prophets of the Eucharistic feast and the taste of Divine love to come. But I hope that this study of Brown's Catholic imagination has made clear that his religious writing goes far beyond the biblical. Brown's body of work can be imagined as a vast stained-glass picture, overcrowded with saints, Reformers, crucifixions, martyrs, spiritually insightful children, poor tinkers, holy mothers, and transformative acts of grace that renew the very soil. Brown's Catholic imagination is not confined to the biblical: it aches for fresh interpretations of very old forms, stories, characters and narrative techniques, so that the apocryphal merges with the midrashic, and the hagiographical coalesces with the folkloric. Brown's religious writing may be anchored in the Gospels, but it reaches towards the numinous by using ceremony, prayer and devotional act as structure and organisational pattern. The theology of time in Brown's writing is not linear – it is frequently God-centred, and, at first glance, anachronistic. The

Divine intervenes in history in totally unexpected ways, and through the mundane materials of bodies, objects and matter.

In these ways, and especially because of Brown's insistence on the validity of miracle, his work is resolutely at odds with the 'condition of Scotland', 'realist' works of his twentieth-century Scottish contemporaries. Alan Bold may argue that Brown is 'not an intellectual poet' and that 'his work is carried along not by an overtly cerebral process', but this is surely a better description of his faith than his writing.[4] Faith cannot be primarily an intellectual exercise – it is also an emotional experience – but Brown's handling of medieval dramatic tropes, encultured faith narratives, and his engagement with other conversion writings shows that he was anything but artless, his writing only a 'spontaneous overflow of powerful feelings'.[5] He stands under the cross, shoulder to shoulder with Greene, Mauriac, Waugh, O'Connor and Spark, as a writer of the Catholic imagination whose grammar of devotion is global.

But Brown was a Scottish, Orcadian Catholic writer, too. He was received into the Church in December 1961, months before the formal opening of the Second Vatican Council in October 1962. Marc Bosco writes that Vatican II 'opened up multiple ways to embrace Catholic belief and practice. After the Council, Catholicism had in fact arrived at its own postmodern moment – Catholics began to situate their faith historically in the various social, political, and regional locations in which their faith was practiced.'[6] Brown's very local Catholic vision of the word has led to dismissive critical assessments of him merely as a 'parochial' writer. But, in fact, his imaginative view of Orkney as a 'small green world in itself' makes him a very determined child of the Second Vatican Council, and one who was committed to making that place, and its religious history, known creatively.[7] Brown's contemporary of the American South, Flannery O'Connor, writes in her essay 'The Catholic Novelist in the Protestant South' that '[t]he Catholic novel that fails is a novel in which there is no sense of place'.[8] Brown's work was committed to his place in the world. This book contends that, far from his case being 'the sad one of a truly great writer who has chosen to live in a room with only one view from its single window', Brown's stained-glass window of Orcadian history shows multifarious and diverse refractions of light and perspective.[9] His work is not limited by geography, but, in fact, derives great creative strength from his commitment to place and Catholic devotion.

However, his devotional perspective has been a defining factor in Brown's critical reviews. Strikingly often, Brown's critics have allowed their own religious beliefs – or lack of these – to intrude into, and to dominate, their assessment of his creative work. This has meant that Brown's writing has been critically framed in incomplete and even damaging ways. Frequently the critic of Brown is hostile to his faithful standpoint, and has refused to discuss his work in a detailed way because it seems romantic, fanciful, and out of step with the grittier social realism and cultural nationalism of contemporaneous Scottish fiction. Sometimes Brown's religious subjects are misread as confusingly 'pagan' – proving that he is, after all, not a 'real' Catholic novelist. The Scottish Catholic novelist appears to be incompatible with the deeply entrenched notion of the Scottish author haunted by Calvin, and, too often, the fertile meeting of Calvinism and Catholicism in Scottish fiction has been dismissed critically. Last, Brown's work has, of late, been the subject of studies by those who knew him personally. He has developed something of a posthumous personality cult, and affectionate portrayals of the man tend to override more sustained examinations of his place as a writer of the Scottish Catholic imaginary. Of course, Brown was instrumental in manufacturing his own myth. He submerged his own devotional works at times – keeping these unpublished, and augmenting them so that they revealed less about his own life. It may be, also, that he saw the monolithic uniformity of early religious readings of Graham Greene – a writer whose private life was constantly drawn into discussion of the representations of faith in his work. This may well have horrified Brown, who was desperate to remain private throughout his career, writing in a letter to Sr Margaret Tournour: 'It may be that abounding fame – such as GG experienced – is one of the worst things that can happen to a person. Bad for his art, too: maybe his best work was done when he was comparatively unknown.'[10] Brown was very reticent to discuss his faith in later life, and reluctant to become another Greene, defined by the label 'Catholic writer'. This book contends that Brown should not solely be seen as a Catholic writer – he is also a writer of the environment, of Scottish and Scandinavian history, and of community (among other things) – but his faith shaped his view of the world. It cannot be discounted in discussion of Brown's rendering of the small green world of Orkney. It is too important.

Ultimately, I suggest in this book that Brown's work can be read as an excellent case study of the neglected Scottish Catholic writer. A wealth of material by Scottish Catholics, particularly of the twentieth century, has yet to be explored. Writers such as Bruce Marshall, George Scott-Moncrieff, Fionn Mac Colla, A. J. Cronin and George Friel still need to be read in light of their Catholicism, and particularly in its Scottish context. While there are major studies on French, English and American Catholic writing, there is very little indeed about post-Reformation Scottish Catholic literature. Patrick Sherry's observation of differences in Catholic writing according to 'the writers' individual temperaments; their personal, especially religious history [and] their nationalities and the history of their countries'[11] should loom large in studies of Scottish Catholic fiction and poetry, so that Muriel Spark's notion of Catholicism varying 'geographically, culturally, and in every way' can be applied to her own nation and its faithful fictions.[12] Brown's work allows us to view the theological characteristics and dramatic tensions of his place as a convert writer of the northern isles, but his body of work has little to say about the literary renderings of Catholic immigrants and their children, of central belt Catholicism, or of Catholic recusancy in the Highlands and the Outer Hebrides. These stories have still to be critically explored.

This does not mean ghettoising the Scottish Catholic writer. Broadening the scope of the Scottish literary-critical lens is an important new step in the fresh and inclusive consideration of all committed writers, regardless of denominational perspective, and it will utterly change the way that religion has been read in Scottish writing until now. As Brown was to write at the end of the manuscript draft of his *Tablet* essay:

> It seems to me that there can never be art without religion. I don't mean that every musician and dancer and writer and weaver and potter has to be Christian or Buddhist or Muslim, but unless there is some awe and wonderment at the things that occur under the sun, little of value will be done, however much it is praised in the galleries and the reviews.
>
> For the artist – and for all men and women – to wonder is to praise.[13]

Notes

1. 'Tablet Essay' (1996), ms [n.p.], OLA D124/2/3/11.
2. Ibid.
3. Smith, 'Tolkien's Catholic Imagination: Mediation and Tradition', p. 75.
4. Bold, *George Mackay Brown*, p. 30.
5. William Wordsworth, 'Preface', in *Lyrical Ballads: The Text of the 1798 Edition with the Additional 1800 Poems and the Prefaces*, ed. by R. L. Brett and A. R. Jones (London: Methuen, 1963), p. 266.
6. Bosco, *Graham Greene's Catholic Imagination*, p. 158.
7. Brown, 'Foreword' to *A Calendar of Love*, [n.p.].
8. O'Connor, *Mystery and Manners*, p. 199.
9. Gifford, 'Scottish Fiction Since 1945', p. 15.
10. Letter of G. M. Brown to Sr Margaret Tournour, 22 September 1994, MFA.
11. Sherry, 'The End of the Catholic Novel?', p. 172.
12. Hosmer, 'An Interview with Dame Muriel Spark'.
13. 'Tablet Essay' (1996), ms [n.p.], OLA D124/2/3/11.

Works Cited

WORKS BY GEORGE MACKAY BROWN

Andrina and Other Stories (London: Triad Grafton Books, 1983).
A Calendar of Love (London: The Hogarth Press, 1967).
The Collected Poems of George Mackay Brown, ed. by Archie Bevan and Brian Murray (London: John Murray, 2005).
Greenvoe (New York: Harcourt Brace Jovanovich, 1972).
Hawkfall (London: The Hogarth Press, 1974; repr. Edinburgh: Polygon, 2004).
The Loom of Light (Nairn: Balnain Books, 1986).
'The Lost Traveller', *The Tablet*, 24.31 (1994), 1648–50.
Magnus (London: The Hogarth Press, 1973).
The Masked Fisherman and Other Stories (London: Grafton Books, 1991).
Northern Lights: A Poet's Sources, ed. by Archie Bevan and Brian Murray (London: John Murray, 1999).
An Orkney Tapestry (London: Victor Gollancz Ltd, 1972).
Pictures in the Cave (London: Pan Books Ltd, 1979).
Poems New and Selected (London: The Hogarth Press, 1971).
Selected Poems (London: The Hogarth Press, 1977).
Selected Poems 1954–1983 (London: John Murray, 1991).
A Spell for Green Corn (London: The Hogarth Press, 1970).
Stained Glass Windows (York: Celtic Cross Press, 1998).
The Sun's Net (Edinburgh: W. & R. Chambers Ltd, 1992).
Three Plays: The Loom of Light, The Well and The Voyage of Saint Brandon (London: The Hogarth Press, 1984).
Time in a Red Coat (London: The Hogarth Press, 1984).
A Time to Keep and Other Stories (London: John Murray, 2000/1969).
Tryst on Egilsay (Wetherby: Celtic Cross, 1989).
Winter Tales (Edinburgh: Polygon, 2006).

Non-fiction by George Mackay Brown
The First Wash of Spring (London: Steve Savage Publishers Ltd, 2006).
For the Islands I Sing (London: John Murray, 1997).
Letters from Hamnavoe (London: Steve Savage Publishers Ltd, 2002).
'The Realms of Gold', *Chapman*, 60 (1990), 24–31.
Rockpools and Daffodils (Edinburgh: Gordon Wright Publishing Ltd, 1992).

Under Brinkie's Bray (London: Steve Savage Publishers Ltd, 2003).
'The Way of Literature: *An apologia by George Mackay Brown*', *The Tablet*, 12 June (1982), 584–5.
'Writer's Shop', *Chapman*, 16 (1976), 21–4.

MANUSCRIPTS, CORRESPONDENCE, ARCHIVE MATERIALS

Orkney Library and Archive

Ernest Walker Marwick Collection
D31/30/1, Press cuttings and notes relating to George Mackay Brown and his work, includes five photographs, 1954–76.
D31/30/2, Typescript copies of poems written by George Mackay Brown, 1944–77.
D31/30/3, Bundle of magazines, booklets, etc., containing articles and poems by George Mackay Brown, 1953–71.
D31/30/4, Letters from George Mackay Brown to Ernest Walker Marwick, 1946–76.

George Mackay Brown Collection
D124/18/1/5, 'A Christmas Holiday: A Short Faction', short story, 9 November 1991, manuscript.
D124/18/1/4, 'The Lost Traveller', short story, November 1991, manuscript.
D124/18/2/6, 'Magnificat', short story, June/July 1994, manuscript.
D124/2/3/11, 'Tablet Essay', 25 March 1996, manuscript.

Centre for Research Collections, Edinburgh University Library
MS 2841.1.1, *Time in a Red Coat* – a play, 1981–2, manuscript drafts.
MS 2841.2–3, *Time in a Red Coat*, a novel, 1982, manuscript drafts.
MS 2843.7.1, *St Magnus*, manuscript and typescript, 19 fols.
MS 2843.9.14, Script for 'The Way of Literature', for *The Tablet*, Winter 1982, manuscript and typescript, 27 fols.
MS 3111.3, *The Loom of Light* – a Saint Magnus Play, manuscript notes, working copies and corrected typescripts.
MS 3115.5.b, *Our Lady of the Fishing Boats*, a play, 1966, manuscript.
MS 3116.1 (a–g), Various poem manuscripts, includes *Vinland* manuscript.
MS 3117.1, Letters from George Mackay Brown to Stella Cartwright, 1963–4.
MS 3119.1–3, Poems 1986–94.

Archival Material belonging to Maggie Fergusson
George Mackay Brown, 'The Magnus miracles were manifold', *The Orcadian*, 3 November 1994, 14.
Letters of George Mackay Brown to Sister Margaret Tournour, 1990–6.

Erik O. Paulsen, 'Well, is St Magnus really a saint?', *The Orcadian*, 13 October 1994, 14.

Maggie Fergusson's transcriptions of letters from George Mackay Brown to:
Kenna Crawford, 1986–92.
Dr Michael Curtis, 1977–85.
Flora MacArthur, 1953–76.
Ian MacArthur, 1955–80.
Renée Simm, 1978–93.

The National Library of Scotland

Acc. 4835.1–20, Manuscripts and typescripts of short stories, 1958–67, n.d., and manuscript drafts for part of the poem cycle *Fishermen with Ploughs*.

Acc. 4847.1, One hundred and two letters, 1947–69, George Mackay Brown from various correspondents.

Acc. 4864.1–8, Poetry 1960–9. Manuscripts, typescripts and corrected typescripts of poems.

Acc. 4864.9, Two manuscripts, 1964, of 'Our Lady of the Fishing Boats', a nativity play.

Acc. 10209.5, Letters from Stella Cartwright to George Mackay Brown, 1961–74.

Secondary Texts

Allitt, Patrick, *Catholic Converts: British and American Intellectuals Turn to Rome* (Ithaca: Cornell University Press, 1997).

Annwn, David, 'Correspondences: An Interview with George Mackay Brown', *Poetry Wales*, 27.2 (1991), 18–21.

   'The Fresh Echo: The Recent Poetry of George Mackay Brown', *Poetry Wales*, 27.2 (1991), 21–4.

Antonsson, Haki, *St Magnús of Orkney: a Scandinavian Martyr-Cult in Context* (Leiden: Brill, 2007).

Atwan, Robert and Laurance Wieder (eds), *Chapters into Verse: Poetry in English Inspired by The Bible*, ii (Oxford: Oxford University Press, 1993).

Atwan, Robert, George Dardess and Peggy Rosenthal (eds), *Divine Inspiration: The Life of Jesus in World Poetry* (New York: Oxford University Press, 1998).

Baker, Timothy C., *George Mackay Brown and the Philosophy of Community* (Edinburgh: Edinburgh University Press, 2009).

   'George Mackay Brown's *Greenvoe* as Impossible Community', *Scottish Studies Review*, 8.1 (2007), 53–66.

Bell, Ian, 'Breaking the Silence', *Scottish Review of Books*, 7 May 2006, 14–15.

Ben, Joseph, 'Description of the Orkney Islands' (1529), *The Belfast Monthly Magazine*, 2.9 (1809), 266–71.

Bicket, Linden, 'George Mackay Brown's "Celia": The Creative Conversion of a Catholic Heroine', *Studies in Scottish Literature*, 40 (2014), 167–82.

Bold, Alan, *George Mackay Brown* (Edinburgh: Oliver & Boyd, 1978).
  Modern Scottish Literature (London: Longman, 1983).
  'Orkneyman', *Scotia Review*, 18 (1977), 15–29.
Bosco SJ, Mark, 'From *The Power and The Glory* to *The Honorary Consul*: The Development of Graham Greene's Catholic Imagination', *Religion and Literature*, 36.2 (2004), 51–74.
  Graham Greene's Catholic Imagination (Oxford: Oxford University Press, 2005).
Boss, Sarah Jane, 'Telling the Beads: The Practice and Symbolism of the Rosary', in Sarah Jane Boss (ed.), *Mary: The Complete Resource* (London and New York: Continuum, 2007), pp. 385–94.
Boyle, Alexander, 'The Novels of Bruce Marshall', *The Irish Monthly*, 76 (1948), 457–63.
Breslin SJ, John B. (ed.), *The Substance of Things Hoped For: Short Fiction by Modern Catholic Authors* (New York: Doubleday & Company, 1987).
Bright, Michael H., 'English Literary Romanticism and the Oxford Movement', *Journal of the History of Ideas*, 40.3 (1979), 385–404.
Brown, David and Ann Loads (eds), *Christ: The Sacramental Word: Incarnation, Sacrament and Poetry* (London: SPCK, 1996).
Brown, Peter, *The Cult of the Saints: Its Rise and Function in Latin Christianity* (London: SCM Press, 1981).
Brown, Stewart J., '"Outside the Covenant": The Scottish Presbyterian Churches and Irish Immigration, 1922–1938', *The Innes Review*, 42.1 (1991), 19–45.
  'Scotland and the Oxford Movement', in Stewart J. Brown and Peter B. Nockles (eds), *The Oxford Movement: Europe and the Wider World 1830–1930* (Cambridge: Cambridge University Press, 2012), pp. 56–77.
Bruzelius, Margaret, 'Mother's Pain, Mother's Voice: Gabriela Mistral, Julia Kristeva, and the Mater Dolorosa', *Tulsa Studies in Women's Literature*, 18.2 (1999), 215–33.
Burnett, David, *Sister Margaret Tournour: With three wood engravings by the artist and a poem dedicated to her by George Mackay Brown* (Durham: Black Cygnet Press, 2003).
Butter, P. H., 'George Mackay Brown and Edwin Muir', *The Yearbook of English Studies*, 17 (1987), 16–30.
Cadegan, Una M., 'The Cultural Work of Catholic Literature: An Exploratory Analysis', *US Catholic Historian*, 17 (1999), 21–34.
Cambridge, Gerry, 'A Thread Too Bright for the Eye: An appreciation of George Mackay Brown', *Chapman Magazine*, 84 (1996), 36–40.
Campbell, Donald, '"Greenness in Every Line: The Drama of George Mackay Brown', *International Journal of Scottish Theatre*, 1.1 (2000), 1–8.
Campbell, Ian, 'The Short Stories', in Hilda D. Spear (ed.), *The Contribution of Orcadian Writer George Mackay Brown: An Introduction and a Bibliography* (Lewiston, NY: Edwin Mellen Press, 2000), pp. 41–62.

Campbell, James P., *Mary and the Saints: Companions on the Journey* (Chicago: Loyola Press, 2001).

Carruthers, Gerard, '"Fully to Savour her Position": Muriel Spark and Scottish Identity', *Modern Fiction Studies*, 54.3 (2008), 487–504.

Scottish Literature (Edinburgh: Edinburgh University Press, 2009).

Carruthers, Gerard and Liam McIlvanney (eds), *The Cambridge Companion to Scottish Literature* (Cambridge: Cambridge University Press, 2012).

Cawley, A.C. (ed.), *Everyman and the Medieval Miracle Plays* (London: J. M. Dent & Sons, 1956).

Chesterton, G. K., *Father Brown Stories* (London: Penguin Books, 1994).

Orthodoxy (Rockville: Serenity Publishers, 2009).

Clancy, Thomas Owen (ed.), *The Triumph Tree: Scotland's Earliest Poetry AD 550–1350* (Edinburgh: Canongate Classics, 1998).

Clouston, J. Storer, *A History of Orkney* (Kirkwall: W. R. Mackintosh, 1932).

Coghill, N., 'The Case for University Drama', *The Universities Quarterly*, 1 (1948), 159–65.

Colby, Robert A., 'The Poetical Structure of Newman's "Apologia pro vita sua"', *The Journal of Religion*, 33 (1953), 47–57.

Coleridge, S. T., *The Statesman's Manual; or the Bible the Best Guide to Political Skill and Foresight* (London: [Gale and Fenner], 1816).

Craig, Cairns, *The History of Scottish Literature*, IV (Aberdeen: Aberdeen University Press, 1987).

The Modern Scottish Novel: Narrative and the National Imagination (Edinburgh: Edinburgh University Press, 1999).

Crawford, Robert, 'In Bloody Orkney', *London Review of Books*, 22 February 2007, pp. 23–5.

Cronin, A. J., *The Keys of the Kingdom* (London: Victor Gollancz, 1942; Kent: Hodder & Stoughton, 1983).

Crowe, Marian E., *Aiming at Heaven, Getting the Earth: The English Catholic Novel Today* (Plymouth: Lexington Books, 2007).

D'Arcy, Julian Meldon, 'George Mackay Brown', in *Scottish Skalds and Sagamen: Old Norse Influence on Scottish Literature* (East Linton: Tuckwell Press, 1996), pp. 242–83.

Davies, Peter Maxwell, 'Pax Orcadiensis', *Tempo*, 119 (1996), 20–2.

De Flon, Nancy, 'Mary In Nineteenth-Century English and American Poetry', in Sarah Jane Boss (ed.), *Mary: The Complete Resource* (London and New York: Continuum, 2007), pp. 503–20.

De Visscher, Eva, 'Marian Devotion in the Latin West in the Later Middle Ages', in Sarah Jane Boss (ed.), *Mary: The Complete Resource* (London and New York: Continuum, 2007), pp. 177–201.

Deane, Seamus, 'Extremes', *London Review of Books*, 7.2 (1985), 12–14: http://www.lrb.co.uk/v07/n02/seamus-deane/extremes (accessed 22 March 2016).

Deboo, James, 'Wordsworth and the Stripping of the Altars', *Religion and the Arts*, 8.3 (2004), 323–43.

Delehaye, Hippolyte, *Legends of the Saints*, trans. Donald Attwater (Dublin: Four Courts Press, 1998).

Donovan, Leslie A., *Women Saints' Lives in Old English Prose* (Cambridge: D. S. Brewer, 1999).

Dorsey, Peter A., *Sacred Estrangement: The Rhetoric of Conversion in Modern American Autobiography* (University Park, PA: Pennsylvania State University Press, 1993).

DuBois, Thomas A. (ed.), *Sanctity in the North: Saints, Lives and Cults in Medieval Scandinavia* (Toronto: University of Toronto Press, 2009).

Duffy, Eamon, *The Stripping of the Altars: Traditional Religion in England 1400–1580*, 2nd edn (New Haven and London: Yale University Press, 1992).

Dulles SJ, Avery Cardinal, *Newman* (London: Continuum, 2002).

'Newman: The Anatomy of a Conversion', in Ian Ker (ed.), *Newman and Conversion*, (Edinburgh: T. & T. Clark, 1997), pp. 21–36.

Dunn, Douglas, 'Inscriptions and Snapshots', *Times Literary Supplement*, 20 January 1984, 54.

'The Poetry: "Finished Fragrance"', in Hilda D. Spear (ed.), *The Contribution of Orcadian Writer George Mackay Brown: an Introduction and a Bibliography* (Lewiston, NY: Edwin Mellen Press, 2000), pp. 19–39.

'The Supernatural Frisson', *Times Literary Supplement*, 1 April 1983, 324.

Dunnett, Roderic, 'George Mackay Brown at Seventy', *Poetry Now Review*, 18.3 (1992), 7–8.

Dunnigan, Sarah, 'The Return of the Repressed', in Gerard Carruthers, David Goldie and Alastair Renfrew (eds), *Beyond Scotland: New Contexts for Twentieth-Century Scottish Literature* (Amsterdam and New York: Rodopi, 2004), pp. 111–31.

Eliot, T. S., *Later Poems 1925–35* (London: Faber & Faber, 1941).

Farrow, Kenneth D., *John Knox: Reformation Rhetoric and the Traditions of Scots Prose, 1490–1570* (Oxford: Peter Lang, 2004).

Ferguson, Ron, *George Mackay Brown: The Wound and the Gift* (Edinburgh: Saint Andrew Press, 2011).

'How true is the Christmas story?', *Sunday Herald*, 19 December 2010, 1–2.

Fergusson, Maggie, *George Mackay Brown: The Life* (London: John Murray, 2006).

'Up vistaed hopes he sped', *The Tablet*, 26 March 2016, 9–10.

Firth, John, *Reminiscences of an Orkney Parish: Together with Old Orkney Words, Riddles and Proverbs* (Stromness: John Rae, 1922).

Fitch, Audrey-Beth, 'Maternal mediators: saintly ideals and secular realities in late medieval Scotland', *Innes Review*, 57.1 (2006), 1–35.

Fleishman, Avrom, *Figures of Autobiography: The Language of Self-Writing in Victorian and Modern England* (Berkeley and London: University of California Press, 1983).

Fraser, James E., 'Hagiography', in Thomas Owen Clancy and Murray Pittock (eds), *The Edinburgh History of Scottish Literature Volume 1: From*

Columba to the Union (until 1707) (Edinburgh: Edinburgh University Press, 2007).

Fraser, Theodore P., *The Modern Catholic Novel in Europe* (New York: Twayne Publishers, 1994).

Friedman, Melvin J. (ed.), *The Vision Obscured: Perceptions of Some Twentieth-Century Catholic Novelists* (New York: Fordham University Press, 1970).

Gable OSB, Mariella, *The Literature of Spiritual Values and Catholic Fiction*, ed. by Nancy Hynes (Maryland: University Press of America, 1996).

Gifford, Douglas, 'Renaissance and Revival', *Books in Scotland*, 50 (1994), 1–7.

'Scottish Fiction Since 1945', in *Scottish Writing and Writers*, ed. by Norman Wilson (Edinburgh: The Ramsay Head Press, 1977), pp. 11–28.

Goodwin, Gregory H., 'Keble and Newman: Tractarian Aesthetics and the Romantic Tradition', *Victorian Studies*, 30.4 (1987), 475–94.

Greeley, Andrew, *The Catholic Imagination* (Berkeley: University of California Press, 2001).

Green, Stanley Roger, 'Diary: Muse to the Makars', *Scottish Review of Books*, 4.4 (2008), 9.

Greene, Graham, *Brighton Rock* (Harmondsworth: Penguin Books, 1970).
The End of the Affair (London: Vintage, 2004).
The Power and the Glory (Harmondsworth: Penguin Books, 1975).

Grieve, C. M., 'Five Sonnets Illustrative of Neo-Catholic Tendencies in Contemporary Scottish Literature', *The Scottish Chapbook*, 1.3, October 1922, 74–6.

'Religion and the Scottish Renaissance Group', *Scots Observer*, 9 June 1932, 8.

Gribben, C. R. A., 'The Literary Cultures of the Scottish Reformation', *The Review of English Studies*, 57.228 (2006), 64–82.

Gribben, Crawford and David George Mullan (eds), *Literature and the Scottish Reformation* (Farnham: Ashgate, 2009).

Griffiths, Richard, *The Pen and the Cross: Catholicism and English Literature 1850–2000* (London: Continuum, 2010).

Gusdorf, Georges, 'Conditions and Limits of Autobiography', trans. James Olney, in James Olney (ed.), *Autobiography: Essays Theoretical and Critical* (Princeton: Princeton University Press, 1980), pp. 28–48.

Hall, Mark A., 'Wo/men only? Marian devotion in medieval Perth', in Steve Boardman and Eila Williamson (eds), *The Cult of Saints and the Virgin Mary in Medieval Scotland* (Woodbridge: Boydell Press, 2009), pp. 105–24.

Hall, Simon W., *The History of Orkney Literature* (Edinburgh: John Donald, 2010).

Harris, Daniel A., 'Language, History and Text in Eliot's "Journey of the Magi"', *PMLA*, 95.5 (1980), 838–56.

Hemingway, Samuel B., *English Nativity Plays* (New York: Russell & Russell, 1964).

Hopkins, Gerard Manley, *The Major Works*, ed. by Catherine Phillips (Oxford: Oxford University Press, 2002).

Hortmann, Wilhelm, 'Graham Greene: The Burnt-Out Catholic', *Twentieth Century Literature*, 10.2 (1964), 64–76.

Hosmer, Robert, 'An Interview with Dame Muriel Spark', *Salmagundi*, 146/147 (2005): http://gateway.proquest.com/openurl/openurl?ctx _ver=Z39.88-2003&xri:pqil:res_ver=0.2&res_id=xri:lion&rft_id=xri:lio n:rec:abell:R03553030 (accessed 12 May 2010).

Huberman, Elizabeth, 'George Mackay Brown's *Magnus*', *Studies in Scottish Literature*, 16 (1981), 122–34.

'In 1999 James MacMillan launched a furious attack on anti-Catholic bigotry. He has not talked to the Scottish press since 2000. Now, as his latest work premieres in New York, the composer is ready to speak out once again', *Sunday Herald*, 15 May 2004: http://www.heraldscotland. com/news/12508472. In_1999_James_MacMillan__launched_a_furi ous_attack_on_anti_Catholic_bigotry___He_has_not_talked_to_the_ Scottish_press_since_2000__Now__as_his_latest_work_premieres_in_ New_York____the_composer_is_ready__to_speak_out_once_again/ (last accessed 24 February 2016).

Jasper, David and Stephen Prickett, *The Bible and Literature: A Reader* (Oxford: Blackwell Publishers, 1999).

Jeffrey, David Lyle (ed.), *A Dictionary of Biblical Tradition in English Literature* (Michigan: Gracewing, 1992).

Jenkins, Robin, *A Would-Be Saint* (1978; repr. Edinburgh: B&W, 1994).

Johnson, Elizabeth A., 'The Marian Tradition and the Reality of Women', in Lawrence Cunningham (ed.), *The Catholic Faith: A Reader* (New York: Paulist Press, 1988), pp. 97–127.

Johnson, Trevor, 'Mary in Early Modern Europe', in Sarah Jane Boss (ed.), *Mary: The Complete Resource* (London and New York: Continuum, 2007), pp. 363–84.

Keble, John, *Lectures on Poetry: 1832–1841*, 2 vols (Oxford: Clarendon, 1912), ii.

Ker, Ian, *Newman and Conversion* (Edinburgh: T. & T. Clark, 1997).

Kidd, Colin, 'Scottish Independence: Literature and Nationalism', *Guardian*, 19 July 2014: http://www.theguardian.com/books/2014/ jul/19/scottish-independence-literature-nationalism (accessed 5 April 2016).

Kuehn, Heinz R., 'Catholic Fiction and the Modern World', *The Sewanee Review*, 101 (1993), 43–65.

Labrie, Ross, 'The Catholic Literary Imagination', *US Catholic Historian*, 17 (1999), 9–20.

Lindsay, Maurice, *The Enemies of Love: Poems 1941–1945* (Glasgow: William MacLellan, 1946).

History of Scottish Literature (London: Robert Hale, 1977).

Lindsay, Maurice and Lesley Duncan (eds), *The Edinburgh Book of Twentieth-*

Century Scottish Poetry (Edinburgh: Edinburgh University Press, 2005).

Litvack, Leon B., 'The Road to Rome: Muriel Spark, Newman and the "Nevertheless Principle"', in David Bevan (ed.), *Literature and the Bible* (Amsterdam: Rodopi, 1993), pp. 29–46.

Livingstone, Elizabeth A., *The Concise Oxford Dictionary of the Christian Church* (Oxford: Oxford University Press, 1977).

Lodge, David, *The Art of Fiction* (London: Penguin Books, 1992).

   The Novelist at the Crossroads: And Other Essays on Fiction and Criticism (London: Routledge & Kegan Paul, 1971).

   The Practice of Writing: Essays, Lectures, Reviews and a Diary (London: Secker & Warburg, 1996).

   Write On: Occasional Essays '65–'85 (London: Secker & Warburg, 1986).

McBrien, Richard P., *Catholicism* (New York: HarperCollins, 1994).

McGonigal, Jim, Donny O'Rourke and Hamish Whyte (eds), *Across the Water: Irishness in Modern Scottish Writing* (Glendaruel: Argyll Publishing, 2000).

McIlvanney, Liam, 'The Scottish Literary Renaissance and the Irish Invasion: Literary Attitudes to Irishness in Inter-War Scotland', *Scottish Studies Review*, 2.1 (2001), 77–89.

Mac Colla, Fionn, *The Albannach* (London: Souvenir Press, 1971).

   Too Long In This Condition: Ro Fhada Mar So A Tha Mi (Thurso: John Humphries, 1975).

MacDiarmid, Hugh, *Albyn: Shorter Books and Monographs*, ed. by Alan Riach (Manchester: Carcanet, 1996).

   The Raucle Tongue: Hitherto Uncollected Prose, Volume II: 1927–1936, ed. by Angus Calder, Glen Murray and Alan Riach (Manchester: Carcanet, 1997).

MacDougall, Carl, *Writing Scotland: How Scotland's Writers Shaped the Nation* (Edinburgh: Polygon, 2004).

MacKay, Marina, 'Catholicism, Character, and the Invention of the Liberal Novel Tradition', *Twentieth Century Literature*, 48 (2002), 215–38.

Mackenzie, Compton, *Catholicism and Scotland* (London: George Routledge & Sons, 1936).

MacLean, Rev. William, 'The Pagan Origin of Christmas: A Reminder', *Free Presbyterian Magazine*, 104 (December 1999), 367–9.

MacMillan, James, 'Scotland's Shame', in T. M. Devine (ed.), *Scotland's Shame? Bigotry and Sectarianism in Modern Scotland* (Edinburgh: Mainstream, 2000), 13–24.

Maritain, Jacques, *Art and Scholasticism and the Frontiers of Poetry*, trans. Joseph W. Evans (London: University of Notre Dame Press, 1974).

Márkus, Gilbert, *The Radical Tradition: Saints in the Struggle for Justice and Peace* (London: Darton, Longman & Todd, 1992).

Marshall, Bruce, *Father Malachy's Miracle: A Heavenly Story with an Earthly Meaning* (London: William Heinemann, 1931; repr. London: Constable, 1947).

Marshall, George, *In a Distant Isle: The Orkney Background of Edwin Muir* (Edinburgh: Scottish Academic Press, 1987).

Marwick, Ernest W., *An Anthology of Orkney Verse* (Kirkwall: W. R. Mackintosh, 1949).

Maunder, Chris, *Our Lady of the Nations: Apparitions of Mary in Twentieth-Century Catholic Europe* (Oxford: Oxford University Press, 2016).

Metcalfe, W. M. (trans.), *Lives of the Scottish Saints: The Lives of Saints Columba, Servanus, Margaret, and Magnus* (Lampeter: Llanerch Enterprises, 1990).

Moffat, Alexander and Alan Riach, *Arts of Resistance: Poets, Portraits and Landscapes of Modern Scotland* (Edinburgh: Luath Press, 2008).

Montgomery, Benilde, 'Spark and Newman: Jean Brodie Reconsidered', *Twentieth Century Literature*, 43 (1997), 94–106.

Mooney, John, *St Magnus, Earl of Orkney* (Kirkwall: W. R. Mackintosh, 1935).

Moore OP, Gareth, *The Body in Context: Sex and Catholicism* (London: Continuum, 2001).

Muir, Edwin, *An Autobiography* (Edinburgh: Canongate, 1993).

    Collected Poems (London: Faber & Faber, 1960).

    John Knox: Portrait of a Calvinist (London: Collins, 1930).

    Scottish Journey (London: William Heinemann; Victor Gollancz, 1935).

Muir, Lynette R., *The Biblical Drama of Medieval Europe* (Cambridge: Cambridge University Press, 1995).

Muir, Willa, *Imagined Selves*, ed. by Kirsty Allen (Edinburgh: Canongate, 1996).

Mullet, Gilbert H., *Nightmares and Visions: Flannery O'Connor and the Catholic Grotesque* (Athens: The University of Georgia Press, 1972).

Murphy, Diane, *Medieval Mystery Plays as Popular Culture: Performing the Lives of Saints* (Lampeter: Edwin Mellen Press, 2006).

Murray, Isobel (ed.), 'Robin Jenkins', in *Scottish Writers Talking 3* (Edinburgh: John Donald, 2006), pp. 101–46.

    'A Sequence of Images: George Mackay Brown', in *Scottish Writers Talking: George Mackay Brown, Jessie Kesson, Norman MacCaig, William McIlvanney, David Toulmin* (East Linton: Tuckwell Press, 1996), pp. 1–54.

Murray, Rowena and Brian Murray, *Interrogation of Silence: The Writings of George Mackay Brown* (London: John Murray, 2004).

Newman, John Henry, *Apologia pro vita sua: Being a History of his Religious Opinions* (London: Longmans, Green & Co., 1890).

    Essays Critical and Historical, 2 vols (London: Basil Montagu Pickering, 1871).

    An Essay in Aid of A Grammar of Assent, ed. by I. T. Ker (Oxford: Clarendon Press, 1985).

    The Letters and Diaries of John Henry Newman, ed. by Ian Ker, 29 vols (Oxford: Clarendon Press, 1979), iii.

    Parochial and Plain Sermons, 8 vols (London: Longmans, Green & Co., 1908), viii.

Nicholson, Colin, 'Unlocking Time's Labyrinth', in *Poem, Purpose and Place: Shaping Identity in Contemporary Scottish Verse* (London: Polygon, 1992), pp. 96–113.

Nilgen, Ursula and Renate Franciscono, 'The Epiphany and the Eucharist: On the Interpretation of Eucharistic Motifs in Medieval Epiphany Scenes', *The Art Bulletin*, 49.4 (1967), 311–16.

O'Brien, Catherine, 'Mary In Modern European Literature', in Sarah Jane Boss (ed.), *Mary: The Complete Resource* (London and New York: Continuum, 2007), pp. 521–31.

O'Connor, Flannery, *Complete Stories* (London: Faber & Faber, 1990).

 The Habit of Being, ed. by Sally Fitzgerald (New York: Farrar, Straus, Giroux, 1979).

 Mystery and Manners, ed. by Sally and Robert Fitzgerald (London: Faber & Faber, 1972).

O'Donnell, Angela Alaimo, 'Seeing Catholicly: Poetry and the Catholic Imagination', in James T. Fisher and Margaret McGuinness (ed.), *The Catholic Studies Reader* (New York: Fordham University Press, 2011), pp. 331–51.

O'Donnell, Donat, *Maria Cross: Imaginative Patterns in a Group of Modern Catholic Writers* (London: Chatto & Windus, 1954).

Orsi, Robert A., 'The Many Names of the Mother of God', in Melissa R. Katz and Robert A. Orsi (eds), *Divine Mirrors: The Virgin Mary in the Visual Arts* (Oxford: Oxford University Press, 2001), pp. 3–18.

Orwell, George, *Inside the Whale and Other Essays* (Harmondsworth: Penguin Books, 1957).

Pacey, Philip, 'The Fire of Images: The Poetry of George Mackay Brown', *Akros*, 11.32 (1976), 61–71.

Pálsson, Herman and Paul Edwards (trans.), *Orkneyinga Saga: The History of the Earls of Orkney* (London: Penguin Books Ltd, 1978).

Pearce, Joseph, *Literary Converts: Spiritual Inspiration in an Age of Unbelief* (London: HarperCollins, 1999).

 Literary Giants, Literary Catholics (San Francisco: Ignatius Press, 2005).

Peterson, Linda H., 'Newman's *Apologia pro vita sua* and the Traditions of the English Spiritual Autobiography', *PMLA*, 100 (1985), 300–14.

Prickett, Stephen, *Romanticism and Religion: The Tradition of Coleridge and Wordsworth in the Victorian Church* (Cambridge: Cambridge University Press, 1976).

Reichardt, Mary R. (ed.), *Between Human and Divine: The Catholic Vision in Contemporary Literature* (Washington, DC: The Catholic University of America Press, 2010).

 Exploring Catholic Literature: A Companion and Resource Guide (Oxford: Rowman & Littlefield Publishers, 2003).

Reilly, Patrick, 'Catholics and Scottish Literature 1878–1978', *Innes Review*, 29 (1978), 183–203.

Rendall, Jocelyn, *Steering the Stone Ships: The Story of Orkney Kirks and People* (Edinburgh: Saint Andrew Press, 2009).

Rubin, Miri, *Mother of God: A History of the Virgin Mary* (London: Penguin Books, 2009).

Ryan, Denise, 'Playing the Midwife's Part in the English Nativity Plays', *The Review of English Studies*, 54.216 (2003), 435–48.

Schmid, Sabine, 'George Mackay Brown: European Poet?', *Chapman*, 93 (1999), 10–17.

 'Keeping the Sources Pure': The Making of George Mackay Brown (Oxford: Peter Lang, 2003).

Schoene, Berthold, 'I Imagined Nine Centuries': Narrative Fragmentation and Mythical Closure in the Shorter Historical Fiction of George Mackay Brown', *Scottish Literary Journal*, 22.2 (1995), 41–59.

 The Making of Orcadia: Narrative Identity in the Prose Work of George Mackay Brown (Frankfurt: Peter Lang, 1995).

 Review of *Interrogation of Silence: The Writings of George Mackay Brown* by Rowena Murray and Brian Murray, *Scottish Studies Review*, 6 (2005), 131–3.

Schwartz, Adam, 'Swords of Honor: The Revival of Orthodox Christianity in Twentieth-Century Britain', *Logos*, 4 (2001), 11–33.

Scott, Tom, 'Orkney As Pairt O An Eternal Mood', *Chapman*, 60 (1990), 32–8.

 The Penguin Book of Scottish Verse (London: Penguin, 1970).

Scott-Moncrieff, George, *Death's Bright Shadow* (London: Allan Wingate, 1948).

 The Mirror and the Cross: Scotland and the Catholic Faith (London: Burns & Oates, 1960).

Sharpton, William, 'Hamnavoe Revisited: An Interview with George Mackay Brown', *Chapman*, 84 (1996), 20–7.

Sherry, Patrick, 'The End of the Catholic Novel?', *Literature & Theology*, 9.2 (1995), 165–78.

Sinanoglou, Leah, 'The Christ Child as Sacrifice: A Medieval Tradition and the Corpus Christi Plays', *Speculum*, 48.3 (1973), 491–509.

Smith, Julia M. H., 'Review Article: Early medieval hagiography in the late twentieth century', *Early Medieval Europe*, 1.1 (1992), 69–76.

Smith, Thomas W., 'Tolkien's Catholic Imagination: Mediation and Tradition', *Religion and Literature*, 38.2 (2006), 73–100.

Spark, Muriel, *The Comforters* (London: Virago Press, 2009).

 Curriculum Vitae (London: Constable, 1992).

 'My Conversion', in Joseph Hynes (ed.), *Critical Essays on Muriel Spark* (New York: G. K. Hall; Oxford: Maxwell Macmillan International, 1992), pp. 24–8.

 The Prime of Miss Jean Brodie (London: Penguin Books, 1961).

Spear, Hilda D. (ed.), *George Mackay Brown: A Survey of His Work and a Full Bibliography* (Lewiston, NY: Edwin Mellen Press, 2000).

Spengemann, William C., *The Forms of Autobiography: Episodes in the History of a Literary Genre* (New Haven and London: Yale University Press, 1980).

Stannard, Martin, *Muriel Spark: The Biography* (London: Weidenfeld & Nicolson, 2009).

Starobinski, Jean, 'The Style of Autobiography', in James Olney (ed.), *Autobiography: Essays Theoretical and Critical* (Princeton: Princeton University Press, 1980), pp. 73–83.

Starr, Mirabai (trans.), *Teresa of Avila: The Book of My Life* (Boston: New Seeds Books, 2007).

Stevenson, Randall and Gavin Wallace (eds), *The Scottish Novel Since the Seventies: New Visions, Old Dreams* (Edinburgh: Edinburgh University Press, 1993).

Stone, Brian (trans.), *Medieval English Verse* (Harmondsworth: Penguin Books, 1964).

Strachey, Lytton, *Eminent Victorians: The Definitive Edition* (London: Continuum, 2003).

Teilhard de Chardin, Pierre, *The Divine Milieu*, trans. Siôn Cowell (Brighton: Sussex Academic Press, 2004).

TeSelle, Sallie McFague, *Speaking in Parables: A Study in Metaphor and Theology* (Philadelphia: Fortress Press, 1975).

Tóibín, Colm, *The Sign of the Cross: Travels in Catholic Europe* (London: Picador, 2001).

Tomany, Maria-Claudia, 'Sacred Non-Violence, Cowardice Profaned: St Magnus of Orkney in Nordic Hagiography and Historiography', in Thomas A. DuBois (ed.), *Sanctity in the North: Saints, Lives and Cults in Medieval Scandinavia* (Toronto: University of Toronto Press, 2009), pp. 128–53.

Tomko, Helena M., *Sacramental Realism: Gertrud von le Fort and German Catholic Literature in the Weimar Republic and Third Reich (1924–46)* (London: Maney Publishing for the Modern Humanities Research Association, 2007).

Towill, Edwin Sprott, *The Saints of Scotland* (Edinburgh: Saint Andrew Press, 1978).

Tracy, David, *The Analogical Imagination: Christian Theology and the Culture of Pluralism* (New York: Crossroad, 1981).

Traherne, Thomas, *Centuries of Meditations* (New York: Cosimo Classics, 2009).

Undset, Sigrid, *Kristin Lavransdatter*, trans. Charles Archer and J. S. Scott (London: Alfred A. Knopf, 1930).

Saga of Saints, trans. E. C. Ramsden (London: Sheed & Ward, 1934).

Vloberg, Maurice, 'The Iconographic Types of the Virgin in Western Art', in Sarah Jane Boss (ed.), *Mary: The Complete Resource* (London and New York: Continuum, 2007), pp. 537–85.

Voragine, Jacobus de, *The Golden Legend: or, Lives of the Saints / as Englished by William Caxton* (New York: AMS Press, 1973).

The Golden Legend: Readings on the Saints, trans. William Granger Ryan (Princeton: Princeton University Press, 1993).

Waldmeir, John C., *Cathedrals of Bone: The Role of the Body in Contemporary Catholic Literature* (New York: Fordham University Press, 2009).

Walker, Marshall, *Scottish Literature Since 1707* (London: Longman, 1996).

Warner, Marina, *Alone of All Her Sex: the Myth and Cult of the Virgin Mary* (London: Pan Books, 1985).

Waugh, Evelyn, *Brideshead Revisited: The Sacred and Profane Memories of Captain Charles Ryder* (London: Penguin Books, 2000).

Weigel, George, *Letters to a young Catholic* (Herefordshire: Gracewing, 2004).

Wells, Robert Preston, Review of *Selected Poems* by George Mackay Brown and *George Mackay Brown* by Alan Bold, *Lines Review*, 70 (1979), 5–14.

Whitehouse, J. C., 'Catholic Writing: Some Basic Notions, Some Criticisms, and a Tentative Reply', *Modern Language Review*, 73.2 (1978), 241–9.

'Men, Women, God, and So Forth', *Logos: A Journal of Catholic Thought and Culture*, 4.1 (2001), 54–75.

Whittaker, Ruth, *The Faith and Fiction of Muriel Spark* (London: Macmillan, 1982).

Whyte, Christopher, *Modern Scottish Poetry* (Edinburgh: Edinburgh University Press, 2004), pp. 149–73.

Wilson, Robert H., 'The "Stanzaic Life of Christ" and the Chester Plays', *Studies in Philology*, 28.3 (1931), 413–32.

Wood, Jeremy, *Themes in Art: The Nativity* (London: Scala Publications Limited, 1992).

Woodman, Thomas, *Faithful Fictions: The Catholic Novel in British Literature* (Buckingham: Open University Press, 1991).

Wordsworth, William, *The Collected Poems of William Wordsworth* (Ware: Wordsworth Editions, 1995).

Lyrical Ballads: The Text of the 1798 Edition with the Additional 1800 Poems and the Prefaces, ed. by R. L. Brett and A. R. Jones (London: Methuen, 1963).

Wright, T. R., 'Newman on Literature: "Thinking Out Into Language"', *Journal of Literature & Theology*, 5.2 (1991), 181–97.

Theology and Literature (Oxford: Basil Blackwell, 1988).

Index

paganism, 2, 4, 5, 11, 35, 38, 40, 81, 121, 142, 145–7, 148–9, 153, 154, 170, 178

Péguy, Charles, 18, 19

Pitcairne, Archibald, 15–16
The Assembly, 15–16

Plymouth Brethren, 22, 27, 51

prayer, 1, 29, 32–3, 50, 55, 60, 64, 65, 75, 79–80, 84, 87–9, 90–1, 97, 100, 123, 128, 130, 136, 143, 151, 152, 159, 160, 168, 176; *see also* Roman Catholic Devotions

Presbyterianism, 1, 12, 16, 17, 21, 22, 33, 35, 48, 50, 52, 60, 62, 68, 69, 70, 71, 72, 75, 91, 147–9, 154, 176; *see also* Calvinism, Church of Scotland

Protestant imagination, 5, 11, 12, 15, 35–6, 37, 17, 112, 127

Protestant Reformation, 1, 9, 10, 22, 33, 35, 116, 126, 145, 147, 148, 154, 162
in Scotland, 1, 2, 4, 5, 6, 7, 9, 10, 11, 15, 18, 21, 22, 25, 41, 52, 69, 70, 71, 80–1, 83, 93

Protestantism, 4, 5, 8, 9, 11, 12, 15, 19, 20, 21, 22, 23, 26, 27, 28, 33, 35, 36, 37, 49, 60, 83

Rendall, Robert, 51–2, 53

Restoration of the Scottish Catholic hierarchy, 14

Robertson, James, 11

Rolfe, Frederick, 18

Roman Catholic devotions, 20, 26, 54, 80, 121, 136, 137–8, 145, 146, 148, 165, 171, 176, 177
Marian devotion *see* Mariology
rosary, 60, 79–80, 89, 90–1, 100, 103
Stations of the Cross, 25, 26, 38, 61, 142, 176

Roman Catholic doctrine
Eucharist and, 4, 62, 91, 124, 146, 151, 152, 155, 156, 159, 163–70
Holy Spirit, 90, 154, 173n
Mass and, 25–6, 33, 49, 53, 55, 60, 62, 79, 83, 99, 116, 124, 132, 133, 143, 148, 156, 163, 165–6, 157, 168, 169, 175, 176

miracles and, 2, 29, 35, 36, 111, 112, 113, 122–3, 124, 126, 127, 128–9, 138, 147, 157, 160, 165, 177
sacraments in, 61, 68, 70, 71, 78n, 96, 98, 152, 153, 156, 165, 167, 175; *see also* grace
Virgin Mary *see* Mariology

Roman Catholic liturgy, 11, 18, 26, 84, 85, 96, 130, 131, 138, 143, 145, 146, 147, 148, 162, 163, 166, 169, 171

romance, 15, 17, 18, 20, 25–6, 33, 34, 138, 177

romanticism, 59, 61–3, 67–8, 73, 75, 135, 136

rosary *see* Roman Catholic devotions

Ross, Alexander, 16

sagas (Icelandic), 9, 72, 112–14, 116, 118, 122, 123, 124, 126, 134, 137, 138; *see also Orkneyinga Saga*

saints, 4, 24, 35–6, 65, 69, 75, 88, 106, 107, 108, 112, 120–1, 176; *see also* hagiography

St Bernard of Clairvaux, 85, 97–8

St Brandon, 125–6

St Cecilia, 121

St Dominic, 103

St Francis, 155

St Gregory, 168

St Joseph, 146

St Lucy, 123

St Magnus, 36, 42, 64, 80, 89, 108, 111–39, 160, 172

St Margaret Clitherow, 118

St Paul, 48, 57, 58, 72, 120

St Sunniva, 118, 121

St Teresa of Avila, 102

St Thomas Becket, 130

St Thomas More, 118

St Tredwell, 121, 123

Salvation Army, 48, 52, 53

Scots College (Rome), 18

Scots language, 10, 15, 16, 23, 94

Scott, Alexander, 6
'Calvinist Sang', 6

Scott, Tom, 6

Scott, Walter, 17, 21
Tales of a Grandfather, 21